SURREY

D1081389

AT WAR

1939-1945

by Bob Ogley

This companion volume to the highly acclaimed *Kent at War* records the momentous events of six years of war in the county of Surrey as seen through the eyes of those who served in the forces, the services, the voluntary occupations, and the civilian population. Their resolve was to beat off the Nazi menace and, in the face of growing adversity, they went about it with great determination, irrepressible humour and unbelievable resilience. Their experiences are recorded in the pages that follow, accompanied by a fascinating selection of contemporary photographs. They cannot fail to stir powerful emotions as they bring back memories of the most dramatic years in Surrey's history.

Published by Froglets Publications

Froglets Publications Ltd

Brasted Chart,
Westerham,
Kent TN16 ILY

Tel: 01959 562972
Fax: 01959 565365

© Bob Ogley 1995

Paperback ISBN 1 872337 65 1
Hardback ISBN 1 872337 70 8

This book was originated by Froglets Publications Ltd and printed and bound by Staples Printers (Rochester) Ltd, Neptune Close, Medway City Estate, Rochester, Kent ME2 4LT.

Back cover illustration:

In 1945 a bomb disposal unit of the Royal Engineers remove a "Satan" which had been buried in the East Surrey Sawmills at Croydon since January 1941. *Imperial War Museum*

If you recognise yourself, a friend or relation in any of the photographs in this book, please let us know. We may be able to include the information in our first reprint.

Jacket design and additional artwork by Alison Clark

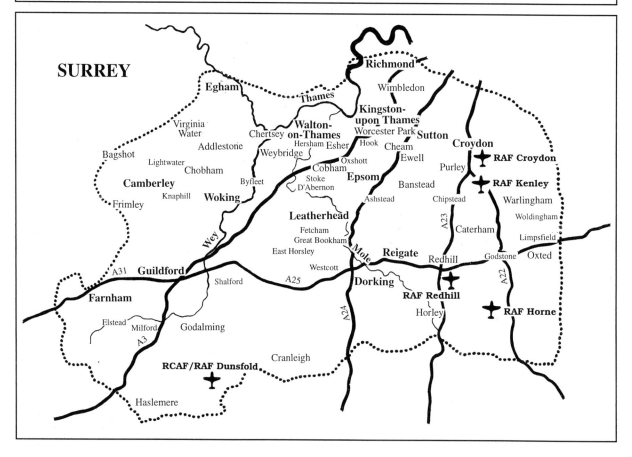

CIVIL DEFENCE IN SURREY: SEPTEMBER 1939

AT the outbreak of war the county of Surrey was divided into two Civil Defence regions (the Eastern and Western Emergency Areas) and each region was sub-divided into districts. The communications system for Civil Defence consisted first of reporting agents, the police and wardens, whose main task was to detail incidents to local report centres. These reports were then sent via control centres to the regional headquarters which, in the case of most Surrey towns, was at Tunbridge Wells, Kent. From here they were sent, usually by teleprinter, to the Home Security war room in London.

UD = Urban District
RD = Rural District
 B = Borough

Western Emergency area:	Eastern Emergency Area (later Group 9 of London CD)
Bagshot RD	Banstead UD
Caterham and Warlingham UD	Barnes B
Chertsey UD	Beddington and Wallington B
Dorking UD	Carlshalton UD
Dorking and Horley RD	Coulsdon and Purley UD
Egham UD	Croydon B
Farnham UD	Epsom and Ewell B
Frimley and Camberley UD	Esher UD
Godalming RD	Kingston B
Guildford B	Malden and Coombe B
Guildford RD	Merton and Morden UD
Hambledon UD	Mitcham B
Leatherhead UD	Sutton and Cheam B
Reigate B	Richmond B
Walton and Weybridge UD	Surbiton B
Woking UD	Wimbledon B

You must remember this...

NEVILLE Chamberlain announced to the nation on Sunday September 3rd, 1939 that war had been declared on Nazi Germany. Immediately, units of the Territorial Army began taking up their wartime positions, followed by thousands of conscripts, the first in British military history. Within months the British Expeditionary Forces were in France and soldiers from the Dominions were sailing to the defence of their Motherland.

Tens of thousands of Canadians settled in Surrey. It was like the Roman occupation except that these men were friendly and were prepared to repulse the German invaders when (rather than if) they arrived. But instead of fighting, life was filled with route marches, demonstrations, lectures and exercises. The real battle was going on overhead and the Canadians stationed on the Surrey hills had a grandstand seat for the Battle of Britain.

RAF Kenley was a vital sector station and the men and women stationed there played a significant part in the Battle of Britain and all air operations which followed. Alongside, Croydon and Redhill were satellite stations and later RAF Dunsfold and Horne joined in the fray as the advantage switched in favour of the Allies.

This photographic history of the war years in Surrey is a hybrid of journalism and history and contains pictures and stories of the momentous events as they unfolded. It includes not only the famous events such as the evacuation of children, Dunkirk, the great battle in the skies and the Blitz but life in the Surrey villages, the county's response to the great appeals, the frantic activity in the great aircraft factories, the heroes of the home front, the soldiers who were overseas and much more.

Special features include a day-by-day diary of the Battle of Britain, all those from Surrey who won the George or Victoria Cross and casualty figures for the county. We describe the role of Surrey's most famous residents — Barnes Wallis and his bouncing bomb, Sydney Camm and his Hawker Hurricane, John Anderson and his shelter, Lord Beaverbrook and his appeal for scrap metal, Leslie Howard and his death in a plane crash.

Much of the information comes from Surrey newspapers, museums, libraries and the general public who took the trouble to write with their own reminiscences, anecdotes and photographs.

Like the rest of England, the spirit of Surrey during the Second World War was of indomitable optimism, quiet courage, enterprise, patience and humour. This spirit was embodied by all those who played a leading part in the battle zones and on the home front. We salute them all.

1939

Time to fuse all warheads

February: The Home Office announced plans to provide shelters to thousands of homes in districts likely to be bombed. Priority was to be given to all London metropolitan boroughs and especially target towns such as Kingston and Croydon.

March: Britain promised to support Poland in the event of a German invasion. Surrey's anti-aircraft batteries were strengthened and the county's territorial units moved onto a war footing.

April: Military conscription was introduced. Surrey's farmers were urged to plough up grazing pastures in a Government drive to increase the proportion of food produced at home. Farmers were asked to provide another 15,000 acres in the county and paid £2 for each additional acre cultivated.

May: Italy and Germany signed the Pact of Steel. Germany also signed a non-aggression pact with Denmark.

June: The RAF were said to be producing 750 aircraft a month. Among these were almost 500 Hurricanes made in the great Hawker factories at Kingston and Brooklands (Weybridge).

July: Communities throughout Surrey took part in a test black-out during the weekend of July 8th-9th. Churchill proposed a military alliance with Russia.

August: British negotiations with Russia broke down and the German Foreign Minister was invited to Moscow to sign the Nazi-Soviet pact. The British Government announced that it stood by its promise to Poland. On August 24th military reservists were called up and ARP services warned to stand ready. Hundreds of refugees throughout Surrey volunteered for National Service. All place names visible from the air, particularly the Hawker factories and others along-

side the Thames, were ordered to be erased. Special attention was given to gasholders which displayed the name of the town in which they stood.

Guildford Education Committee rejected a proposal for ARP protection in schools and the chairman, Sir Claud de la Fosse promptly resigned. He wanted concrete lined trenches giving protection for 2,400 children costing approximately £5,700. The meeting decided that nothing but deep bomb-proof shelters were adequate and it was decided in the event of war not to open schools until such precautions were provided.

The shadows of war were affecting entries for sports and social events across the county. Several events in the skiff club regatta at Teddington Reach had to be cancelled and village cricket clubs were finding it impossible to raise sides as many of their men had enrolled for National Service. Several ladies volunteered to fill the vacancies.

September: Miss Joan Russell, an East Moseley dancer, who was on tour with her company and appearing at the Scala, Leipzig was among the last British subjects ordered to leave Germany. She and her colleagues had to pool money in order to buy food on their journey to the frontier. She was eventually reunited with her parents at 4 Hurst Lane, East Moseley.

Well-known Fleet Street journalist, Mr Walter Swaffer, brother of Hannen Swaffer was one of the first Surrey people to be killed in the black-out. Mr Swaffer of Liverpool Road, Kingston was in a head-on collision with a tramcar on September 2nd.

Special meetings were held in towns throughout Surrey to form food control committees, made up of traders and consumers. Efforts were being made by local councils to establish first aid posts and complete the erection of garden Anderson shelters.

German troops invaded Poland on September 1st. Black-out began in Surrey on the same day and thousands of children, mothers, teachers and the disabled from metropolitan Surrey moved to reception centres to prepare for evacuation.

Mr A.B. Griffiths French master of Kingston Grammar School was arrested as a spy while cycling in Germany. He was turned over to the Gestapo who believed his story. A Nazi member took him to lunch and then drove the fortunate teacher to the frontier at Saarbruken.

The Surrey Comet called for the Kingston town clock to be silenced forthwith. Apparently it struck every 15 minutes, so loudly, that there was a danger air raid sirens would not be heard.

Gas masks were issued to everyone and there were special baby bags (respirators) for infants. The author was among those children to be issued with a gas "helmet" and used to emerge as red as a beetroot from its clammy confines.

Orders were given to organise mock gas attacks for the Government was convinced that poisonous gases would be a feature of this modern conflict. Public health demonstrations were also held, such as this one at the civil defence headquarters in South Norwood. The men are gamely demonstrating a method of decontamination.

When Surrey teetered on the brink

THE weeks leading up to the outbreak of war were hectic and confusing for the people of Surrey. Air raid precautions had been discussed at county level for more than three years and many exercises had been held. In addition shelters had been built, decontamination centres opened and refuge rooms gas proofed in hundreds of homes. Everyone was convinced that the poisonous gases used in the trenches in 1917 were likely to be a feature of this modern conflict, so an order was made to issue gas masks to everybody.

In many places there were not enough to go around. A census in Leatherhead indicated there were 700 babies under the age of two and 800 between two and four. Families were asked to be as patient as possible; delivery could not be expected until the end of August. In Banstead there was a shortage of baby bags (respirators for infants) so, if parents were required to evacuate their homes on account of a gas attack, they were advised to lay a damp cloth lightly across the child's face and wrap the child securely in a blanket.

Surrey was one of 15 counties to take part in a test blackout during Saturday night and Sunday morning, July 8th-9th, 1939. Local authorities throughout the county arranged exercises and sounded the air-raid sirens at regular intervals. Road beacons were covered with sacks, motorists drove with sidelights only, householders screened their windows and traffic lights were deflected away from the sky. The following month an even greater black-out trial was held and the public was warned that stiff penalties faced those who failed to comply with the regulations.

Many Jewish refugees, who fled from Hitler earlier in 1939, made their homes in Surrey and were greeted sympathetically. Some were living in Egham where the vicar, the Rev. A.C.Tranter said they could use the parish church as a synagogue on Saturday mornings. They declined this offer but accepted the parish rooms where Hebrew classes were also arranged.

As the deepening crisis in Europe began to intrude on everyday life, German nationals living in Surrey were warned they would be handed over to military escorts and interned if war broke out.

One of them, Mr H.A.Kluthe wrote to the *Surrey Advertiser*: "It came as a shock to many Guildford residents — most of whom are sincere friends of this country — to see themselves suddenly classed as enemy aliens. However, this unpleasant, though inevitable, formality has been made more tolerable by the splendid attitude of the people of Surrey. Instead of looking at us with suspicion we have met only kindness and sympathy."

As the county teetered on the brink of war, Surrey County Council elected its War Executive Committee, to be known as "The Big Six". They were Sir Philip Henriques (chairman), Sir Richard J.Meller MP, Mrs J.Chuter Ede MP, Sir Laurence Halsey, Mr S.H.Marshall and Capt. E.H.Tuckwell. Sir Philip appealed to the county: "Surrey has only a small place in the struggles ahead but I'm proud to be chairman in a county so strong and so united. We will pull together to win freedom from tyranny".

At parochial levels, town halls were converted into control rooms and strengthened. At Farnham the staff were established as two officers in charge, two message supervisors, two plotting officers, two plotting clerks, two record clerks, eight women telephonists and numerous dispatch riders. Here the stage was set. The tables, the maps, the plotting flags, the switchboard plugs were all in place. The motorbikes were outside. Farnham was prepared for war.

On the day that German troops invaded Poland, the county council and all local authorities made their plans to receive evacuated children from London. Properties were requisitioned such as The Mount in Gatton Road, Reigate to be used as a maternity unit for expectant mothers. Billeting surveys were carried out to find what accommodation was available and which householders would be willing to take charge of unaccompanied children. With the help of the Women's Voluntary Services (WVS), they made arrangements to store blankets and bedding, pay the householders and supply emergency rations. Reception centres were earmarked and billeting officers appointed.

In a stirring speech to some of his constituents at Frimley Warren, Mr Godfrey Nicholson MP for Farnham said Britain was well prepared for any eventuality. "The Navy is the most potent factor for peace and is more formidable than ever", he said. "The RAF, if not numerically the strongest, is second to none in quality of personnel and material and the Army is so rapidly taking shape that there are now more than a million men."

Surrey didn't want to go to war for the memories of the slaughter of 1917 were too fresh in the mind. Thirty of those who came through the bloodiest conflict of all — members of the Guildford branch of the Old Contemptibles Association — must have had mixed emotions as they joined colleagues from all over the country on their annual pilgrimage to Ypres to remember, as one put it "the old unhappy far off things and battles long ago". The Guildford veterans went to Passchendaele Ridge. It took them two minutes to traverse a piece of country which some of them recalled having taken months to cross when "the air was rent by the devastating sounds of war".

No, Surrey didn't want to go to war but time was running out. The identical British and French ultimatum telling Hitler to withdraw his troops from Poland "or a state of war would exist" was timed to expire at 11am on Sunday September 3rd.

With the proximity of the fighter stations at Croydon and Kenley, the numerous factories already working for the "war effort" and the size of the borough (243,000 population in 1939) it was inevitable that Croydon would be in the thick of the battle should the war follow its expected course. The Civil Defence forces staged a mock exhibition showing models of a heavily bombed borough (see picture) and the action that should be taken to bring out casualties, render first aid and tackle the bombs. Nobody really imagined that it could be so bad; in fact the Government declared that Croydon was not in the category of maximum risk, a decision that led to a protest from the council, an interview at the Ministry and a change of heart at Whitehall. Croydon, it was agreed, might be subject to heavy bombardment.

Sandbags, piled around doors and windows to deflect blast were a feature of those early days of the war. Priority was given to hospitals and public buildings and here Red Cross nurses and doctors at Pelham House, Harestone Valley, Caterham take a break from the arduous task of filling the bags to pose for a photograph.

A gas chamber in the vicarage

THE people of Surrey gathered round their radio sets on that fateful Sunday morning of September 3rd and, at Kenley and Croydon airfields, Dowding's pilots basked in the warm sunshine. At 11.15 am, they heard through loudspeakers the voice of a tired Prime Minister, his voice cracking with strain: "This morning the British Ambassador in Berlin handed the German Government a final note stating that unless we heard from them by 11 o'clock that they were prepared at once to withdraw their troops from Poland, a state of war would exist between us... I have to tell you now that no such undertaking has been received and that consequently this country is at war with Germany."

Families checked their black-out screens, their gas masks and their shelters in the back garden. A nervous tension was discernible in the eyes and in the gait of everyone. Britain was at war and Hitler's deadly air force, its destructive powers amply demonstrated in Poland would soon be threatening the lives of everyone.

Chamberlain asked the people to play their part "with calmness and courage". His historic words had hardly faded away

before the first air raid warning put his appeal to the test. The time was 11.30 am and a raider was reported coming from the south. People made their way quietly to the shelters and waited for the All Clear.

Among them was the vicar of St Luke's Church, Kingston, the Rev L.A.H.Isaac who was in the pulpit when the wailing began. Without panic he stopped the service and invited the congregation to take refuge in the gas chamber in the vicarage. There was not room for all, so many went to the boiler room.

As the "raider" flew across the Channel towards the Thames Estuary, a tell-tale blip in the radio-location stations gave warning of its approach. In Surrey it was picked up by the vigilant men of the Observer Corps and the defence network sprang into life.

The "suspect" landed at Croydon Airport — it was a French transport aircraft bringing a party of staff officers to London, the pilot unaware that he had been the first to test Fighter Command's complex defence system and had almost been blown out of the sky!

First war victims were two lions

IN those first few days of the war, there was frantic activity in Surrey. Many families began to move from vulnerable areas into the countryside and some of the wealthier people from the "stockbroker belt" elected to travel overseas, principally to the United States. Those who chose to face Hitler and his mighty Luftwaffe passed the time perfecting their defences and digging more air-raid shelters. Food offices were set up, ration books issued and a fuel office controlled the amount of coal and petrol used.

The initials ARP (for Air Raid Precautions) became commonplace in towns and villages alike. Those actively engaged were given uniforms; there were special tunics for wardens, auxiliary firemen, fire ladies, women ambulance drivers. nursing auxiliaries, rescue and demolition parties. In Kingston there was an appeal for 200 more wardens to bring them up to full strength. In Guildford camp beds were desperately required for first aid posts. ARP Wardens' posts were set up everywhere. In Redhill, the famous Market Hall drinking fountain was removed to make way for one.

In Woking every single store stocking torches and batteries exhausted its supply. One shopkeeper estimated that he sold 50,000 torch batteries in one week. The introduction of petrol rationing and the strain of car driving at night caused a record sale of pedal cycles. One person stepped into a Woking shop from a Rolls Royce and went off on a bicycle.

Carriers for gas masks were also in demand.

The Lord Lieutenant of Surrey, Sir Malcolm Fraser issued a challenge to the county. In a letter to the *Surrey Advertiser* he said: "In searching the records of the last war it will be found that few counties equalled and none exceeded the contribution made by Surrey to the general welfare and safety of the Realm. In military and charitable work Surrey set a standard which must and will be beaten this time".

Unbelievably hasty was the decision to slaughter two young lions at Chessington. It was considered that danger might result from their escape in an air raid. Two tigers were sent to another zoo but the future of the penguins and sealions was not decided. Ironically, on the day war broke out, local hero Mr Peter Massey of Anyards Road, Cobham, holder of the Mons Star and badly injured in the 1914-18 war, died. He was 66.

The Territorial Army (TA) units had long since moved onto a war footing and the army was growing in strength by the day. Police reservists of more than 1,300 men were inspected by Sir Malcolm Fraser at a special rally on Ranmore Common, Guildford.

The lack of men and the spectre of war, however, meant the cancellation of sporting events and this was a real blow to Guildford FC who led the Southern League and had hopes of winning the championship pennant.

In Shamley Green the main group of evacuees came from the Gerard Road LCC school in Earlsfield. They were accompanied by their head teacher, Mr Crosskey, (centre) and one other teacher, Miss Storey, (left). They attended lessons at the Chapel and later moved to the Church room. In this picture a group of the children are seen outside the Chapel with their teachers and Sid Killick.

'Little hooligans' made Surrey smile

THE mass evacuation of children from London to reception areas in Surrey considered safe from air attack began on September 1st, the day German troops invaded Poland. It was a cultural shock for the children, who were suddenly transported from urban areas of Lewisham to rural Lingfield, and for the billeting families who were to find their young guests both funny and infuriating.

The *Surrey Advertiser* wrote: "If some of the pleasant residences in Guildford differ from the conditions to which the town's young guests are accustomed, then they do not have the effect of overawing them. The Cockney adaptability and talent for rising to the occasion has repaid in laughter and friendliness any inconvenience householders may have suffered through billeting. The mental picture of 'Little London hooligans' has been pleasantly disillusioned".

By the evening of September 3rd, hundreds of London children were safe and sound in their strange homes. The children who had travelled into the Surrey towns and villages with their teachers were marshalled at railway stations, bus terminals and market places. Each child was labelled with name, address and school number and carried a gas mask, nightwear and the necessary clothing. No destination was given; parents were informed that they would be notified of this as soon as possible.

In Redhill, small but sympathetic groups of spectators watched the arrival of the advance guard of evacuees. They were taken to the Odeon Cinema where their "iron" rations were distributed by a number of voluntary helpers. They were then taken to various centres in the district where they waited "to be chosen". This was the most humiliating experience of all, for people who had volunteered to have children in their care claimed those who most appealed to them.

The village of Headley was one to receive its full quota of evacuees. In most homes the only organised entertainment was Children's Hour on the wireless from 5 to 6 pm and it took the little refugees some time to be fully integrated into a country way of life. The tiny village school had to be shared with the pupils of Sydenham Secondary — so the children of Headley went to school in the morning and the Londoners in the afternoon. This continued for some months until new premises could be organised.

Wonderful stories of Cockney humour became quite a feature of those uncertain days at the start of the war. The first inquiry from two small girls in East Clandon was straight to the point — "where's the cinema?" A kid from Fulham told a schoolmate in Onslow village: "Coo, I ain't arf livin' in a posh ahse". A five-year-old boy called Tommy arrived at his billet in Guildford and was told that he could have a bath immediately. He replied somewhat tersely: "I don't av barves". Pressed to comply, Tommy consented. The lady of the house took him to the bathroom and waited. "Well git art", he expostulated, his five-year-old masculinity outraged.

On their first night in Cranleigh, two little boys were given a candle and told to go to bed. Moments later their beds were checked but found to be undisturbed. A casual search failed to find them. They had disappeared. Eventually they were discovered — under the bed — where they always slept at home!

Surrey had actually made plans to receive many thousands of evacuees but in reality, due in part to worried mothers refusing to send them, only a fraction arrived and many were to return home to London as the "phoney war" took its grip.

Evacuees at Westborough School, Southway, Guildford in the autumn of 1939.

Children from Merton Infants School on their way to the station. In every district throughout Surrey, evacuation plans were co-ordinated by the WVS who appointed two evacuation officers — Lady Grieg of Richmond Park and Mrs Helen Lloyd of Albury. Secretaries were chosen for each area and the WVS laid on trains, coaches, arranged clearing stations, set up canteens and dealt with all billeting arrangements.

Page five of The Surrey Comet *contained this report of evacuation arrangements in the area, on Wednesday September 6th, 1939.*

Children Calm When Air Raid Sirens Sounded

SO advanced was the evacuation of school children and others from the London districts that it was found possible to notify Wimbledon evacuation officer, Mr E.G.Hodges on Saturday afternoon that evacuation in his area would take place the following day by means of motor coaches.

However, at night this arrangement was cancelled so that the children and expectant mothers should travel to their destination by train on Sunday morning and children under school age in the afternoon.

This meant that the officer, his staff, school teachers and helpers were kept busy until very late on Saturday night but with the willing assistance of parents and guardians everything was promptly made ready for the evacuation.

The manner in which the mothers and their children assembled, the departure from schools and the implicit following of instructions throughout showed how perfectly the work had been organised. Although Mitcham children were being evacuated from Wimbledon station at the same time the scheme went off according to plan.

Only one untoward circumstance occurred. While the children were waiting at the station the air raid sirens sounded shortly after 11 o'clock, Everyone rose to the occasion splendidly and complete calm prevailed. The children were led to the Town Hall where community singing took place until the "raiders" passed. The children, now aware that war had been officially declared, were then marched back to the station and were soon being entrained for their unknown destinations.

Pilots, ground crews, pets and Hurricanes at Kenley on May 23rd, 1938.

Kenley welcomes the Hurricane

The photograph of Kenley airfield was taken in May 1938, before Neville Chamberlain's confident declaration of "peace in our time" and before this senior sector station of No 11 Group Fighter Command had moved onto a wartime footing. This picture is evocative. It shows pilots, ground crews and two pilot's dogs (there were always a few pet dogs on every major airfield) of No 3 Squadron in front of the Signals Square.

In the background, a camouflaged Demon taxies towards the watch office while the airmen discuss the new techniques and procedures planned for that day. There is a buzz of excitement, and no wonder. Lined up behind them are eight Hawker Hurricanes (Mark1), built at Kingston-upon-Thames and assem-

bled at Brooklands — an aircraft that was then superior to any other in the world.

It was in May 1938 that *The Times* wrote: "The fastest 'plane in any air force in the world was yesterday removed from the Air Ministry's semi-secret list. The Hurricane is outstanding in its class in respect of duration as well as speed".

By the beginning of 1939, 3 Squadron shared the facilities at Kenley with 17 Squadron (flying Gauntlets) and 615 (Tudors and Hectors). The pilots put in many flying hours and took part in some vigorous training exercises in preparation for what might be. For the pilots of nearby Biggin Hill one of these training flights became a tragedy when a young flying officer crashed his Hur-

ricane in the Surrey countryside, not far from Tatsfield. As it was such a wild and stormy night a second pilot, also from Biggin Hill, volunteered to drop a marker flare near the scene of the crash. To the great horror of both Biggin and Kenley control the second pilot also crashed; the bodies of the men and the completely wrecked Hurricanes were found barely 100 yards apart.

Two pilots and two Hurricanes had been lost. It was a tragedy that was to have even greater significance on August 24th when RAF stations were instructed to mobilise and all leave was cancelled. Kenley, however, was not among them for the aerodrome was out of commission while new runways and perimeter tracks were constructed and the old hangars replaced.

This aerial picture of Croydon was taken before the war after the new-look aerodrome had been formally opened by the then Secretary for Air, Sir Samuel Hoare. It shows the new buildings (left centre) and the old buildings (right centre) bisected by Plough Lane which had just been closed to traffic. In its place was a new road between Wallington and Purley.

By the end of the year with the "phoney war" well established, Kenley was ready for action. There were two new runways over 1,000 yards long, fuel storage for 35,000 gallons of aviation spirit and 1.25 million rounds of small arms ammunition. Four 40mm Bofors guns manned by the 31st Light AA Battery were defending the airfield alongside two 3 inch guns operated by the 148th Light and 20 Lewis guns in a dual ground-air role. Kenley also had a secret weapon that was to play its part in the Battle of Britain — a parachute device which fired a cable 600 feet in the air into the path of low-flying aircraft (see page 53) in a bid to drag them down.

Croydon, steeped in civil aviation history and London's main airport, was becoming increasingly unsuitable for such a role. It was now earmarked as a wartime satellite for Kenley with facilities that were outstanding. The terminal building became the administration block and the 30-bedroom Aerodrome Hotel was taken over as the pilots' mess and accommodation. Four landing areas were specifically laid out on the grass surface and two fighter squadrons were instructed to take up station there.

No 3 Squadron, who had moved from Kenley to Biggin Hill, flew their Hurricanes to Croydon. They were joined by No 615 (County of Surrey Auxiliary Squadron) who had swapped their

Tudors and Hectors for Gladiators. Redhill was established as an alternative airfield for Croydon and the little satellite at Gatwick was to be used if Kenley had to be evacuated.

In October, 145 Squadron was reformed as a day and night fighter unit and in December, 3 Squadron left for the forward base at Hawkinge. In their place came 92, full of panache and vigour, a squadron due to convert to a new aircraft, the Spitfire 1 — more advanced than the Hurricane, with a slimmer fuselage and wings of great strength, narrow depth and memorable grace. An aircraft, like the Squadron who flew it, destined to become the most famous in Fighter Command.

'Put those bloody lights out' cried the wardens

BY mid-September 1939 the "black-out", which the Chief Constable of Surrey had demanded, was virtually complete. Windows of all homes were screened, motorists drove with only their sidelights on, road beacons were covered in sacks and traffic lights had hoods fitted to deflect the light downwards. Wardens toured the streets urging those who contravened to "put those bloody lights out".

Black-out material had virtually disppeared from the shops. So had brown paper, black paint, drawing pins and torch batteries, for the people of Surrey were aware that even the slightest chink of light could lead to a heavy fine.

Trains ran at night with their blinds drawn, each compartment illuminated by a blue pinpoint. The windows of buses were covered for the black-out and remained covered in daytime to protect passengers in the event of flying glass. There was a small slit in the material to allow passengers to identify their stops.

Road casualties began to escalate and the Government decided to ease vehicle lighting restrictions by allowing one headlight to be lit and introducing white lines on major routes to help drivers. Even so, pedestrians stumbling through blacked out streets had great difficulty in avoiding cars and buses with dimmed headlights and there was chaos in some of the bigger towns. Eventually pedestrians were allowed to use hand torches provided they were muffled and turned off in a raid.

One of the first tragedies occurred in Newchapel Road, Lingfield when 85-year-old William Stanford, a veteran of the Boer Wars, was knocked down and killed on September lst. The driver, Gilbert Brooks, said it was a foggy night and he had driven his car at just 10 miles an hour with the offside wheels just over the white line. He had suddenly felt a bump and found Mr Stanford lying at an angle in the road.

The *Surrey Mirror* told how a well-known Coulsdon resident, "holding an important post in the Auxiliary Fire Service" was driving his car along the Brighton Road during a thunderstorm. "There came a vivid flash of lightning and to his astonishment he saw in front of him two elephants. The driver, a tee-totaller, discovered that the animals were being evacuated from London and were led by a man with a dimmed red light."

Epsom and Ewell had no trouble in recruiting men and women into the ARP service. By the outbreak of war more than 600 had enrolled and the figures continued to grow throughout September. Here are the men and women of the ARP post in Plough Lane, West Ewell.

Coroners in Surrey commented that motorists who hugged white lines in the centre of the road were bound to have accidents and called for kerbs to be painted white. They were, and here, on the Kingston by-pass, one man was engaged on kerb-painting duty. At the rate of half-a-mile a day it was a back-breaking job but he completed it.

This report appeared in The Surrey Mirror *on September 15th, 1939.*

ESCAPED FROM GESTAPO: Austrian Jew's story at Godstone Court

CHARGED as aliens, two Austrian Jews, Paul Haas (39), export agent and his wife, Else Haas who have been living at The Cottage, Detillens Lane, Limpsfield, were charged at Godstone Sessions on Monday (September 11th) with failing to comply with the condition to leave the country on July 18th.

When an application was made for a remand in custody, Haas produced a lengthy document and asked permission to say something in his own defence. Speaking with great emotion he said the accusation of being in this country illegally was due to a terrible mistake. He and his wife lived in Vienna. In November last year they were attacked by German Nazi Storm Troops and were plundered of their money and other valuables. They escaped from home and were hidden every night with a friend. In January they escaped without the permission of the Gestapo.

The Jewish Aid Committee gave them a guarantee for their safe conduct and "praise God" said the defendant, "we were able to come to Limpsfield in wonderful and free England. Our native country has been robbed of us", Haas said, "and all that is left to us is our honour".

The clerk told Haas he had already been in touch with the Jewish Aid Committee in London and was told records had been removed to Ascot. Supt King said: "I have nothing to say about the matter now. They are Jews and will not be sent back to Austria. We are satisfied with their character and behaviour in this country."

The chairman, Mr F. Kimber Bull said to Haas: "We are bound to remand you in custody and we think you will be treated with every consideration. There is no disgrace at all in going to prison in the circumstances. Remember, we are fighting for you as well as for ourselves and the Poles."

As magistrates courts throughout Surrey continued to be packed with cases of black-out infringements, there were some rather unusual practices introduced into both rural and town life. White stripes were painted on cows so they could be found and milked without difficulty during the early-morning darkness. During a court case in Sutton, it was reported that the only beneficiaries of the black-out were burglars and courting couples.

No war yet and no poisonous gases but there was no let up in gas mask assembly at this factory in Redhill. These girls must have wondered — would they ever have to be used?

Women and children die in the war at sea

TWO young women — one from Guildford and the other from Chertsey — were among the first casualties of the war. Mrs Betty Adam who had been living with an aunt at Guildford and Mrs Gertrude Read of Abbey Road, Chertsey were on board the 13,500-ton liner *Athenia*, sailing from Glasgow to Montreal when it was attacked by a German U-Boat on the first day of the war. There were 1,418 people on board and 112 passengers and crew died. It was a blunder that embarrassed the Nazis, for the commander of the U-Boat thought he was torpedoing a British armed merchantman.

More liners and cargo ships were to go down in the first few weeks of hostilities and many more people from Surrey lost their lives. Dangerous magnetic mines were laid in British waters and U-Boats continued to torpedo vessels regardless of the chances for women and children to escape.

On September 17th, HMS *Courageous*, one of the navy's oldest aircraft carriers was torpedoed in the Hebrides. It sank in 15 minutes and half of the 1,000 strong crew were drowned including Ernest Baker, formerly a Kingston postman who lived with his wife and daughter at Matlock Way, New Malden. A veteran of the 1914-18 war, Mr Baker was a stoker on Royal Naval Reserve and had been recalled to service a few weeks before war was declared.

Battleships were also attacked including the 29,150-ton *Royal Oak,* the pride of the British fleet, which was sunk at anchor in Scapa Flow on October 14th. This tragedy was felt particularly badly in Leatherhead. Four local men, two of whom were cousins, were serving on the battleship and two men from Farnham also died when a U-boat, on the surface, blatantly sailed into the harbour and fired seven torpedoes. The *Royal Oak* rolled over and capsized and 800 of the 1,224 crew perished.

Distressing news of casualties from the war at sea continued to affect many Surrey families. Mr F.A. Elkins, formerly an employee with Farnham Council went down with the ill-fated HMS *Exmouth* and two children from Richmond were among 85 to die when an evacuee ship taking them to safety in America was sunk by a U-Boat.

Meanwhile, back at home there were more sandbags to fill and here the office staff at John Sainsbury, play their part in trying to protect the premises of the well-known grocers, before the wartime move from Stanford Street, Blackfriars to the greater safety of Castle Parade, Ewell.

The air raid shelters were named after Sir John Anderson, Home Secretary who lived at Rockshaw Road, Merstham. Here they are being delivered to citizens lucky enough to have gardens.

"Haw Haw" warns Croydon: 'we will bomb your airfield'

AS the people of Surrey watched and waited for the war to begin there were periods of great anxiety. On October 26th those who tuned in to *Germany Calling*, the propaganda wireless station in Hamburg heard this warning. "Croydon must beware. She is the second line of defence. We know the aerodrome is camouflaged but we know just what kind of camouflage it is. We shall bomb it and bomb it to a finish and we would advise the people there to evacuate the area next weekend as we shall do the job thoroughly. But we shall be merciful and use only incendiary bombs."

The speaker who later won the sobriquet of "Lord Haw Haw" because of his superior English drawl , frightened some Croydonians but the majority did not seem to be unduly perturbed.

No-one knew quite what to expect when (and if) the air raids began so they continued with the task of gas proofing refuge rooms and utilising whatever convenient natural shelters they could find elsewhere. One innovation was the Anderson shelter, issued free of charge to all those earning less than £250 a year and at a charge of £7 for those with higher incomes.

In Banstead, the local ARP indented for 1,920 Anderson shelters and held an evening demonstration to show how they should be erected. Only 29 people turned up. Another attempt to interest Banstead in the steel shelters attracted an attendance of 15.

The ARP services were involved in intensive training during the early weeks of the war. The residents of Lorne Avenue, Shirley watched an exercise in how to deal with incendiary bombs.

Explosions and sirens — but no sign of war

AS the winter approached there was an air of unreality about the war. RAF Bomber Command were actually dropping leaflets rather than bombs on Germany, an activity which later prompted Air Marshal Arthur Harris, of Bomber Command to observe: "At least it provided the people of Germany with several years free toilet paper".

So little was happening in Surrey that an air raid warning earned considerable space in the newspapers; but even when no raid actually took place there were tragedies. A woman from King's Avenue, New Malden died of shock soon after the siren sounded and there were several reports of people who committed suicide by drowning in the Thames.

More and more people, however, were beginning to appear in police courts for allowing lights to show during blackout hours and there were several court hearings of soldiers marrying bigamously. ARP exercises continued to be organised with great vigour.

The photograph shows a large scale practice in dealing with incendiary bombs, should they ever be dropped. The venue for this exercise was Lorne Gardens, Shirley — an area that was destined to receive a dramatic pounding from all kinds of devices, particularly in the latter years of the war.

There was a flurry of activity in another area — not the skies or the streets, but the churches. Couples were determined that Hitler was not going to stop them marrying, even if they could not have the wedding of their dreams. In October, the *Surrey Comet* reported that, on one Saturday alone there were 24 marriages in Kingston Register Office. The Superintendent had never been so busy; by the end of the following week that total had risen to more than 100.

The calmest marriage of all, however, took place at St. Peter's Church, Norbiton between two Labour supporters, Mr Stanley Bell and Miss Dora Berry. During the service the air raid siren sounded but the vicar continued and not a member of the congregation moved. It later transpired that all parties concerned thought it was the All Clear signal!

By November fewer and fewer people went out with their gas masks. Cinemas and theatres, closed at the outbreak of war, were reopening and doing a brisk trade. However, evacuees continued to pour out of London and, on Ditton Marsh, a marquee was erected to provide them with food and help.

The Hawker Hurricane Mark I takes shape. The strength of the aircraft was in the centre and cockpit area.

Hawker Hurricane — already a legend

AS the Surrey airfields settled into the "phoney war" of the winter of 1939/40 with routine and uneventful patrols, the production teams at Kingston-on-Thames and Brooklands, Weybridge continued to build and assemble, in great numbers, the aircraft that was already known as a "British legend".

The Hawker Aircraft Group's Hurricane Mark I had set incredible standards in fighter performance. With its stressed-skin construction, retractable undercarriages, variable-pitch propellers and a Rolls Royce Merlin engine, it had a top speed of 315 mph and had earned glowing tributes for the ease and simplicity with which it could be flown.

The first production Hurricane had been built at Kingston and flown from Brooklands in 1937. During the following year the first RAF unit to receive the aircraft was 111 Squadron, then at Northolt but destined to be stationed at Croydon for the start of the Battle of Britain.

Re-equipment of squadrons with Hurricanes continued throughout 1938 and 1939 and, by the outbreak of war, the RAF proudly fielded 19 fully-equipped Hurricane squadrons.

continued from page 20

— in all a total of 1,350.

The aces who flew the machines had a great variety of descriptions for them. Bob Stanford Tuck compared the Hurricane to a great lumbering stallion. Robert Doe provided an earthier remark — "like a brick-built shithouse". Others commented on the steadiness of the Hurricane and its wonderful gun platform and how it could turn on a sixpence. To the ground-crews the Hurricane was a dream machine — "a go anywhere, do anything plane", a defensive fighter and a workhorse".

During and after the Battle of Britain, the Spitfire stole the laurels but the Hurricane played the major part. At the end of August 1940, — the peak of the Battle — there were 372 Spitfires and 709 Hurricanes available for front-line operations. Hawker Hurricane squadrons totalled 33.

Imagine the delight of the Brooklands team when the news came through that a Hurricane of No 1 Squadron had claimed the first German aircraft shot down on October 30, 1939. Some weeks later a Dornier 17 was shot down by 'Cobber' Kain of 73 Squadron. He was flying at 27,000 feet which was a record height for any fighter.

Sydney Camm was among the world's greatest aircraft designers and his career encompassed one technical breakthrough after another — biplanes, monoplanes, jet engines and vertical take off. He is best known, however, as chief designer for Hawker's military aircraft and the man who designed the legendary Hurricane. The photograph of young Sydney is a classic. It was taken at Windsor where he was a passionate member of the local model flying club. By 1966 when Sir Sydney Camm died, aged 72, he had designed 52 different types of aircraft.

The huge RFD balloon factory at Catteshall Lane, Godalming which was turning out five barrage balloons a week during the early months of the war. Production could not keep pace with demand.

The large testing shed was capable of holding four inflated balloons. Here the women worked, sewing together the fabric and fully aware that they were playing a vital role in helping to win the war.

The passive monsters of Godalming

IN his book *The Last Enemy,* Richard Hilary gave a vivid description of the London Balloon Barrage — the passive, seemingly innocuous sight in the sky to which people in North Surrey had become accustomed by Christmas 1939. He wrote: "London wore its usual pallor of yellow fog and from time to time a balloon would poke its head grotesquely through the mist as though looking for possible victims before falling back like some tired monster".

The monsters were a vital part of Britain's air defence and, in December, more than 400 were flying around the capital. Manned by the men of RAF Balloon Command they were filled with hydrogen and winched to the required height — the idea being to force enemy raiders to fly higher and, given the limited technology at the time, bomb far less accurately. The tough steel cable which kept the balloon tethered to the ground was another defence aid, for it could amputate the wings of any bomber which flew too low. There was an unfortunate by-product; it was also lethal to our own aircraft.

One of the largest "balloon factories" (the RFD Company) in the country was at Godalming where a work force of more than 600 produced many hundreds. The employees were mainly women and among them was Marjory Spreadbury who remembers the intricate work

of measuring and marking diagrams on what seemed like miles and miles of silver fabric. "The markings were the positions for the patches that would hold the cables and hawsers for anchoring the balloon. This was done on the floor because of the large space needed and it was very hard on the knees."

Tom Vince was an RFD inspector who recalled that several types of balloons were made in the factory at Godalming. "The largest was the barrage balloon of which some five a week were completed on average. Another was the convoy balloon used for the protection of ships against low-flying attack and a third was a spherical single ply fabric balloon made for meteorological forecasting. The fabric was high quality cotton coated with rubber and aluminium." Tom, who has now died, said there was a large testing shed capable of holding four inflated barrage balloons and here they were inspected before being handed over to Balloon Command.

Many of the women in the factory hated the work because of the diabolical smell and there was a considerable staff turnover. Unfortunately production was unable to keep pace with demand; 444 flying around London and 180 elsewhere was not, at the time, enough to keep Balloon Command fully occupied.

All over Surrey, first aid posts, rest centres and feeding points were being established to nurse, accommodate and feed those whose homes might be hit when, and if, the bombing began. Here, near Croydon, meals for the homeless were prepared on an open fire. It was just an exercise, but the real thing was not many months away!

1940

From the phoney war to the Battle of Britain

January 1st: Following a Royal Proclamation a total of two million men between the ages of 20 and 27 were now liable for call-up into the armed services.

January 5th: A British ship named after the famous viewpoint on the North Downs, *SS Box Hill,* 5,600 tons, hit a mine and sank in the North Sea with the loss of 20 lives.

January 8th: Housewives had to register with retailers as rationing was introduced for butter, sugar and bacon.

January 31st: Flying at Kenley recommenced even before the runways, taxi-ing tracks and other rebuilding work had been completed. The construction work had been hampered by one of the most severe frosts ever known in Surrey but all mention of the weather had been censored until 15 days after the event.

February 6th: A nationwide campaign was launched to stamp out war gossip under the slogan: "Careless talk costs lives".

February 13th: The number of evacuees in Redhill and Reigate, which had amounted to 5,000 in September, had fallen to less than 3,000. As the phoney war continued children and their teachers gradually returned home to London.

February 26th: Lord Haw Haw's propaganda broadcasts from Hamburg were attracting a BBC listening audience of more than six million. He referred often to the location of Kenley and Croydon airfields and the great aircraft factories at Kingston and Weybridge.

February 28th: Churches throughout Surrey, which had replaced their evening services with afternoon ones, reverted to the normal evening service. Shops which had closed at dusk were told they could now remain open until 8 pm.

March 1st: Baby protective helmets — in which infants were protected from the horrors of poison gas — were available for distribution throughout Surrey. It was emphasised that these expensive items must be returned when the child reached the age of two.

March 8th: 92 Squadron at Croydon converted to Spitfire 1 A's, much to the delight of its pilots and the envy of 145 Squadron who was later to exchange its Blenheims for the hump-backed Hawker Hurricanes.

April 1st: Two battalions of the East Surrey Regiment, the 1/6th and the 2/6th, both territorials, were dispatched to France as part of the British Expeditionary Force. The 1st Surreys had been fighting in France since March.

April 10th: Allied forces evacuated Norway and Germany's blitzkrieg in the form of parachutists and heavy panzers rolled into the Low Countries annihilating the Dutch and Belgians.

April 23rd: More than 400 babies' anti-gas helmets were returned to the authorities in Dorking. Inside they found such articles as breadcrumbs, sticky sweets, playing cards, wooden pegs, glasses, bus tickets, partly cooked meat and a postcard.

May 25th: The British Expeditionary Forces, which included the three battalions of the East Surreys were trapped in a pocket of land surrounding the port of Dunkirk. It was decided to evacuate the troops.

May 26th-June 3rd: In nine days 338,682 men were evacuated from the beaches of Dunkirk in what the Prime Minister described as a "miracle of deliverance". The dead, wounded or missing numbered 68,000. All told 222 naval vessels and 800 civilian craft joined the operation.

June 10th: Benito Mussolini, Italy's fascist dictator joined Hitler's victorious panzers and declared war on the Allies.

July: King George VI came to Kenley and decorated Squadron Leader Kayll of 615 Squadron with the DSO and DFC. His colleague Flight Lieutenant Sanders received the DFC.

July 13th: Hitler announced his plans for the invasion of Britain and issued a directive to the effect that Germany must first gain superiority over the RAF. On the same day Lord Beaverbrook appealed for aluminium which could be turned into fighter aircraft.

August 15th: Luftwaffe bombers, intent on attacking Kenley, lost their way in the summer haze and dropped their bombs on Croydon airfield. Many buildings were destroyed and 62 people killed. Six enemy aircraft were destroyed by the pilots of 111 and 32 Squadrons.

August 18th: Kenley was attacked at last in a three-pronged assault. Hangars, administrative buildings and the Ops Room were destroyed as 100 high explosives hit the airfield. Nine people died. The bombers paid dearly for this assault; five Dorniers and their crews were lost.

August 20th: The Surrey airfields had taken a terrible battering as the Luftwaffe's bid to destroy the RAF moved into top gear. The relentless and intensive fighting against overwhelming odds continued and many Kenley and Croydon-based pilots lost their lives in the heroic struggle.

August 31st: Against advice from his generals Hitler gave orders for the invasion of England to go ahead. The invasion plans were codenamed Operation Sealion.

September 7th: An enormous wave of German bombers attacked the London docks. The people of Surrey now thought the invasion was imminent and church bells were rung throughout the county. The Home Guard was put on stand-by to help repel the raiders.

September 9th: The second evacuation of children began in the wake of continued bombing.

September 15th: The pilots of the RAF were now gaining the upper hand and Kenley and Croydon were playing a vital part in the Battle of Britain. Many enemy aircraft had crashed in the county as the demoralised enemy attempted to scamper back to their bases in France.

September 17th: Operation Sealion was postponed by Hitler.

September 28th: There were many casualties in Croydon as two landmines fell on the town.

December 18th: Hitler ordered his generals to prepare for the invasion of Russia.

From January 1st to 26th, Croydon and Kenley aerodromes were icebound and deep snow-drifts covered most of Surrey. The photograph shows a Blenheim of 92 Squadron warming up its engines while the snow-clearing gangs work on. On January 28th, after another heavy snowfall during the previous night, a party of officers set off for Box Hill with their toboggans. There was just one problem — no snow at Box Hill!

Just an exercise but ARP was ready for the real invaders

CROYDON Auxiliary Fire Service, regular and reserve police, wardens and stretcher party units followed by demolition squads, drilled into action on February 18th to deal with "5,000 casualties" and "fires that stretched from Shirley to South Norwood".

This was an exercise to see how the services in the Croydon Borough would respond in the event of a severe raid and similar tests were held in towns all over Surrey. Dummy figures were dropped in Guildford, every type of damage possible was simulated in Sutton and dummy bombs were dropped on Farnham. Dorking was able to show off its new auxiliary fire tender — a Rolls Royce loaned to the Fire Brigade Committee by Mr B.T. Pearce of Abinger.

Those taking part in the exercise were served with steaming cups of tea, currant buns and rousing speeches by chief wardens who all said there was more to ARP than throwing darts, smoking cigarettes and shouting at people who infringed the black-out.

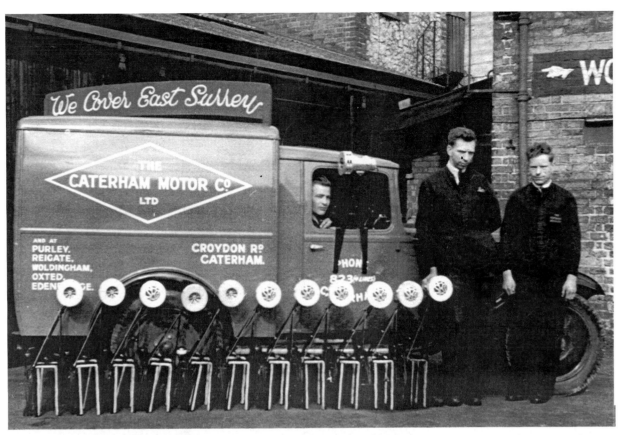

Drivers employed by the Caterham Motor Company prepare to deliver air raid sirens to posts in the locality.

The Marley Tile arch shelter could accommodate up to six people — but not in comfort.

First Surrey fatalities were in Croydon

THE first civilian wartime fatalities in Surrey occurred in Foresters Drive, Croydon on the night of Sunday February 25th, 1940, when a Blenheim taking off from Croydon aerodrome crashed into the rear garden of No 45, killing Mrs Doris Bridge and her daughter.

It was one of many, almost inevitable, aviation accidents that were to become commonplace during those early months of 1940 as the pilots attempted to come to terms with navigational aids for flying at night.

The black-out didn't help and imposed more terrifying hazards. One night alone at Croydon, four accidents involving Hurricanes took place. Two collided with each other while taxi-ing to the take-off point while another taxied into a searchlight position. A fourth, having become airborne suffered engine failure and crashed into the grounds of Purley Hospital.

Holland, Belgium, France invaded: England next

THE phoney war ended abruptly in April, the month in which Chamberlain declared that "Hitler had missed the bus". By April the Führer had occupied Denmark and invaded Norway. In a debate in the House of Commons, MP Leo Amery said to Chamberlain: "In the name of God, go". The Prime Minister resigned and was succeeded by Churchill who went to bed in the small hours of April 11th "conscious of a profound sense of relief". "At last", he wrote later, "I had the authority to give directions over the whole scene. I felt as if I were walking with destiny."

On the day of Churchill's appointment, Germany attacked Holland and Belgium and their advance was awesome. On May 13th they crossed the Ijssel and Maas, outflanked the Dutch fortification line, pressed down through the Ardennes and occupied Liege. Rotterdam was devastated, the Queen of Holland with her family fled to England and the Dutch surrendered on May 15th. Neither the Belgians nor the French were able to stop the sweep of the German armoured forces. They captured Amiens and Antwerp, defeated the 9th French army and took Arras.

By May 21st they had reached Boulogne and were surrounding the Belgian army, the French forces and most of the BEF. Churchill and his Coalition Government knew that France would soon fall and then only the Channel waters would divide the enemy from an imminent invasion of Britain.

All signposts in southern England were removed or painted out. The expected wave of German paratroopers were not to know where they had landed.

The phoney war was now well and truly over. Every day wireless sets in Surrey homes crackled with the tragic news from the Continent where thousands of local men were serving. Events moved rapidly and reports were confusing. The Whitsun holiday came and went, almost without anyone noticing. Wardens throughout the county distributed new instructions for invasion precautions. Car owners were ordered to immobilise cars at night. Town halls and all wardens' posts and depots were staffed day and night. By now the road signs were down and carefully stored away.

Certain now that Hitler was about to invade, road blocks were hurriedly constructed on all main roads and many side roads in the country. Bridges were mined and all kinds of obstacles — steam rollers, water carts, concrete posts and barbed wire — were placed in the way of the advancing army. At Oxted old motor cars were lined up on what looked like an ideal landing strip. The Luftwaffe was not going to land here!

LDF recruits in Croydon, wearing their armbands, march in an orderly fashion from the recruiting office. These were men over the age of 40 and they were getting ready for the invaders.

Thousands join the great civilian army

IN their retreat towards the coast, the British Expeditionary Forces had abandoned most of their heavy equipment in France. The majority of the forces were in the Middle East, Gibraltar, Malta, Singapore, India and Burma. In Britain there was a desperate shortage of fully trained men and the country was now alone, facing the enemy.

It was on May 14th that Churchill's new War Secretary, Anthony Eden spoke about the threat of German parachutists. He then gave his clarion call for men "not presently engaged in military service between the ages of 17 and 65 to come forward and offer their services".

Before he had finished his broadcast, the first volunteers were arriving at local police stations in Surrey. One village bobby saw what looked like an angry mob descending on his station from the direction of the local pub and they appeared to be armed. He was relieved to find that they were signing on.

Within 24 hours, 800 men had registered for service in Reigate and Redhill and 48 hours after Eden's broadcast they were running observation posts. Dorking responded with more than 500 volunteers of which 234 veterans of the Great War were recruited for immediate

duties. The hardy men of Croydon rallied to the call in a remarkable way. Hundreds poured into the appointed stations and within days Major Norman Gillett, a retired officer of the Royal Tank Corps was organising his Croydon army into sub zones, which included Purley, Addington, Coulsdon and Warlingham.

Throughout the county the officers in charge worked day and night in surveying their areas, marking out sectors, fixing observation posts, rendezvous and patrol areas and pursuing new applications. Each group was promised 50 rifles and the authority to recruit three men per rifle.

The new army was known as the Local Defence Force, rechristened "Parashots" in some rural areas of Surrey. Uniforms were scarce but good use was made of anything available. The men carried a great array of weaponry — aged rifles, shotguns, cutlasses and broomsticks converted into pikes. It was the first citizen's army since Napoleon had threatened invasion in 1803.

By July, when the LDF had democratically elected its officers, Winston Churchill referred to them in a speech as the Home Guard. This was to become their new and lasting name.

Norwegian sailors join the Egham Home Guard

FOLLOWING the German occupation of Norway, radio messages were sent from England to Norwegian ships at sea telling them to sail immediately to England. This led to the creation of the Norwegian Shipping and Trade Mission which occupied a large house, Shrubs Hill Place on the main road at Sunningdale. On arrival, the Norwegian sailors expressed a wish to join the Home Guard which, as friendly aliens, they were entitled to do. A platoon was formed attached to B Company of the 10th Surrey Battalion stationed at Egham and granted the special privilege of wearing the Norwegian flag below the flash on their uniform. The platoon strength grew to 50 and, on one occasion, one of them piloted the Royal Navy on the raid of the Lofoten Islands. In June they were visited by the King who saw them practising with dummy hand grenades across the bunkers at Wentworth.

The men and boys of Epsom Home Guard take a break during an exercise on Epsom Down Racecourse.

Dad's Army, or perhaps Grandad's Army at Ranmore, Dorking in 1940.

The men of Chaldon who answered Anthony Eden's clarion call.

The men of Chertsey answered the call to defend their home area against Hitler's attackers — and here they are — members of Chertsey Company 6th Battalion East Surrey Home Guard outside the Drill Hall which had been built in 1902. Among them is Ray Lowther, subsequently a long-serving Chertsey councillor (fourth from left in front row) who recalled: "Everyone was extremely enthusiastic. We mounted guard at the Drill Hall, St Peter's Church Tower, the telephone exchange in Guildford Street, the waterworks and at Woburn Hill not far from the anti-aircraft battery." In addition there was a bicycle patrol through Chertsey, Thorpe and Lyne — the Home Guardsmen determined to give Hitler's Panzer Division a torrid time!

Among the troops stranded on the beach at Dunkirk were the 1st and 1/6th Battalion of the East Surreys. One by one they were picked up by small boats on June 1st and then taken home through the dangerous Channel waters to waiting trains. The volunteers who crewed the Little Ships played a big part in saving the men, and Britain.

On the retreat in France and Belgium

THREE battalions of the East Surrey Regiment were among the troops of the British Expeditionary Force in France and Belgium who found themselves hopelessly placed and greatly outnumbered as Hitler's blitzkrieg, having overwhelmed Denmark, rolled into the Low Countries and then outflanked the Maginot Line in which the French had taken so much misplaced pride.

As ground forces, 200,000 strong — backed by heavy panzers and Stuka dive bombers — crushed Holland and Luxembourg, the British Government ordered the immediate evacuation of as many men as possible. In a plan codenamed *Operation Dynamo* and led by Vice-Admiral Bertram Ramsay from his headquarters deep within the white cliffs of Dover it was hoped that 30,000 men a day could be taken from the ports of Boulogne, Calais and Dunkirk.

As the Germans advanced, the 1st and the 1/6th Battalions of the East Surreys who had been fighting in Brussels were ordered to retreat to the beaches. They had no choice but to go to Dunkirk for Boulogne had been captured on May 25th and the following day Calais fell. As the Surreys left the Belgian capital — the last troops to do so — they found the roads thronged with thousands of refugees who were hoping to join the vast queues that now snaked across the Dunkirk beaches to the moles.

The third Battalion of the East Surreys were facing different problems. As part of a small mobile force they had been ordered to Boulogne to help defend the port but could not get through and became involved with other units in the heavy fighting around Abbeville. The odds against them were enormous; as a junior Territorial battalion the men had no 3 inch mortars, carriers, grenades or revolvers and carried only 500 rounds of .303 for its 20 Bren guns.

As one company of the Battalion was overrun by the German 5th Armoured Division, Major-General Victor Fortune, serving under French orders, was obliged to surrender at the small Channel port of St Valery-en-Caux. One complete British army Division and its attached units which included the 2/6th Surreys were marched into captivity, its men destined to spend the rest of the war in PoW camps.

One Surrey soldier on the road to Dunkirk with the other Battalions was Private Hersey who had met and married a French girl at Tourcoing before the advance into Belgium. As his Company was retreating through Roncq the girl found her husband and begged to be allowed to return with him to England. It was definitely not allowed but the officer in command of the company gave her a battledress and took her back to Dunkirk in his truck. She joined the men on the beaches who were under constant attack and waited for the rescue.

OPERATION DYNAMO: MAY 26TH - JUNE 3RD

Special welcome in Redhill for the heroes of Dunkirk

ON Sunday morning May 24th, people in the Dorking area saw what looked like a white figure over the Ranmore Hills slowly descending from the sky. The cry went up that a German invasion had begun, calls were made to the local police stations to that effect and LDF units were alerted. All was well. The "figure" was a vagrant barrage balloon which had been riddled with bullets by an anxious gunner at Leatherhead and deflated. It floated harmlessly to earth near Polesden Lacey; one of many scares during those anxious days. On May 26th churches throughout Surrey were packed for a day of National Prayer. It was a dark time in British history.

At Dover and Southampton 15 passenger ferries and a force of destroyers, corvettes, minesweepers and naval trawlers were assembling for a desperate bid to embark as many troops as they could from the quays of Dunkirk where the BEF was under constant attack. Vice-Admiral Ramsay believed he had two days before the Germans overran the beacheads. In that time he had to keep the channel clear of mines, bombard the German batteries at Calais, drive off U-Boats and hope the RAF could hold back the Luftwaffe.

Ramsay's aim was to rescue at least 45,000 troops but what he achieved was much, much more. Against a lurid backcloth of a burning town and under relentless attack, a staggering 338,226 British and Allied troops were plucked from the beaches of Dunkirk and taken to England. And the county of Surrey played a major part in what Churchill later described as "a miracle of deliverance".

The military manoeuvre, unprecedented in history, took seven days to complete. Eventually 222 naval vessels and 800 civilian craft joined the operation. Six destroyers and 243 ships were sunk and the killed, missing or wounded numbered 68,000.

The Little Ships sailed at 2200 hours on May 29th. Among them were lifeboats, fishing smacks, dredgers, drifters and trawlers. A mudhopper joined the party and so did a paddle steamer. Tugs came from the London Docks and cockleboats from Leigh-on-Sea.

There were many heroic acts during the seven days but none greater than that achieved by the crew of a small pleasure boat which in peacetime had plied the Thames between Hampton Court and Richmond. *The Tigress* made four trips to the beaches and took off nearly 800 British and French soldiers. The skipper was Henry Hastings, a 27-year-old married lighterman from The Gloucester Arms, Kingston and his crew consisted of just two others, Warren Hastings and Bill Clarke.

Henry told the *Surrey Comet* that when they first arrived hundreds of troops were waiting on the beaches being shelled and bombed mercilessly all the time. "I got the boat as near to the shore as possible and it quickly filled up, some clinging on to the sides. On one occasion a bomb dropped very close and I was thrown overboard but we managed to push off and take the troops to a naval ship lying out to sea. We were going back for a fifth load when a bomb dropped astern and blew in some of the planks. We had to abandon *The Tigress* about a mile from shore and jump in the sea. We were picked up by another small boat."

The skipper said he and his crew reached Kingston on Saturday morning June 1st. "I had never taken *The Tigress* further than Tilbury before", he told the *Comet*. The pleasure steamer, the *Medway Queen* was another Little Ship with a Surrey man in charge. Lieut Commander A.T. Cook of Avon Close, Worcester Park, who had retired from the Merchant Navy in 1935, made eight trips in seven days, picking up 800 troops, many of them floundering in the water.

The destroyers, ferries and minesweepers with their accompanying flotilla restored to Britain four fifths of the British army and more than 100,000 French and Belgian soldiers. They made several journeys to the Kent ports where they berthed and unloaded the troops. The men, hungry and exhausted, many still soaking wet after walking or swimming in the sea, were given food and clothing. Trains were waiting at the Kent stations to take the men away and then return for more.

Southern Railway played a major part in Operation Dynamo. A total of 620 special trains, pulling 7,000 coaches, moved 319,056 troops. The first train left the Kent coast at 4 am on May 27th and the last at 4 pm on June 4th. And along the routes out of "Hellfire Corner" (East Kent) there were welcome food stops.

Redhill station was at the heart of this gigantic movement of soldiers. More than 80 per cent of the engines which left Kent for various destinations called at Redhill to be coaled and watered. Labourers were imported from around the county and more than 300 tons of ashes accumulated at the station during those nine hectic days. Some trains were cleared in just four minutes and one changed engines and set off again in two minutes 30 seconds.

Other wounded soldiers were taken to Botley's Hospital, Ottershaw and every Thursday afternoon for several weeks some of them would be collected by Joan Jacottet and her sisters and given tea at their parents' home at Addlestone Park Road. Photograph shows them at "beer time" accompanied by "Baba and Joan Jacottet". With such care and kindness they recovered quickly from their injuries.

continued from page 35

Bernard Darwin in *War on the Line* wrote: "Never had England seen such scenes as were witnessed at Redhill station. As the troop trains came from the Tonbridge lines, crossed over the down main metals and drew up on the platform, greatcoats and tunics were hanging from the carriage doors to dry from the soaking they had received on the Dunkirk shores. The carriages were packed with men and regiments were intermingled. Many were tired, some bandaged but they all cheered."

The soldiers had not eaten for days and were delighted to see the WVS and members of Redhill and Reigate Rotary Clubs serving sandwiches, cakes and fruit. People living near the station clambered down the embankment to hand postcards and pencils to the men so they could send messages to their loved ones. To many Surrey people those trainloads of courageous men, snatched from the hell of Dunkirk, vividly brought home the realities of war.

Many soldiers threw slips of paper out of the carriage windows which contained their name and address. With it was a note asking for their next of kin to be informed of their safety. On one of the trains was Don Hall, Surveyor Class 2 Royal Artillery who had waited on the beach at Dunkirk for four days with just a tin of cherries to eat. He was eventually rescued and slept soundly until his ship was shelled. He was rescued again, eventually reached England and was put on a train. Don actually travelled through his own home station of Nutfield and, at Redhill, he passed a note to a station worker. Less than an hour later his mum was woken up and told that her son was alive, weary and on his way to Wales.

The Station Master at Redhill, Mr P. Harrow estimated that a quarter of a million troops passed through his station. There had been little pre-arranged planning; it was a triumph of improvisation and, as Churchill put it, a miracle of deliverance.

Many of the sick and wounded men were taken off the trains at Redhill and transferred to hospitals in Surrey.

Among them were 78 casualties who were taken to the Blind School Hospital at Leatherhead. and the town's Cottage Hospital in Poplar Road.

Soldiers, shaken by the army's defeat, feared a hostile reception back in England. That was not the case. In Surrey, as elsewhere, the Dunkirk evacuees were given an overwhelming welcome. At Merton, accompanied by wives and girlfriends, they enjoyed a tea party given by Cllr Baker, chairman of Merton and Morden.

Soldiers of the Royal Corps of Signals, airmen and others who arrived home from Dunkirk at Wimbledon station.

Good news and bad news for "Dunkirk family"

WHERE is the RAF? This was the frequent and bitter cry from the troops on the beaches at Dunkirk who knew little at the time of the furious air battles being fought out of their sight. It was a period of intense activity and the resident squadrons at Kenley made an important contribution to the air cover, holding off the Luftwaffe. In fact there were seven squadrons operating from the Kenley sector and for the first time the RAF and the Luftwaffe were meeting on equal terms.

One young airman flying from Croydon was to distinguish himself during the Dunkirk evacuation. Robert Roland Stanford Tuck, a Flight Commander with 92 Squadron, claimed two Messerschmitt 110s and a 109 on May 23rd and two Dornier 17s on May 24th. On May

Bob Stanford Tuck, one of the heroes of Dunkirk.

25th he shared a Dornier 17 and on June 2nd he claimed a Heinkel 111 and a Messerschmitt 109. The following week he earned this tribute from the *Surrey Comet:* *"Rewarding a display of great dash and gallantry the award of the DFC has been made to a young Walton airman, younger son of Mr and Mrs S.L. Tuck of Claremont, Garrick Close, Walton. But while his parents have been experiencing feelings of pride over his exploits they have been anxious about an elder son, Gunner John Gordon Tuck, reported wounded and missing on the road to Dunkirk".*

In seven days, Goering lost 107 aircraft and Fighter Command 106. "there was a victory inside this deliverance", said Churchill. "It was gained by the Royal Air Force."

Apart from the British, French and Belgian soldiers who had been rescued from the beaches there were now many soldiers from the Dominions in Surrey. Here are some of the men of the New Zealand Expeditionary Force (Anzacs) who had arrived in the county to help repel Hitler's invaders. They had their priorities and one of them was a boat trip on the Thames in the sunshine of June 1940.

A clear line of fire on the Epsom Downs

AWARE that France had now fallen, armistice terms had been signed and the invasion of Britain was imminent, the people of Surrey frantically continued to strengthen their defences. Thousands of gun emplacements, pillboxes, scaffolding and concrete blocks were constructed. Barbed wire was everywhere, designed to make landing difficult for the first wave of German paratroopers and glider pilots.

In the small Surrey town of Banstead, for example, there were numerous physical signs of the measures being taken to hold up Hitler's invaders. Pillboxes were built at intervals along the Belmont to Epsom Downs railway line. Tank traps were dug adjacent to the Brighton Road and all the way down the highway heavy steel cables were secured to pylons to prevent roadway landings. Tons and tons of chalk were excavated to create a wall, fanning out over the Downs, to prevent tanks advancing from the south. Slots in which curved steel rails could be inserted were made in the road surface of the bridge over the railway line. Epsom Downs was cleared of undergrowth to give defenders a clear line of fire.

However, Hitler would have stood a good chance of success in those days immediately after Dunkirk despite the determination of the people and their crude defences for the British army had abandoned most of its modern equipment in France and was ill prepared.

Although the Fuhrer was still hoping for peace with England, he had an invasion plan — to clear the sea route of mines, bring in the big guns to protect the coastal front and to put 20 divisions ashore between Ramsgate and Lyme Regis. He saw the invasion as a river crossing on a broad front, and in place of bridging operations, the navy would keep the sea lanes secure against British attacks.

One attack plan involved a landing on the Sussex coast that would then drive northward through the Guildford gap to outflank London. In the way of the would-be attackers was the "GHQ Stopline", a deep anti-tank ditch overlooked by a chain of concrete pillboxes all along the North Downs.

Croydon children who had been evacuated to South Coast towns were "recalled" while the town's authorities considered a plan for the evacuation of the whole civilian population. Even in this crisis, people remained calm and life went on, but it was far from normal. Rationing became more severe, shelters were strengthened and old men and boys rallied to join the various Surrey units of the Home Guard.

Operation Sealion, as the invasion plan was called, was set for September 21st. With France at his feet Hitler, sure of the overwhelming might of the Luftwaffe and incensed by the refusal of Britain to listen "to the voice of reason", gave simple instructions to Hermann Goering. Now knock out the RAF!

Airmen attached to 111 Squadron which arrived at Croydon in June, seen here picnicking in the garden of the first house, next to Croydon Airport, in Foresters Drive, in August 1940, a time of many tragedies for the squadron. Believed to be (left to right) Jimmy Thrush, 'Lofty' Gardner, Charles Cooper and Tony Wilson.

THE BATTLE OF BRITAIN

HISTORIANS have decreed that the Battle of Britain officially began in July, 1940 and ended on October 31st and only the aircrew involved in operations between those dates qualified for a Battle of Britain clasp. It was, without doubt, the greatest air battle in modern history and claimed the lives of many young men from both sides.

The main battleground was in the skies above Kent where the orchards, fields and villages below were strewn with crashed aircraft. But the aerial combats frequently moved into Surrey as the Luftwaffe strove to destroy the aerodromes at Kenley, Croydon and Redhill, the great aircraft factories at Kingston and Weybridge and, just as important, the morale of the people below.

Because of the enormous scale of the battle it is impossible to give a full picture in a book which covers the whole war in Surrey. However, the next few pages contain a diary of the main events during those 16 critical weeks when the existence of the free world hung in the balance. Here are the squadrons, the scrambles, the combats and the casualties as they affected the county; profiles of some of the great aces who flew from Kenley or Croydon; the bombing of the Surrey towns and many tragic yet provocative photographs of the horrors and the heroes, the action and the aftermath.

High above the fields that summer, the RAF aircrew fought with unsurpassed courage and skill. Scores of pilots died in the narrow confines of the cockpit while their fighter dived to the earth below, struggling to release a trapped limb or jammed hood. Many watched the sea close over them, some were burned alive, helpless and alone. To others, death was at the end of a parachute descent — the horror when one didn't open and the eternity of terror in the fall. Some plunged into overhead hazards or buildings and many lingered in hospital before dying of their wounds.

Those who fought in the Battle of Britain included the pilots from the Dominions and the young men from the over-run nations of Europe. It was a national crusade that united the British people in a way that they had never been united before. And it was followed with great anxiety by everyone in the Western world.

Churchill's immortal words were spoken at the conclusion of the battle:

"The gratitude of every home in our island, in our Empire, and indeed throughout the free world, except in the abodes of the guilty, goes out to the British airmen who, undaunted by odds, unwearied in their constant challenge and mortal danger, turned the tide of the world war by their prowess and by their devotion. Never in the field of human conflict was so much owed by so many to so few."

A Spitfire of 616 Squadron, whose pilots flew in to Kenley in August at the height of the Battle of Britain and suffered some terrible tragedies.

RAF SQUADRONS AT CROYDON: MAY '40 TO DEC '40

No 145 Squadron
Sq Ldr J.D. Miller

Arrived 10-10-39. Reformed at Croydon. Bristol Blenheims Mk 1 and Hawker Hurricanes Mk 1. Departed 9-5-40. Code SO.

No 92 Squadron
Sq Ldr Roger Bushell

Arrived 30-12-39 with Bristol Blenheims Mk1 and 1 Miles Magister Converted to Spitfires Mk 1. Departed 8-5-40. Code GR.

No 2 Squadron
Wing Cdr A.J.W.Geddes

Army Co-operation Wing. Arrived 20-5-40 with Westland Lysander Mk1 and 11. Left the following day.

No 607 Squadron (return)
Sq Ldr J.A.Vick

Arrived 22-5-40 with Gladiators Mks 1 and 11. Departed 4-6-40. Code AF.

No 111 Squadron
Sq Ldr J.M.Thompson

Arrived 4-6-40 with Hawker Hurricanes Mk 1. Departed 19-8-40. JU.

No 501 Squadron
Sq Ldr M.V.M.Clube
Sq Ldr Harry Hogan
(from 29-6-40)

Arrived 21-6-40 with Hawker Hurricanes Mk 1. Departed 4-7-40. Code SD.

No 401 Squadron
(No 1 Sqd RCAF)
Sq Ldr E.A.McNabb

This Squadron was training under battle conditions. Arrived 5-7-40 with Hawker Hurricanes Mk 1. Departed 16-8-40. Code YO.

No 85 Squadron
Sq Ldr Peter Townsend

Arrived 19-8-40 with Hawker Hurricanes Mk 1. Departed 3-9-40. Code VY.

No 72 Squadron
Sq Ldr A.R.Collins
Sq Ldr E.Graham
(from 2-9-40)

Arrived 1-9-40. Vickers Supermarine Spitfires Mk 1. Departed 12-9-40. Code RN.

No 111 Squadron (return)
Sq Ldr J.M.Thompson

Arrived 3-9-40. Hawker Hurricanes Mk 1. Departed 8-9-40. Code JU.

No 605 Squadron
Sq Ldr Walter Churchill
Flt Lt Archie McKellar
(from 29-9-40)
3 Flt Lt Chris Currant
(from 1-11-40)
Sq Ldr G.R. Edge
(from 29-11-40)

Arrived 7-9-40 with Hawker Hurricanes Mk 1 and 11. Departed 25-2-41. Code UP.

Note: With the departure of 111 Squadron on 8-9-40, 605 Squadron was in sole possession of Croydon until the end of the Battle of Britain.

BATTLE ORDERS FOR KENLEY FROM MAY '40

No 64 Squadron
CO Sq Ldr Aeneas MacDonnell

Arrived on 16-5-40 from Usworth with Supermarine Spitfires Mk 1. Departed 19-8-40. Code SH.

No 615 Squadron
Sq Ldr Joe Kayll

County of Surrey Auxiliary Squadron. Arrived 20-5-40 from Belgium with Hawker Hurricanes Mk 1 Departed 30-8-40. Code KW.

No 616 Squadron
Sq Ldr Marcus Robinson

Arrived 19-8-40 from Leconfield. Supermarine Spitfires. Departed 3-9-40. Code QJ.

No 253 Squadron
Sq Ldr Harold Starr
& Sq Ldr Tom Gleave

Arrived 30-8-40 from Prestwick with Hawker Hurricanes. Departed for Leconfield 3-1-41. Code SW.

No 66 Squadron
Sq Ldr Rupert Leigh

Arrived 3-9-40 from Coltishall with Supermarine Spitfires. Departed 11-9-40. Code LZ.

No 501 Squadron
Sq Ldr Harry Hogan

Arrived from Gravesend 10-9-40. Hawker Hurricanes. Departed 17-12-40. Code SD.

King George VI at Kenley in the summer of 1940.

Desperate days — A battle diary for Surrey

IN the blue skies of this splendid English summer, the greatest air battle in history was fought — for those whom Churchill called 'The Few' were attempting to thwart Hitler's preparation for an invasion of Britain.

This diary begins on Wednesday July 10th, the date chosen by historians as the first official day of the battle, and continues to October 31st. It tells briefly of the dramatic days with more detailed accounts of the bigger raids.

Based at Croydon was 111 Squadron, whose pilots had already been heavily engaged in patrols and air battles over the evacuation ports of France and Belgium. Alongside them was No 1 Royal Canadian Air Force Squadron — non-operational while modifications were carried out on their Hurricanes.

At Kenley the aircraft of Nos 64 and 615 Squadrons had also returned from France and a flight from 229 Squadron had arrived to form a Squadron with 253. It was on July 12th that Winston Churchill inspected 615 (County of Surrey) Squadron at Kenley.

During the next hectic 15 weeks the pilots from the Kenley and Croydon Squadrons played their part in this great aerial battle. There were many losses, of both men and machines. As the Luftwaffe mounted attack after attack and the resources of Fighter Command were stretched to the limit, the exhausted squadrons were withdrawn and others came to take their place.

By September. the constant strain and relentless attrition suffered by the pilots together with a series of devastating attacks on the two airfields heralded the beginning of the end. The capacity to resist much longer was wearing thin.

Wednesday July 10th: (1300 hours) Flying Officer Tom Higgs was the first Croydon-based pilot to lose his life in the Battle of Britain. The Hurricanes of 111 Squadron, Croydon were scrambled to protect shipping in the Channel off Folkestone and Higgs collided with a Dornier 17 at 6,000 feet. He baled out but died in the Channel and his body was washed ashore at Noordwijk just over a month later. The Dornier crashed near Dungeness. In the same combat, Hurricanes flown by Flying Officer Henry Ferriss, Sergeant Ralph Carnall and Fly-

Squadron Leader Joe Kayll of 615 Squadron, already credited with nine enemy aircraft destroyed, received a well-earned double when the King visited Kenley on June 28th — the DFC and the DSO.

ing Officer Basil Fisher were also damaged.

Friday July 12th: Sergeant Sydney Ireland suffered the cruel fate of being the first pilot to be killed in Surrey. Ireland of 610 Squadron, Biggin Hill lost control in a dive through cloud during dogfight practice and crashed at Titsey Park, near Westerham. His Spitfire was a write-off.

Saturday July 13th: The pilots of 610 Squadron, stunned by the death of Sydney Ireland, lost another colleague — this time during routine patrol. The Spitfire flown by Sergeant Patrick Watson-Parker crashed at Skid House, Tatsfield. He was buried in the nearby churchyard of Cudham in Kent.

Sunday July 14th: 615 Squadron, Kenley was scrambled to protect a convoy off Dover in the

early afternoon. Yellow Section (Flying Officers Gayner and Collard and Pilot Officer Hugo) shot down a Junkers 88 killing two crew. In the same combat Pilot Officer Michael Mudie baled out of his blazing Hurricane, badly wounded. He was rescued from the sea by the Navy but died in Dover Hospital the following day. Mudie. 24, is buried in Esher Cemetery, East Moseley.

Wednesday July 17th: In a surprise solo attack over the Channel, Flying Officer Donald Taylor of 64 Squadron, Kenley was shot down and taken, badly wounded, to Eastbourne Hospital. His Spitfire was damaged but repairable.

Wednesday July 24th: Water mains and 10 houses damaged at Walton-on-Thames as Dorniers attack aircraft factories and other key points near Weybridge. No serious casualties.

August 10th was the day nominated by Hitler as Adlertag, "Eagle Day" which was to be the commencement of the annihilation of the RAF. Because of bad weather it was postponed until August 13th when the Luftwaffe began to appear in great force and attack the fighter stations, including Croydon and Kenley.

Thursday July 25th: Fierce fighting took place in the early afternoon over a west-bound convoy which entered the Dover Straits around midday — and 64 Squadron from Kenley was right in the thick of the action. Stuka dive-bombers, operating with strong fighter cover, demonstrated the vulnerability of large naval targets. Flying Officer Alistair Jeffrey was one who failed to return to Kenley when his Spitfire crashed in the sea. A second Spitfire pilot was lost minutes later. Sub Lieutenant Francis Paul had been 'loaned' to the RAF by the Fleet Air Arm. He joined 64 Squadron on July 1st and in 25 days of hectic action shot down nine enemy aircraft. At 5.45pm on the 25th, Paul was shot down in the Channel. He was picked up by a German U-Boat but died in captivity nine days later.

Monday August 5th: Six pilots from 64 Squadron, Kenley, despatched for a dawn patrol over the Kent coast, were jumped by Messerschmitt 109s who appeared unannounced out of the early morning mist. Cannon shells ripped into the fuselage of the Spitfire flown by American-born Pilot Officer Arthur Donahue but he managed to land at Hawkinge with his aircraft seriously damaged. Sergeant Lewis Isaac was not so lucky. His Spitfire was sent plunging into the Channel and the 24-year-old Welshman was never seen again.

Thursday August 8th: Another tragic day for 64 Squadron, again on patrol over the Channel. Peter Kennard-Davis who joined the Squadron on August 3rd found himself in fierce combat with 109s. His aircraft caught fire and Kennard-Davis baled out, seriously wounded. He was taken to the Royal Victoria Hospital, East Grinstead and died there two days later. Kennard-Davis was just 19. He is buried in Brookwood Cemetery. Another victim of this surprise attack was Sergeant John Squier who made a forced-landing and was also severely burned. He, too, went to Queen Victoria Hospital, survived his injuries and became one of the Guinea Pig Club.

Sergeant Lewis Isaac, 24, of 64 Squadron left Kenley on August 5th for a dawn patrol over the Kent coast and never returned. His Spitfire was sent hurtling into the Channel.

Sergeant Robert Sim of 111 Squadron, heavily engaged against overwhelming odds on August 11th, became separated from his unit and was shot down in the sea. No trace of him was ever found.

Tragic day for 111: four pilots killed

AS a precursor to Adlertag — **Sunday August 11th** saw the hardest fighting so far. For 111 Squadron it was a day of one tragedy after another.

On that morning two 20-year-old sergeant pilots, bursting with enthusiasm, drove into Croydon from their operational training unit with a minimum of experience on Hurricanes. Squadron Leader John Thompson welcomed them to the unit and explained he had no time to give them the simulated battle experience they would have expected. As the Squadron was likely to be scrambled later that morning he had no alternative but to commit them to action. A few hours later one was dead and the other in hospital wounded, shocked into such a state of amnesia that he could not remember his own name.

The improvement in the weather had given the Luftwaffe an opportunity to attack the naval installations at Weymouth and Portland, the balloon barrage at Dover and the Chain Home RDF stations at Dunkirk (Kent), Dover, Rye and Pevensey. It was the latter raid that occupied the attention of 111 Squadron.

Scrambled soon after lunch the Hurricanes, using their well-trusted, extremely courageous combat tactics of a head-on attack with the whole of the formation flying in line abreast, met the Dornier-escorted Messerschmitt 109s over Margate. During a hectic dogfight against overwhelming odds 27-year-old Pilot Officer Jack Copeman was shot down and killed at 2.20 pm. His aircraft crashed into the Channel. Pilot Officer John McKenzie followed, just seconds later. His Hurricane crashed into the sea and McKenzie, just 20, was reported "missing".

As the drama continued one of the young sergeants, Harry Newton found himself in the thick of the fray and fast running out of fuel. With the last drop gone Newton crash-landed on the marshes at Boyton, near Martlesham Heath, Suffolk and scrambled out of the wreckage with severe concussion. His Hurricane was a write-off.

The build up of cloud failed to help the beleaguered pilots of 111 Squadron and, in these conditions, the second sergeant pilot Robert Sim found himself separated from his unit and facing a gaggle of enemy fighters. Sim lost the battle and his life. He was shot down in the sea and no trace of him or his aircraft was ever found.

In just a few minutes three pilots had been killed and four Hurricanes lost. The remainder of the exhausted squadron limped back to Croydon to report the crippling losses, knowing their capacity to resist much longer was wearing thin. The effective strength of 111 Squadron was down to nine experienced pilots. For them and many others in Fighter Command, this was the beginning of the end. Surely it was just a matter of days.

Back at base there was more bad news. Canadian Pilot Officer Roy Wilson, another 20-year-old, had also failed to return. No-one knew of his fate and it was presumed that he, like his colleagues, had gone into "the drink".

Despite the advantage in numbers it was a bad day also for the Luftwaffe with 37 aircraft and many pilots lost.

The high summer of 1940 was perfect and, in August particularly, England basked in warm sunshine which often turned to haze as the evening approached. And so it was on Thursday August 15th when the Luftwaffe launched its greatest assault of the whole battle. Under cloudless blue skies more than 500 enemy bombers escorted by 1,256 fighters set off from France to attack British airfields in five massive assaults. All day long the skies above Kent and Surrey were flecked with vapour trails left behind by the wheeling snarling fray. As the evening sunshine turned to haze the foe returned for a final assault — and this time Kenley was on the menu. The low-flying bandits completely foiled the complex defence system for there was no warning of their approach and no sirens to send people scurrying to the shelters until the bombs actually started falling. Here, a group of men in Croydon, eyes straining for a clearer view, saw the Germans on their way.

The aftermath of the raid on Croydon. As the All-Clear sounded scores of young people pedalled furiously to the scene of the drama.

Monday August 12th: With the launch of Adlertag now scheduled for the following day, the Luftwaffe attacked the coastal RDF stations while continuing to bomb shipping and harbours. 111 Squadron, still licking their wounds, had a welcome day off but a constant reminder of the previous day's battle was there for all to see. Parked on the apron at Croydon was an old car with unpacked baggage still inside. It belonged to two young sergeants. Kenley's 64 Squadron were in action losing one Spitfire when Pilot Officer Arthur Donahue was shot down over Sellindge, Kent. He was taken to hospital badly burned. Flight Lieutenant Lawrence Henstock was also pounced on by 109s but his damaged Spitfire landed safely at Hawkinge. There was drama in Godstone where a Junkers 88 crashed killing one of its crew. Three baled out and were captured.

Tuesday August 13th: 111 Squadron returned to the fray soon after dawn to deal with Dorniers assigned to bomb Sheerness and Eastchurch airfield. To the surprise of all, the raiders arrived without escort and quickly fell foul of Thompson and his avengers. The Squadron Leader dealt with one Dornier which force-landed at Stodmarsh and the crew were captured. Pilot Officer James Walker and Flight Lieutenant Henry Ferris claimed two more Dorniers. On this day the Luftwaffe lost 44 aircraft on operations and 36 returned to their bases with serious battle damage. There were no pilot losses for 111 Squadron but three Hurricanes were in need of repair.

German fighters hit wrong target in the summer haze

AS evening fell on that memorable summer day — August 15th, 1940 — 23 aircraft of the precision attack specialists, Erprobungsgruppe 210, crossed the Kent coast near Dungeness and headed for the Surrey border where they swung north. The target was Kenley and the objective was a fast, strafing run in which they would release their bombs and then head for home hopefully before Fighter Command knew what was happening.

It all went terribly wrong. In the summer evening haze the 23 Messerschmitt 109s and 110s failed to find their target and instead delivered a devastating attack on a group of buildings at Croydon Airfield. They were then so heavily engaged by British fighters that the Gruppe lost seven aircraft including its charismatic Kommandeur, Hauptmann Walter Rubensdorffer.

For the Luftwaffe, it was a terrible

price to pay for a navigational error and, for the people of Croydon, it was a tragedy; sixty two were killed, 37 seriously injured and 137 hurt. The Redwing Aircraft factory and the NSF (formerly Nuremburg Schraube Fabrik, by then British NSF) were destroyed and, in the latter, every member of the management team was killed. Other buildings around the airfield were transformed into gaping black skeletons of twisted girders. Bombs fell in Crowley Crescent and Coldharbour Way with fatal casualties and in Foss Avenue and Waddon Way.

Other bombs fell on a Hurricane repair plant, the armoury, hangars and the south wing of the famous terminal building. Next to the airfield The Purley Way was strewn with lumps of chalk and plaster and fragments of glass. Passengers in a bus, travelling down the Purley Way. were uninjured but they had a terrifying

continued overleaf

62 die in devastating raid on Croydon

continued from page 45

front-line view of the attack as did a few soldiers in the streets.

The aircraft had exploded out of the haze at 6.29 pm with machine guns blazing. From what appeared to be a thousand feet the leading aircraft dropped their bombs followed, in rapid succession, by the others. As the airfield defences went into action, the bus passengers and the soldiers saw the most welcome sight of all — nine Hurricanes of 111 Squadron, diving down from 10,000 feet led by their CO, Squadron Leader Tommy Thompson. There followed one of the greatest running skirmishes of the Battle of Britain.

Thompson gained his Squadron's first success. Attacking a 110 in a near-vertical climb he blew large chunks from the port engine and wing and watched as the plane, wheels up, made a brilliant skidding landing in a nearby field, the crew uninjured.

111 Squadron were heavily outnumbered but reinforcements arrived in the shape of 32 Squadron from Biggin Hill forcing Erpro 210 into defensive circles from which individual aircraft could break free as cloud cover allowed. The 109s were the first to make a dash and

all but one of them got away, the unfortunate exception crashing in flames at Lightlands Farm, Frant, Sussex at 7.10 pm. The pilot baled out and was captured unhurt.

For the slower 110s, time and fuel were running out. One of them attempted to escape from the circle and was immediately chased by Thompson across the undulating farmland of Surrey and Sussex. Turning and twisting only feet above the ground the Swiss-born German pilot could not shake off his attacker and, close to Rotherfield, the Messerschmitt 110 fell to earth and exploded. Both pilot and gunner were killed.

Five more aircraft of Erpro 210 fell that day — all to the pilots of 111 and 32 Squadrons. One burned out at Redhill aerodrome and another at School Farm, Hooe. A third, chased by Flight Lieutenant Stanley Connors and Sergeant T.Y. Wallace of 111 Squadron crashed at Broadbridge Farm, Smallfield, Horley and a fourth was shot down by Squadron Leader John Worrall and Flight Lieutenant Mike Crossley of 32 Squadron at Ightham. The fifth force-landed at Hawkhurst and the crew were captured.

The raid on Croydon had lasted less than 10 minutes and the air raid siren did

not sound until after the bombs had dropped and the great chase across the rooftops was underway. By that time dense smoke from the blazing armoury filled the sky and the first aid teams were rushing to the airfield. Within minutes the casualty service, the fire brigade, the police and the Home Guard were at work and stretcher parties were quickly organised. Before those who were trapped could be released tons of debris had to be removed. There was also a danger from falling iron or brickwork and, until the police cordoned off some of the roads and diverted traffic, there were crowds of sight-seers who got in the way of the rescue operation.

Shelter had to be found for 180 people. The rescuers worked through the long evening and into the night while the canteens of the Salvation Army and YMCA stood by. The search for bodies did not cease until the evening of Saturday August 17th.

So ended Eagle Day or 'Black Thursday'. In all the Luftwaffe lost 75 bombers and fighters on operations and another 15 returned to base damaged.

For the RAF and Anti-Aircraft Command it was their biggest haul of the Battle of Britain. Dowding lost 30 fighters and 13 pilots.

Mr. J. Coster (left, bandaged), a factory manager, was among those injured in the raid of August 15th.

A dramatic scene at Croydon after the raid on August 15th. Children view an Anderson shelter which saved five lives.

The Aerodrome Hotel, Croydon before the war.

Gunners on the roof saw the bombs fall around them

MR Walter Martin lived in Old Coulsdon in 1940 and, after a period as stretcher party leader with the ARP, he volunteered for the Royal Artillery, trained at Walton-on-Thames and was sent on active service to Croydon Airport with 148 Battery. Here, he and his colleagues were stationed on the roof of the Aerodrome Hotel and given a 40mm Bofors. They also acquired eight Lewis machine guns. Walter was on duty on the afternoon of Thursday August 15th. This is his story:

"We were in the mess room at Croydon when the tannoy yelled 'one, one, one', come to readiness, followed by 'Scramble'. By the time I reached my station only one plane was left on the field. I heard a whistling noise, just as I had heard in the Talkies and my immediate feeling was disbelief. A moment later I was convinced. Everything shook as the bomb exploded on Purley Way, on the footpath in front of a public surface shelter. While the debris was still shooting skywards there was a second whistling and a bomb was aimed right at the back of my neck. It fell against the hotel wall beneath us.

"The whistling and exploding continued in rapid order, and all seemed very close indeed. Any moment the next one would exterminate us, seeing that we were sitting on top of the target. Ready to shoot, we looked up and saw two white twin-engined planes, one of which was diving directly towards us. At that moment the huge cloud of dust and smoke drifted over. We were in a dense fog and could not see a thing. We craned our necks and swung the gun around looking for a chance to shoot but the chance never came. It was bad, standing there, waiting to be blown to pieces and not being able to hit back. We diso-

beyed orders and fired blind.

"Silence descended and the smoke began to clear. It was all over. There was a strong smell of cordite and the roof of the hotel was covered with earth and debris. We had suffered no casualties but we were very shaken. As we remained poised, waiting for the return of the raiders, the air raid warning sounded. So we had every right to expect another blasting. We didn't have one. The 'all clear' sounded some minutes later but it was a long time before we were allowed to 'stand down'.

"Some members of our troop had a narrow escape. A bomb had come down between two gun pits, broken through the concrete roof, gone down to the basement and set off ammunition which exploded like firecrackers. Five airmen had been killed. "Rollasons aircraft repair works was blazing and I could feel the heat on my face. Most of the damage seemed to be among the works and hangars. A red bus stood askew in Purley Way and looked as if it had been thrown aside by the force of the explosion

"The following day we were taken off the roofs of the hotel and placed in the playing field on the other side of Purley Way. Our eight Lewis guns were put onto quadruple mountings so we now had two gunsites to a man. Large sections of concrete sewer piping had been placed all over the field to prevent Junkers landing and disgorging well-armed and highly trained troops ahead of advancing armies.

"I began to dig a slit trench at the corner of the fence. By Sunday (and the attack on Kenley) it was still not deep enough to get into"

A machine gun emplacement manned by members of 615 Squadron at Croydon.. This picture was actually taken in 1939.

The twisted, almost unrecognisable remains of the Messerschmitt 110 which was scattered across Redhill aerodrome, south of Croydon. It was shot down by Sgt Dymond of 111 Squadron and Sgt Pearce of 32 Squadron.

Reigate watched the aerial battle

REIGATE received its baptism of fire on the evening of August 15th when 125 bombs fell in the borough causing injury only to three cyclists who were thrown from their machines by the blast of the explosion. In describing this incident the *Surrey Mirror* said: "Great was the excitement as three enemy aircraft were seen to come hurtling earthwards not far from Redhill, an excitement that reached its topmost pitch when a German Dornier fell with a British fighter on its tail.

"Three of the crew provided the excited onlookers with their first demonstration of bailing out, the British airman doing the Victory Roll at his triumph."

The spectators from Redhill and Reigate were watching the aerial activity that accompanied the raid on Croydon. Because of the censorship that existed at the time they were unaware that the airfield had been so badly damaged. The Reigate bombing left 18 craters and many houses damaged, including Salfords School which fared the worst.

One of the three hangars at Kenley, destroyed in the raid of August 18th, 1940. Cars and aircraft were lost.

Luftwaffe war correspondent, Rolf von Pebal, aboard one of the Dorniers, took this dramatic picture en route to RAF Kenley at lunchtime on Sunday August 18th. This shot shows how low they were as they roared over the rooftops of Burgess Hill, Sussex. The spinner cone of the port propeller can be seen on the left.

Kenley pounded by low-level Dorniers

SATURDAY August 17th was ominously quiet. The forward bases at Hawkinge, Manston, Lympne and Tangmere had been methodically pounded by Junkers bombers and Croydon was still reeling from the devastating attack on the 15th. Few buildings in these airfields were habitable and, at Manston, pilots were forced to shave in the swimming pool. Morale was at its lowest ebb and everyone at Kenley felt that it must be their turn next.

As a sector station Kenley was a vital link in the inner ring of RAF airfields protecting the capital and it was certainly the Luftwaffe's intention to "knock it out". As commonly predicted, the welcome respite on Saturday turned out to be the calm before the storm for Kampfgeschwader 76 from their headquarters north-west of Paris were planning a three-pronged assault on Kenley — precision dive-bombing on the station buildings, a high-level attack by Dorniers and then a surprise low-level raid by nine Dorniers who would fly all the way to

the target at little more than tree-top height.

The low-level specialists arrived first. They had received no more opposition than a few bursts of machine gun fire from a naval patrol boat and had raced north in wide line-abreast at 100 feet or lower, following the Southern Railway electric line from Lewes to London as their route guide. They were spotted by the Observer Corps heading for the white chalk quarry that marked out Kenley and homing in so fast that no scramble could possibly be ordered by No 11 Group headquarters.

Kenley's controller, Squadron Leader Anthony Norman acted on his own initiative. "Battle bowlers" (tin hats), he ordered everyone and to 64 Squadron "Freema Squadron, scramble, patrol base, angels 20". Similar orders had gone to the Hurricanes of 615 Squadron, Kenley, 111 Squadron, Croydon and 32 Squadron, Biggin Hill.

Three minutes after the departure of the low-level Dorniers, hotly pursued by 111 and 615 Squadrons, came the intense

Another photograph of Kenley taken by the Luftwaffe war correspondent from the cockpit of the Dornier. Now the airfield is on fire and high explosives are raining down on the buildings below. Picture shows 1: one wrecked aircraft. 2: hangars on fire and 3: a crater on the runway. There are also fires to the rear of the airfield.

high-level attack — the bombers and their escorts protected from the anti-aircraft gunners by the thick smoke and dust below.

In a matter of seconds, Kenley was blitzed. Three hangars were destroyed and six more damaged, the Ops room was put out of action and numerous buildings reduced to trembling shells. Not far from the Ops Room, an airman shouted to some WAAFs in a shelter that there were unexploded bombs outside. As the girls coolly climbed out and marched away the high-level attack began, sending them scurrying to another shelter.

When they emerged once again they saw that Kenley was ablaze and the fires raged unchecked because there was no water supply. More than 100 high explosives had fallen, of which 24 were delayed action. Four Hurricanes and a Blenheim on the ground were destroyed and there were 19 human casualties, including nine dead. There were also large fires in the oil and petrol stores and extensive damage to houses in Purley Way.

For this attack on Kenley, Bomber Group 76 paid dearly. Five Dorniers and the crews were lost. They crashed at Leaves Green, Kenley village and Hurst Green. Two limped back only to crash into the sea. A sixth was hit by ground fire and the pilot mortally wounded. It was heroically flown back to Norrent

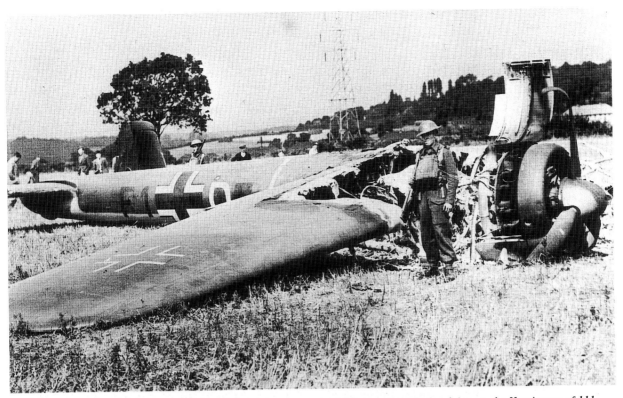

The Dornier which crashed at Leaves Green after meeting the full force of the Kenley defences, the Hurricanes of 111 Squadron and then the Addington Home Guard (see page 55).

Fontes by the navigator. A seventh limped back to Calais after a terrifying return journey and an eighth just made it to Abbeville. The barrage of Bofors, 3-inch machine gun fire, aiming blindly through the clouds of dust managed a few hits, but it was one of the parachute and cable launchers which made the greatest impact. One Dornier, already on fire, struck one of the electrically fired cables and plummeted down to crash outside the northern perimeter of the airfield.

Squadron Leader John Thompson of 111 Squadron wrote later that he was almost a casualty himself. "No-one had warned us that PAC rockets would be snaking upwards at 40 feet a second to grapple the wings with steel wire. I thought if one of those hits me, I'm finished."

Sadly there was one RAF casualty of "friendly" fire. Flight Lieutenant Stanley Connors, having claimed one Dornier, was caught in the anti-aircraft fire and his blazing Hurricane was believed to have crashed in The Oaks, Wallington. Connors was buried in his native town of North Berwick. Another Hurricane force-landed on Woodcote Park Golf Course, Epsom Downs and a third crashed at Oxted. Pilot Officer Peter Simpson and Sergeant Albert Deacon, both of 111 Squadron, baled out safely. Minutes later the Hurricane flown by Sergeant Harry Newton was set alight by return fire and the pilot was forced to abandon his aircraft over Botley Hill Farm, Tatsfield. He too was unhurt.

As the drama continued another effective fighter attack came from 32 Squadron whose pilots caught sight of a swarm of Dorniers approaching Kenley, 12,000 feet high. Squadron Leader Mike Crossley, leading A Flight, ordered his six Hurri-canes to attack the 50 escorted bombers head-on at a closing speed well in excess of 400 mph. The formation broke up, the bombing run was abandoned and Dorniers dropped their loads haphazardly onto the Surrey countryside.

615 Squadron's pilots were not having things all their own way. Outnumbered at least five to one by Messerschmitt 109s they lost four Hurricanes in the air (as well as six on the ground). Flight Lieutenant Lionel Gaunce, a Canadian, baled out over Sevenoaks with slight burns and his Hurricane crashed in Robsacks Wood, Sevenoaks Weald. Pilot Officer Petrus Hugo, the brilliant South African ace, crash landed at Orpington and was taken to hospital. Pilot Officer David Looker had a double dose of action. As his Hurricane, severely damaged, forced-landed at Croydon the station battery opened up. He was admitted to hospital with severe shock.

Sergeant Peter Walley, 20 years old, was killed. Shot down in flames he was unable to escape and his Hurricane crashed on Morden Park golf course with the pilot still inside. Sgt Walley was buried in Kenley's churchyard at Whyteleafe.

Meanwhile the scene on the ground was appalling. Hangars were still ablaze, planes on the airfield were burning and the rescue squads were tearing frantically at collapsed buildings. A few hours later, Edmund R. Murrow, covering the day's attack for CBS said this of the WAAFs coming on duty at Kenley to replace those caught up in the raid. "Most of them are girls with blonde hair and plenty of make-up. They are marching well, right arms thrust forward and snapping smartly down after the fashion of the Guards. Some of them are probably frightened but every head is up and most of them are smiling".

Kenley's anti-aircraft defences brought down a Dornier 17 during the low-level raid on August 18th. It crashed in the village at Golf Road and completely destroyed a detached house called Sunnycroft. Five men in the Dornier were killed including the navigator and captain, Oberleutnant Ahrend and an official war correspondent. Mr Turner-Smith was in his house at the time and miraculously escaped serious injury.

Cinema warning at Wimbledon, then 14 die

FROM their observation post high on the roof of Wimbledon Town Hall the air raid wardens on duty could clearly see white vapour trails in the blue sky and then a massive pall of drifting smoke, during the August 15th attack on Croydon airfield. As there were few buildings or industries of great importance they must have wondered if the Luftwaffe would bother about their Borough. Twenty four hours later they were to find out.

The siren, which had sounded frequently to indicate the imminent arrival of raiders, went off at 5.15 in the evening and people trooped to their shelters. At the Elite Cinema, crowded with children on holiday, the film *Just William* was halted while a warning was given on stage. Five minutes later 14 people were killed by bombs which fell just a few hundred yards from the cinema.

Homes in Cecil, Montague, Russell, Gladstone and Palmerston Roads were completely wrecked or damaged by blast. The worst single incident was at the Wimbledon Tyre Company where seven people died. All over this area of Wimbledon there were fires and the smell of burning rubber. And to add insult to injury St Andrew's Church in Herbert Road was hit by machine gun bullets and all electricity cables and gas and water mains were shattered.

Dornier meets fusilade from Addington Home Guard

A SECOND Dornier, piloted by Rudolf Lamberty, was also hit by a Bofors shell from the Kenley defences on August 18th— and then attacked by Sergeants Dymond and Brown of 111 Squadron. As a port wing exploded and blazed furiously, two of the crew jumped out but their parachutes failed and they crashed to their deaths in the Surrey countryside.

With his aircraft losing height rapidly, Lamberty decided to crash-land as best as he could but, as the blazing Dornier limped over the village of Addington, he ran into a massive fusilade of fire from the local Home Guard who later claimed that they pumped 180 rounds into the plane's belly.

Lamberty brought his Dornier down with a bump in the village of Leaves Green and both he and Hauptmann J. Roth crawled out badly burned to be captured immediately and taken to the Guard Room at nearby RAF Biggin Hill. The following day the newspapers credited the kill to the men of the Home Guard, declaring it was the first time that the part-time soldiers had achieved such a feat.

The pilots from Biggin Hill cut the Swastika from the fin of the Dornier and proudly displayed it with other relics in the Mess. It was later presented to the RAF Museum at Hendon where it remains today. There are plenty of bullet holes in the Swastika — courtesy of the Lee Enfields of the Addington Home Guard!

THE AIR BATTLES OVER BRITAIN—*VIVID PICTURES*

THE WAR

No. 45

3D WEEKLY

HOME GUARD SHOOT DOWN NAZI RAIDER

The Berlin Press has sneered at the Home Guard as "hedge-snipers." But last week members of the Home Guard proved that they could "snipe" to some effect when they brought down a Dornier bomber by rifle fire. The Nazi plane was machine-gunning a common in a South London suburb. Twenty Home Guards in an emplacement near by "let him have it" with 180 rounds. The Dornier was hit and crashed. This impression by a WAR WEEKLY artist shows our "spare-time soldiers" at it.

Pilot Officer Petrus Hendrik Hugo was one of the heroes of Kenley — outnumbered but right in the thick of the action. Hugo, from Cape Province, South Africa crash-landed his blazing Hurricane at Orpington and was taken to hospital there with wounds to the face. Five days later he was awarded the DFC and returned to the fray with 615 Squadron gaining more kills and winning a bar to his DFC. In November 1941 Hugo was given command of 41 Squadron at Merston.

Merton received its first taste of bombing in August 1940.

Life in Malden during the war was one of continuous hazard. Many bombs dropped in the locality including this one, on August 16th 1940, which left Nos 17 and 19 Graham Road completely devastated.

The Surrey Comet

and

South Middlesex News

8 PAGES
No. 6578 87th Year

WEDNESDAY AUGUST 21 1940

ONE PENNY
Postage 1d

NAZI FRIGHTFULNESS IN SURREY

Many Houses Damaged in Lightning Raid

TRAIN AND CHILDREN MACHINE-GUNNED

Civil Defence Workers Among Number of Casualties

SURREY had its first taste of Nazi frightfulness last Friday, when German planes bombed and machine-gunned three residential areas in south-western London.

A number of people were killed and injured. No damage of military value was done, but a number of private houses, a clinic and a church were demolished, and the railway line had some remarkable escapes. In one town the track of the bombs is in a rough semi-circle and it is estimated that a very large number of bombs were rained on the houses all in the space of 30 seconds.

Among the casualties were a member of the Home Guard, a stretcher party leader, and two rescue squad men: all were killed while hurrying to duty after the sounding of the warning. A number of railwaymen at the station also lost their lives when a bomb fell on the booking hall and blew in the wall of the stairway leading to the up local platform. Some men who were on the stairs were also killed by the same bomb, but other people who were sheltering only a foot or two away, but round the corner of a brick wall, escaped with nothing more serious than a bad shaking.

A quarter of a mile from the station another bomb fell plumb between the

In another road a large bomb fell partly in the street and partly on the pavement not more than ten feet from an old house built of wood. The house was unscathed except for one pane of glass cracked, but a brick-built house nearby had had its front blown in.

Always Take Cover

"The first lesson of the raid," an A.R.P. official told the "Surrey Comet," "is that wise people take cover and stay there. We have had only two casualties from Anderson shelters. In one case it was a direct hit, and in the other two bombs fell, one on either side of the shelter."

"The second lesson is that the A.R.P. services stood up to the test wonderfully well. Our casualty services were on the spot, and at work in some cases within three minutes of

our arms round each other, saying we would go together, expecting another bomb every second. Happily none came near.

"When I opened the door I was met with a perfect hurricane of wind and dust. The house opposite the side door had crumpled like a pack of cards. I could hear my neighbour shouting.

Saved by Kitchen Table

"He and his wife, elderly people, had taken refuge under a strong table in the kitchen. The roof had caved in and crashed through the bedroom floor on top of them but the table saved their lives although it was a long time before they could be got out to be taken to hospital, badly shaken and bruised. Of the house on the other side practically only the front wall remained. A mother and her two young children died there. My house in the middle escaped. I thank God."

South Coast Trader's Misfortune

An inspector employed by a dairy firm left his shop when the siren sounded to cycle to his wife and two children a few hundred yards down the road. Hardly had he gone fifty yards when the bombs began to fall. A tradesman standing at the door of his lock-up furniture shop saw the milk inspector alight from his bicycle, apparently meaning to take cover.

"I called to him to come into the shop," said the trader. "As I did so my wife, who was just behind me in the shop, was flung to the floor by the concussion from a bomb. I dashed back to hold her and as I did so a machine gun bullet or small piece of shrapnel carved a hole through the doorpost, killing the inspector first, the shot passing through his head. He was killed at the spot where I had stood a few seconds earlier."

This trader, incidentally, had practically all his stock of antique furniture and china ruined. He had only opened the business a fortnight earlier after being evacuated from a south-east coast town !

Postman's Treasured Teacup

There is a postman who is keeping a tea cup as a souvenir. He says it saved his life. He was in charge of a post office van which he left by the kerb whilst he collected the mail from a sub-post office at a little general stores. When he was about to start off he was called back for another parcel. Then the warning siren came. Invited to take cover in the shop the postman replied that he would remain

---

Tea dances, blackout news, shopping bargains and "Nazi Frightfulness". This is how the Surrey Comet reported the first big raid on a residential area in Surrey. A few people in Kingston were killed, a train was machine-gunned and there were many stories of resourcefulness, courage and remarkable escapes. Because of the censorship no locations could be given but this did not stop newspapers from giving vivid descriptions of the raids and the reactions.

The Luftwaffe lost about 110 men in the furious fighting of August 18th and the RAF, 15. The Junkers 87 was the greatest casualty and was proving so vulnerable that Luftwaffe High Command made the decision to virtually withdraw it from the Battle. There was damage also to the Hurricanes of 111 and 615 Squadron including the one above which went back to the repair shop.

Pilot Officer George Moberley of 616 Squadron whose body was recovered from the sea and buried in Caterham and Warlingham burial ground.

Sunday August 25th: Another attack on Croydon Airport with relatively little damage. Sergeant Thomas Emrys Westmoreland of 616 Squadron, now based at Kenley, failed to return from combat with Messerschmitt 109s over Canterbury. Another Spitfire pilot who went missing on this day was Sergeant Thomas Wareing, shot down in the sea. A few days later his colleagues of 616 Squadron heard he was a PoW in Germany. Wareing was destined to be interned in Schukin camp, 150 miles west of Warsaw, from where in 1942 he made a most daring escape. After many adventures he stowed away on a Swedish ship and eventually reached Stockholm. The British Legation arranged for his repatriation to England where he rejoined the RAF.

Monday August 26th: Bad day for Kenley. A large formation of over 100 German fighter bombers crossed the coast to attack Folkestone, Margate and Broadstairs and was met by the Hurricanes of 615 Squadron. First to be shot down was Pilot Officer John McClintock who baled out unhurt but his aircraft was lost in the sea. McClintock survived until November 25th when he and Pilot Officer Anthony Truran, flying in a Magister, lost a wing at 2,000 feet. It crashed at Sunningdale and both men were killed. Another pilot to be shot down on August 26th was Flight Lieutenant Lionel Gaunce who was rescued from the sea west of Herne Bay pier. Pilot Officer Douglas Hone and Flying Officer John Gayner both crash-landed and were taken to hospital and their Hurricanes were lost.

On August 26th 616 Squadron had an even more tragic day. In the skirmish above Dover and Folkestone, Pilot Officer William Walker baled out in the sea, Flying Officer John Bell force-landed at Bekesbourne, Kent, Flying Officer E.F. St Aubin crash-landed near Eastchurch, Sergeant Percy Copeland force-landed at Wye and Pilot Officer Roy Marples was wounded in the leg by cannon splinters. In each case the Hurricanes were lost and all but Bell were taken to hospital.

Flying Officer George Moberley and Sergeant Marmaduke Ridley were not so lucky. Both pilots were shot down in the sea off Dover and killed.

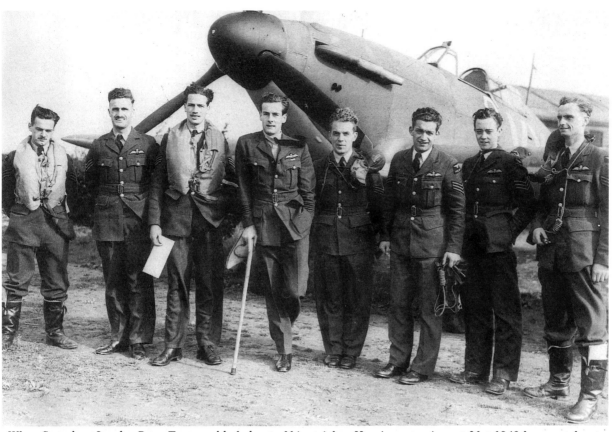

When Squadron Leader Peter Townsend baled out of his stricken Hurricane on August 31st 1940 he was taken to Hawkhurst Hospital, Kent and then transferred to Croydon where his left big toe was amputated. In the photograph above Townsend, back at base with a stick to help him walk, is with his pilots of 85 Squadron.

Peter Townsend joins the fray at Croydon

JOHN Thompson's battle-scarred warriors of 111 Squadron hastily left Croydon on Monday August 19th for a brief respite at Debden. They just had time to exchange the time of day with the Hurricane pilots of 85 Squadron who were replacing them, warning their CO, Squadron Leader Peter Townsend that a "blitzy" time awaited his men.

The newcomers were given a dispersal area on the western side of the airfield close to Plough Lane North and told to make use of a set of vacant villas as rest rooms. The 18 pilots and their ground crews settled in quietly — for five days of cloudy weather followed, giving everyone at the station a welcome break.

It was on Monday August 26th that the cloud cover broke and the Luftwaffe returned — not in vast numbers as before but with a solitary aircraft which dived down from a great height dropping incendiaries on the station. Bombs fell close to Forester's Drive, some near a public shelter and others between the gun posts. More fell in the vicinity of Waddon and, on the airfield, a Hurricane was destroyed by fire and two more damaged.

The lone raider scored one sensational hit. A bomb completely destroyed the Bourjois scent factory at Waddon and for many days afterwards the air around Croydon was filled with the sweet smelling *Evening in Paris*.

Peter Townsend's "blitzy" day came on Saturday August 31st when 12 of his Hurricanes were scrambled to intercept a formation of approaching Dorniers and their Messerschmitt escorts. The bombers reached Croydon as the Hurricanes took off and blasts from the ground shook the aircraft as they climbed heavenwards.

The attack on the airfield from 2,000 feet lasted barely six minutes but was long enough to destroy a hangar belonging to Redwing Aircraft Company and cause several craters on the landing ground. The airman's cookhouse was strafed by machine gun bullets and a bomb landed in the middle of Purley Way where a Dennis 30 cwt lorry was destroyed. There was just one injury — to a soldier of the Royal Artillery on aerodrome defence.

Meanwhile the Hurricanes had tightened up their formation and gained the all-important height advantage only to find the Dorniers were streaking home. 85 Squadron caught up with the Messerschmitts, intercepted them at 9,000 feet and a fierce battle took place over Tunbridge Wells. The Hurricane pilots destroyed two 109s and one 110 but the score finished all-square. Pilot Officer Piers Worrall crashed near Northiam, Pilot Officer William Hodgson crash-landed at Shotgate and Squadron Leader Peter Townsend came down at Goudhurst. He baled out wounded and was taken to Hawkhurst Hospital.

Scores of people flocked to Manor Avenue to see the burning remains of the Heinkel.

Crewless Heinkel crashes in Caterham

THIS is one incident that the people of Caterham still talk about. A massive 'Hindenburg' Heinkel bomber crashed into the rear garden of a bungalow at 21 Manor Avenue in the early hours of Tuesday morning August 27th after an incident-filled return journey from a bombing mission over Coventry. The bungalow, occupied at the time by a retired schoolmaster and his wife, was partly demolished as the blazing hulk exploded, awakening the entire Surrey village.

The bomber of KG1 had set out from its base at Mondidier for the West Mid-

lands and delivered its deadly cargo. On the way home it was caught in the searchlights and shot down by Sergeant Longman of the 148th Anti-Aircraft Battery. With its port engine out of action and the starboard engine running rough it began to lose height and, over Surrey, the Gruppenkommandeur Major Willibald Fanelsa gave orders for his crew to bale out. The burning aircraft hit the ground, ploughed its way across Queen's Park, Caterham and came to rest in Manor Avenue.

One of the crew who had baled out near Kenley walked into a house and then

quickly out again as he noticed RAF coats hanging in the hall. It was Grove House, then in use as WAAF's quarters. When challenged he repeatedly asked for the police. Another 17-year-old crewman broke his leg and was treated by Dr Lewis who said the young man was gripped in a state of complete terror.

All five were interrogated and taken to PoW camps. Major Fanelsa found himself at the only PoW officers' camp in Britain. Grizedale Hall near Ambleside — where he and two others formed the 'Altestenrat' (council of elders) which also acted as the escape committee.

It was not uncommon for aircraft to collide during combat and this is exactly what occurred over the Surrey countryside on the morning of August 30th 1940. Two Messerschmitt 109s, harried by RAF fighters south of Biggin Hill flew straight into each other. Both pilots baled out and were captured immediately. One landed at Layham's Farm, near Addington and the other crashed at Oxted. Photograph shows Flight Lieutenant/Acting Squadron Leader John Ellis of 610 Squadron, holding the notebook, with airmen and gunners sifting through the wreckage at Layham's Farm.

The Bourjois scent factory at Waddon, Croydon continued to burn after being hit by a single German raider. Perfume filled the air for many days.

Buy a new fighter: Surrey takes up the challenge

AS the Battle of Britain raged and RAF losses increased, the challenge went out to every sizeable town in Surrey to raise enough money to buy a Spitfire or Hurricane. The fighters were priced at £5,000 and any town or group giving that amount could have the name of its choice on the new aircraft.

Guildford, having now abandoned the raising of money for a new Cathedral to be built on the hill above the town, was among the first to take up the challenge. The mayor, Alderman R.H.Tribe opened the Spitfire fund on August 12th, 1940 by unveiling an indicator in the High Street which had a model Spitfire as a marker. Twelve days later he proudly pushed the aircraft to the top of the indicator, announced that the total stood at £6,611 and declared that a second fund was to be opened immediately,

Donations again began to pour in. House-to-house collections were augmented by whist drives and beetle drives. A sizeable donation came from Guildford in Australia and, on the Castle Green, a bowls match was played between two teams of Old Contemptibles aged between 70 and 80. They raised the princely sum of £5.

Every single town in Surrey exceeded their own target and many villages made their own collections. In Croydon, a Messerschmitt 109, was on display with a card bearing the words "Made in Germany — finished in England. All proceeds go to the local Spitfire Fund". In West Horsley the Home Guard took the boot from a dead German airman and used it to collect cash donations.

It would have been disloyal for the people of Kingston to collect for a Spitfire, but they had a Hurricane Fund and the lead was given by the giant department store, Bentalls who promised to double each individual donation whether a penny or £1,000. Outside the store was a Junkers 88 and a battle-scarred Hurricane with admission to view.

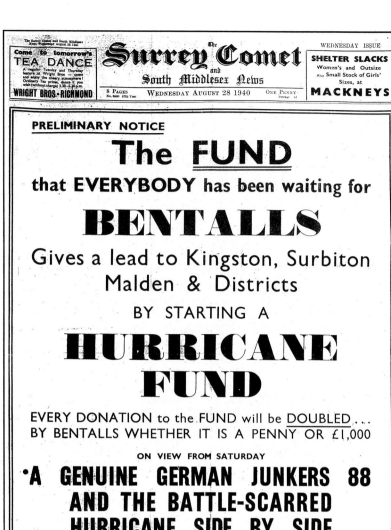

Courageous Croydon — the town that could save

Alongside the Spitfire Fund and other money raising efforts, the Government set up a National Savings Campaign and Croydon's enthusiasm was such that the Borough became the first in England to start a street savings group and introduce a special "Savings Week".

The mayor appealed in the Press and speeches were made in all 14 local cinemas. An indicator in St Katherine's Street showed all the new groups that were being formed and the total subscribed. The week raised an incredible £286,439 and, in the six months after the Mayor's appeal for National Savings, Croydon raised over one and a half million pounds.

Even in the middle of 1940 with the war just a year old, the contribution by the people of Croydon to final victory was legendary. Not once did their courageous, wholehearted efforts wane, even though they were to suffer more attacks than any other south London borough.

This Heinkel was displayed on Mitcham Common to help raise money for the Spitfire Fund

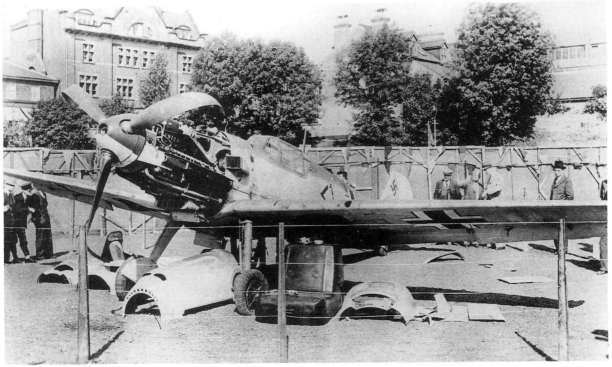

The Croydon Messerschmitt 109. "Made in Germany — finished in England."

The remains of Teddy Morris's Hurricane at Lodge Farm, South Holmwood.

Pilot rams Heinkel in battle over Reigate

S HORTLY before noon on Friday August 30th, 150 German bombers, escorted by a similar number of fighters swept over Surrey en route for the aerodrome at Farnborough. Radio-location and the Observer Corps gave ample warning and, at Biggin Hill, the Controller was able to get his squadrons airborne.

Among them was Flying Officer Edward (Teddy) James Morris, a South African who had been with 79 Squadron at Biggin Hill for more than 18 months and was renowned for his nerves of steel. On this day, in the middle of the most deadly phase of the Battle of Britain, facing a black swarm of bombers and fighters Teddy Morris needed more than just sheer courage. He needed good luck — and he got it.

The South African had been well briefed on the form of warfare his squadron was to adopt — a head-on attack, getting sight of the enemy at 600 yards and pressing the firing button at 300 yards. This gave the pilots just one second to break away, but the effect on the bomber formation could be devastating.

Teddy Morris bravely bore into the huge formation of Hindenburg Heinkel 111s but failed to evade in time and, right over Reigate, bounced off the nose of a 111. The two machines simultaneously began to plunge earthwards. Morris extricated himself from his straps, pulled the ripcord and jumped. He landed at Dorking breaking his leg and his Hurricane crashed at Lodge Farm, South Holmwood and exploded.

The Heinkel with a crew of five plummeted into the earth at Swires Farm, Capel less than a mile to the south. Three were killed, one badly wounded and the fifth captured.

As the Heinkel came down a squad of soldiers rushed across a field to it in a lorry. As they arrived the Heinkel exploded, the soldiers scattered but the army lorry and some trees caught fire.

In sick quarters the pilots of 79 went to see Teddy Morris who said he thought the Heinkels would break formation if he pressed home a good frontal attack. So he just flew straight at them.

"No, Teddy", said one of his colleagues, Donald Stones. "A Heinkel wouldn't break if the pilot is dead. You are supposed to allow for that."

"How the hell do you know if he's dead or not?"

"The way you did", seemed to be the only answer!

Army personnel triumphantly display a section of the wing of the Heinkel 111 which crashed at Swires Farm, Capel.

August 30th 1940: There was more drama in Surrey on the day that Teddy Morris introduced his hazardous new method of destroying German bombers. Sergeant Geoffrey Allard of 85 Squadron shot down a Heinkel 111 which crashed at Mannings Heath, killing two of the crew of five. And Pilot Officer John Greenwood of 253 Squadron shot down an He 111 which force-landed at Haxted Farm, Lingfield. A third Heinkel crashed in Sussex. All three bombers were on the same mission to attack Farnborough.

Tom and Harry take over at Kenley

SQUADRON Leader Joe Kayll, who had been given the double award of DSO and DFC by the King when he visited Kenley, knew more about air combat than most having survived a demoralising onslaught in France and then leading a shattered 615 Squadron through the deadliest weeks of the Battle of Britain.

Kayll, already credited with nine enemy aircraft destroyed, took his battle weary warriors out of the front line to rest and train at Prestwick and, in their place came 253 Squadron — unique in that two pilots of equal rank, Squadron Leaders Harold Starr and Tom Gleave shared the running of the squadron.

On August 30th, their first day at Kenley, both Starr and Gleave were quickly into action. Gleave claimed three 109s while Starr was forced to manoeuvre his damaged Hurricane to base after being hit over Nutley. Two other pilots of 253 were killed, 19-year-old Pilot Officer Colin Francis and Sergeant John Dickenson who was just 21. Less than 24 hours later, Harry Starr was also dead and Tom Gleave lay in hospital grievously burned.

Meanwhile Joe Kayll, the charismatic leader of 615 Squadron (see page 42) survived combat for another year before being shot down in France and taken PoW. He escaped in a mass breakout in 1942 and was recaptured. By May 1943 he was in charge of the Escape Committee for the East Compound of Stalag Luft 111.

Miss A. Blackburn (now Mrs Coles) has sent this photograph, by Frank Dann, of the remains of the home in Richmond where she and her brothers and sisters lived with their parents. This is her story.

The night a landmine fell in our road

"WHEN talk of war was in the air in 1938 my mother, a woman of vision, used her insurance endowment to buy a cabin-cruiser on the Thames. It cost £60, had four berths and for my family proved to be an enduring and infinite source of safety and pleasure. During the Battle of Britain we spent many days and nights on the boat and watched the "dog fights" over London. On occasions we had to leave the boat when river police warned us of unexploded bombs but we felt secure on board.

In August 1940 daylight bombing by the Germans started and on one occasion when we returned from the boat we found all the windows in our house blown out. That afternoon a young mother and her two toddlers were killed.

Richmond was of no military importance. In peacetime it had been a favourite weekend place for trippers to the river and public gardens. It had a theatre, cinemas, historic houses, a huge park and a thriving shopping centre. Why it should have been the target of enemy action is a mystery.

The night a landmine fell on our road, my twin brother and I, my older sister and my mother were in the Anderson shelter in the garden. My older brother had returned to his naval base and my father was firewatching. The All Clear had gone. I was awakened by a huge booming sound and soil in my mouth. There was the sound of crashing masonry and glass shattering, then silence. My mother struggled to the entrance of the Anderson and said: "Next door's house is down and OUR house is down. They're all down". Then the cries started, really terrible cries, and the noise of more falling bricks and crashing timbers.

The day before the bomb fell my mother had been talking to her neighbour who told her that as it had been so quiet she and her four children were going to forget the war and sleep at home that night. This was on my mother's mind as she stepped into the debris outside. An ARP warden told her to return to the shelter but she insisted on going into the bombed house next door where she found a little boy, alive, but terrified. He had been sheltering in a cupboard under the stairs. In the front room they found his three sisters, unmarked but dead. The mother was alive but the medical people had to cut her out and she didn't survive.

My mother continued looking for people. There were huge gaping trenches where the drains and sewers had collapsed. She found another woman whose mother was still in the ruins. We sat in our shelter, terribly shocked. We could hear the voices of the rescuers calling to each other outside and every so often they would peer inside to give a word of encouragement. They had huge torches and wore tin hats. Eventually we were taken to the school hall where we sat with the victims of a large block of nearby flats which had also been hit.

During the days that followed my father and sister went back to our road to see what they could find. They found our bicycle, two mugs undamaged and a little box with a padded seat. That's all.

Twenty people were killed that night in our road of 49 houses and more died in the block of luxury flats which had been commandeered to house refugees. I lived in Richmond, went to school and worked there for 15 years but I never saw or heard of anyone from our road again."

Sunday September 1st: Two waves of enemy aircraft crossed the coast during the day intent on attacking Kenley and Biggin Hill and 85 Squadron were dispatched to meet them. In the whirling dog-fight which ensued five Hurricanes were damaged or written off and there were more tragedies. The first to be killed was Pilot Officer Patrick Woods-Scawen who baled out over Kenley but his parachute failed to open and he landed in the grounds of The Ivies, Kenley Lane. Twenty four hours later Patrick's brother Charles, flying with 43 Squadron, was also killed. Distinguished Flying Crosses were awarded posthumously to the boys by the King. They were buried at their home town of Farnborough where a simple epitaph was placed on their headstone: 'Thy Will Be Done. RIP'. On that day two people on the ground were killed when 25 bombs fell on New Addington.

September 3rd: In the morning the shattered remains of 616 Squadron were withdrawn from Kenley to make way for 13 Spitfires of 66 Squadron from Coltishall. In the afternoon the airfield's new emergency operations centre was opened for business in the middle of Caterham. For many days GPO engineers had been transferring the complex telephone system of Fighter Control from the aerodrome to a little shop at 11 Godstone Road which still bore the name of Spice and Wallis, butcher. The new Ops Room was to receive many distinguished visitors including Churchill who slipped through the back door of the "shop" to watch the progress of the Battle.

September 5th: There were scattered raids in Kent and Surrey throughout the day. 72 Squadron, now at Croydon, were called to defend the station and lost two pilots, Doug Winter and 20-year-old Sergeant Malcolm Gray. A third, Flying Officer Doug Sheen, baled out wounded.

A team of nurses with their mobile first aid unit, part of the ARP Auxiliary Ambulance Service. Note the hospital windows protected by sandbags.

Tom Gleave — first of the guinea pigs

THE pilots of Kenley's 253 Squadron were also in the thick of action on Saturday August 31st. Scrambled to attack a formation of bombers which were closing in on Biggin Hill, they were led by Squadron Leader Tom Gleave who had already sorted out four 109s on an earlier sortie.

Gleave formulated his attacks in a series of barrel rolls from beneath the enemy but then he heard a metallic click above the roar of his engine. "A sudden burst of heat struck my face and I looked down into the cockpit. A long spout of flame was issuing from the hollow starboard wing root...I had some crazy notion that if I rocked the aircraft and skidded, losing speed the fire might go out. Not a bit of it; the flames increased until the cockpit was like the centre of a blowlamp nozzle. I had to bale out."

Gleave ripped off his helmet and oxygen mask, exposing his head and face to the inferno. As he opened the cockpit the now inverted aircraft exploded and he was thrown clear. Tom descended into a field adjoining Mace Farm in Cudham. Unable to see clearly because burnt skin from his forehead had fallen across his eyes and with his hands and legs burnt and ripped open, he stumbled towards a gate where a farmer and his son were running towards him.

He was taken to Orpington and then transferred to the Queen Victoria Hospital, East Grinstead where he learned that his great friend Harold Starr of 253 Squadron had been shot down and killed. Tom was put in the care of the brilliant specialist Archie McIndoe who grafted new skin to his face and even sculptured a new nose for the pilot, taking skin from his forehead.

Tom Gleave, who was in hospital for 11 months before continuing with a distinguished career in the RAF, later wrote: "From that moment in East Grinstead I started to accumulate a debt that mounted daily and still mounts; a debt I can never repay, against which human thanks seem utterly inadequate. Every time I see a nurse or doctor now I feel a hidden sense of humility, prompted not only by the ceaseless care and attention I received and still receive from them, but also what I saw them do for others far worse than myself, all but dead casualties who have become living miracles."

In that Burns Unit at East Grinstead, less than a year after his crash, Tom Gleave and other patients of Archie McIndoe formed the exclusive Guinea Pig Club. It was to be renowned all over the world.

Battle of Britain looked good from the summit of Box Hill

THE German bombers were attacking not only airfields and other installations but towns of little military importance. Leatherhead received its first visit from the Luftwaffe on August 27th when 20 high explosives were dropped near the Common. Several houses were damaged but there was only one casualty. Three days later, in a daylight raid, 60 high explosives fell in a line from Yarm Court to Crampshaw Lane, Ashstead and five people died. On September 6th, Leatherhead Golf Course received a direct hit and, on the 10th, a bomb exploded 30 yards from two cyclists who were thrown into the air with their machines, but luckily survived to tell the tale.

In scores of other towns the peril was ever present. There was damage and loss of life. Events crowded one another, communications were interrupted but there was no weakening of the impulse. There above them with machine guns rattling were the RAF, tearing into the enemy formations like a glittering swarm of angry flies.

With the sky so full of flying missiles, debris, shell splinters and other lethal objects the majority of people took cover. The summit of Box Hill, Dorking, however, provided an ideal vantage point from which to witness the Battle of Britain — and many did.

On one famous Saturday scores of people climbed the summit to watch the battle reach its great climax. And they cheered wildly as one RAF pilot executed a well-known rolling manoeuvre signifying his claim to have shot down an enemy aircraft.

September 6th: In a six-hour raid on the Croydon area, 200 plus incendiary bombs and a few high explosives fell. Electricity, water, gas and other service mains were disrupted over a wide area and three people were killed. Among the pilots to lose their life on this day was 22-year-old Hugh Adams from Oxted who had completed his flying training on July 17th. His commission was actually gazetted on the day he was killed. He is buried in St Peter's Churchyard, Tandridge.

September 8th: Great drama at Redhill when Operations suddenly lost R/T contact with a Blenheim of 600 Squadron which was on a straightforward night patrol. The aircraft, petrol exhausted, was abandoned at 6,000 feet over Basingstoke. Pilot Officer H.B.L.Hough, Sergeants E.C.Barnard and Smith baled out unhurt and made their way back to the station.

September 9th: A great wave of bombers attempted to penetrate the defences and hit London dropping incendiaries and two heavy

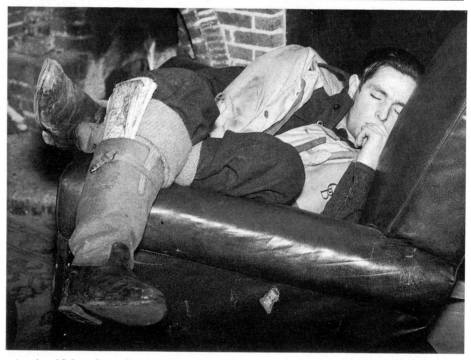

Another 85 Squadron pilot in action on September 1st was Sergeant Glendon Bulmar Booth, of Sydenham. He was shot down in the afternoon and baled out with his parachute alight. Booth, severely burned, came down in Tunbridge Wells and his pilotless Hurricane crashed at Kingswood, Sanderstead. Booth, just 20, was taken to Purley Hospital where he lingered in agony for five months. He died in February 1941.

calibre bombs on Croydon. Homes in many roads were damaged, 13 people died and 15 were injured. This was the forerunner to several days of successive attacks on the town. Before the end of the month there were scarcely 500 square yards of Croydon upon which something lethal had not fallen.

It was a sad day for 310 Squadron, scrambled to intercept the Croydon raiders. At 5.35 pm, Flying Officer John Boulton collided with his friend Flight Lieutenant Gordon Sinclair and bounced onto a Dornier 215 hitting the bomber amidships. Boulton crashed in Ninehams Road, Kenley and was killed. Sinclair, however, managed to bale out. He came down in a wood at Caterham and his Hurricane fell near the Purley Way. In the same combat Pilot Officer Rypl ran out of fuel and was forced to crash-land at Oxted. Another pilot to lose his life was Pilot Officer

continued on page 73

Pilot Officer Bob Doe with his Hurricane and ground crew in 1940.

When a mascot monkey drank the Sergeant Major's pint

BY the beginning of September the little satellite airfield at Redhill which had been operational only in emergencies, suddenly burst into life when a detachment of specialist night-fighters from 600 Squadron arrived with Blenheims and one newly delivered Beaufighter. The aerodrome was equipped with only basic runway lighting, no navigational aids were available for the crews and conditions generally were appalling.

The Squadron brought their mascot with them, a monkey called Mini, who was always dressed in full RAF uniform when she accompanied the pilots to the local pub. In his book *Redhill at War* Geoffrey Tait tells how Mini leapt onto the bar one evening and quickly downed a pint which, unfortunately, belonged to a burly tough Sergeant Major of a Canadian Scottish Regiment camped nearby.

The soldier grabbed at Mini but, demonstrating her agility, she leapt out of harm's way leaving members of the 600 Squadron wishing they could follow suit.

On another occasion a sergeant pilot was sent north for a rest leaving behind his pet duck, which always lived in the static water tank at Redhill. Geoffrey Tait explains how the pilot flew down from Carlisle to collect his feathered friend only to discover that, the previous day, it had made a wonderful supper. His heartless informant then added: "Had you come down yesterday, you could have had some yourself".

Three in one day for the lad from Reigate

A YOUNG pilot officer who was born in Reigate, worked as an office boy for the *News of the World* and completed his elementary flying training at Redhill, was the toast of his Squadron (and his family) on September 4th, 1940. Bob Doe, just 20 years old, was with 234 Squadron at Middle Wallop when he brought down three Messerschmitt 110s to bring his own total of enemy aircraft destroyed to nine.

Doe himself was shot down on October 10th. His Hurricane crashed near Corfe Castle and he spent some time in Poole Hospital before rejoining his Squadron in December.

A few days into the New Year Doe was flying at night when the oil in the cooler froze and his engine stopped at 6,000 feet. He glided to Warmwell and attempted a crash landing on the snow-covered airfield. His harness broke on the impact and smashed his face against the reflector sight.

The officer, with his face badly injured, went to Park Prewitt Hospital in the care of another distinguished plastic surgeon, Harold Gillies. After 22 operations he joined 66 Squadron, survived the war and enjoyed a distinguished military career.

83 killed in raid on Brooklands

THE people who worked in the great aircraft factories at Kingston and Brooklands knew it was the intention of the invader to wipe them and their machines off the map. There was such an acute shortage of Hurricanes and Spitfires that any serious damage to the production would have swung the battle measurably in the Luftwaffe's favour.

The big Brooklands raid that everyone expected came on September 4th just after lunch as workers of the afternoon shift were waiting to clock in and others were milling outside the gates of the factory in the sunshine. There had been no siren and the sound of approaching aircraft caused no undue concern.

A worker near the time office at the Hawker shed saw the twin-engined long range fighters, Me 110s suddenly dive out of the sun. He slammed his hand on the klaxon which was just outside the main entrance to the assembly shed. The great horn blower was the one-minute warning signal but it came too late. Bombs rained down, not on the Hawker factory, but on and around the Vickers works. One scored a direct hit on an air-shelter, another hit the old racing grandstand which still stood at The Fork and a third fell inside the repair hangar.

The bomb that caused the most damage fell through the factory roof. Stephen Flower in his book *Raiders Overhead* wrote: "Crashing through the stairwell leading from the first-floor canteen, it landed on top of a heavy press in the machine shop and exploded close to the time clock killing many queuing workers.

"In anticipation of the raids, the Vickers Drawing Office had already been moved to the golf clubhouse at Burhill a few miles away. Norman 'Spud' Boorer, caught in the middle of lunchtime revolver practice with the Home Guard, was glad of that move as he watched the diving 110s attack. Some of his colleagues had narrow escapes. David James, a stressman had been driving with a friend to Burhill as the 110s passed above. Reaching the junction of the Brooklands and Byfleet Roads they hurriedly leapt into the gutter as several bombs fell short."

The attack had taken just three minutes and it was carried out by 14 Me110s from Erprobungsgruppe 210 who had taken off shortly after noon with an escort of more 110s who took a different route. Leading the main group from the forward base at Calais-Marck was Hauptmann Karl von Boltenstern who did not even reach the English coast. Attempting to avoid RAF fighters his aircraft crashed into the Channel killing him and his gunner.

The first German group was spotted flying up from the Cobham area and the second followed the railway line and then turned back from Walton to approach Brooklands from the north-west. They met no resistance from the anti-aircraft guns and the majority of the RAF fighters had been drawn into battle on the south coast.

Kenley's 253 Squadron, however, were patrolling the Croydon area when the bombs began to fall on Vickers and the nine Hurricanes led by Flight Lieutenant William Cambridge turned for Brooklands and climbed to 12,000 feet well above any opposition that might be sighted.

AS the Germans headed for home, it was the turn of the Hurricanes to dive out of the sun and, at 6,000 feet, a huge battle developed. Cambridge picked out a target and sent it crashing down in flames. It hit the ground and burnt out at Waterloo Farm, West Horsley, some six miles from Brooklands. The pilot was killed and the gunner wounded. Another was credited to Flight Lieutenant John Wedgewood. This came down at Upper Common, Netley, near Dorking with both the crew killed.

253 Squadron were having a field day. Pilot Officers W.M.C. Samolinski, T Nowak and A.H.Corkett all claimed successes. Sergeant A.S. Dredge saw smoke burst from the fuselage of a 110 that he attacked and Sergeant R.A.S. Innes and Flying Officer R.D.H.Watts each believed they had silenced the rear gunner of two more 110s. Post-war research showed that some of the claims were rather optimistic.

However, the Hurricane pilots suffered no damage and no losses. They flew back to Kenley unaware that they had taken a huge toll of the escort aircraft while the attackers had streaked back home at full speed.

Brooklands also paid a heavy price for this attack. It was the worst single incident so far in the Battle with 83 dead and 419 wounded. The Brooklands mortuary was unable to take all the dead so Mount Felix Hall in Weybridge was utilised. The gruesome task of removing the bodies from the factory and tending to the injured was carried out by the staff of both Hawkers and Vickers, soldiers of the Royal Artillery search-light battery and others from the 20th Guards Brigade. The Home Guard brought in their armoured cars as temporary hearses. Some bodies were never identified, including factory girls in the shelter which had received a direct hit.

There is no doubt the bombers intended to attack the Hawker factory which was producing a large number of Hurricanes and was protected by balloons. The pilots either didn't like the balloons or were wrongly briefed and, tragically for Vickers, they put six 500 kg bombs into their machine shops instead.

Hurricane of 253 Squadron crashes in Banstead

One member of 253 who didn't take part in the Brooklands battle was the popular Canadian pilot, Alec Trueman who had been with the Squadron since July 20th. Trueman, patrolling above Kenley at 10 am on the morning of September 4th was shot down and killed, his Hurricane crashing at Tudor Close, Banstead. Aged 26 he was buried in St Luke's Church, Whyteleaf.

Many of the victims of the Vickers raid were buried at Burvale Cemetery on September 9th, 1940.

Six tragic days at Kenley for 66 Squadron

WHILE 253 Squadron was in combat over Brooklands, 66 Squadron, having arrived at Kenley the previous afternoon, had another battle — against freelance raiders on the south coast. The pilots hardly had time to unpack their bags before they were climbing into the cockpits of their Spitfires and screaming over the sunbaked ground to meet their foe in the hostile skies of Kent and Sussex. It was a disastrous debut. By tea-time on September 4th, ten Spitfires had been lost, one pilot killed, two seriously wounded and several others suffered minor injuries and deep shock.

The first victim was Pilot Officer Alexander Appleford who crashed near Purleigh and baled out slightly wounded at 9.50 am. Minutes later Sergeant Arthur Smith was shot down near Mersham. He too baled out and was admitted to the Casualty Clearing Station at Benenden, badly hurt.

Among the others, Flight Lieutenant Felix Dunworth force-landed at Billericay and was slightly wounded, Pilot Officer Peter King limped back to base, Flight Lieutenant G.P. Christie was wounded over Thanet and Pilot Officer Charles Cooke

crashed at Chequertree Farm, Aldington.

The pilot who died was Arthur Smith who had only flown with 66 Squadron since July. Aged 22 he was buried in St Luke's churchyard, Whyteleafe.

There was no respite. The following day Christie, in another Spitfire, was shot down again and King, whose aircraft had been repaired, baled out over the Medway but tragically his parachute failed to open. Two more pilots, Pilot Officers Hubert Allen and John Mather force-landed.

For 66 Squadron this maniacal flirtation with life and death continued. On September 7th, Arthur Bodie and Ian Cruikshanks were able to land their badly damaged Spitfires and on the 9th, Pilot Officer George Corbett abandoned his aircraft over East Grinstead. None were seriously hurt, but it meant that ten out of the 13 pilots had baled out or force-landed.

Little wonder their tenure at Kenley was so brief. After just six days of fierce combat the remnants of 66 Squadron changed places at Gravesend with a Hurricane Squadron, 501 destined to be one of Kenley's best known.

Reprieve for the airfields as Hitler attacks London

With the attacks on airfields, RDF stations and vital installations increasing and RAF losses mounting, Fighter Command had reached crisis point. The constant strain and relentless attrition suffered by the British pilots was such that exhausted squadrons were quickly withdrawn from the front line and those who had suffered crippling losses were henceforth to be classified as training units. This was the beginning of the end of Britain's capacity to resist much longer. It was now just a matter of days.

On Friday September 6th, the Luftwaffe lost 30 aircraft on operations. Hitler, incensed by the bombing raids on Berlin switched his point of attack and demanded reprisals. On September 7th the daylight bombing offensive switched to London and the pressure was taken off Kenley, Croydon and the other heavily attacked airfields in Kent.

Dorking fire crew is called to the docks

IN a massive daylight raid on September 7th a great wave of German bombers dropped more than 300 tons of high explosive and incendiary bombs on the streets and docklands of East London. More than 450 people were killed and 1,600 injured.

The attack was directed by Goering from a clifftop in France from where he watched the 350 bombers escorted by 650 fighters stream across the Channel. A few fanned out to attack Croydon and the towns and villages of north Surrey. The others droned on to London where they dropped bombs on bonded warehouses sending blazing rum, paint and sugar floating down the Thames.

London's blazing docks. Dorking firemen went into this mouth of hell.

Many Eastenders were evacuated by boat. "Send all the pumps you've got", pleaded one fire officer. "The whole bloody world's on fire".

One of the first Surrey towns to respond was Dorking. A fire crew with a heavy trailer pump drawn by their Rolls Royce car which had been converted into a fire tender was summoned to join the other crews and appliances at the docks. The call had been received by the Dorking Chief Officer who set off with his crew along country roads which were exceedingly dark. Among them was Mr A.G. Williams, sub officer of the Dorking Auxiliary who saw a huge glow in the sky beyond Box Hill.

In his book *Dorking at Wartime,* David Knight relates the story as told by Mr Williams: "On our way to dockland we passed the Monument — the memorial to that other great London fire — and we passed over London Bridge. The streets were deserted. Enemy raiders were still overhead and anti-aircraft guns were sending up occasional bursts but the searchlight beams were almost lost in the glow of the fires.

"We passed demolished buildings, gaunt ghosts of a horrible night. Once we nearly came to grief, the nearside wheels of our tender were within an inch of the edge of a bomb crater. We turned into the docks entrance and 200 yards ahead was a blazing ship and an inferno of flames. Bombs fell and we took cover and waited for orders to be called into action.

"Eventually we were told to take our pump alongside one of the dock basins and pump water onto stacks of blazing timber to prevent the flames from spreading. We worked for six hours. It was tiring work and hot and thirsty too. We had to move quickly because around us were the pillars of what had been open timber sheds. Iron girders remained and we had to be careful they didn't fall on top of us.

"Occasionally a smouldering craneman's hut on a moveable hosing crane would burst into flames again and we had to redirect a jet of water onto it. We stood ankle deep in a mixture of charred timber, ashes and water".

The story continued of more air raid alerts, more bombing, more dramas and many casualties among the firemen. But the Dorking men came through safely and, in the morning, drove back to the town and returned to their civilian occupations. The experience was one they would never forget.

The battle-hardened pilots of 501 Squadron moved to Kenley on September 10th. There was an accommodation problem at the time so many were given rooms at a local hotel. The pilot standing seventh from left is Squadron Leader Hogan who used the ground floor of Flintfield House as his squadron office. Among the men in this picture are some the great aces including Ken Mackenzie, Ginger Lacey, Robert Dafforn, Kenneth Lee and two Polish pilots. Flying Officer Dafforn was the tallest man in Fighter Command and had great difficulty in fitting into his Hurricane. Steve Woltanski was a Pole who never spoke English and Ginger Lacey went on to become one of the highest-scoring pilots in the Battle of Britain.

continued from page 68

George Forrester of 605 Squadron, Croydon who was shot by crossfire from two Heinkels over Farnborough, collided with a third aircraft, lost a starboard wing and crashed at Southfield Farm, Alton.

Carshalton was robbed of two historic landmarks on September 9th when the 18th century King's Arms pub and the ancient Haydon's butcher's shop each received a direct hit. On the same day a churchyard, cottages, shops and villas at Sutton were struck and mother-of-three Mrs Bryant killed. Miraculously her children, who were sleeping in the same room, escaped. There was more confusion in Sutton when a stick of high explosives came whistling down and there was a thud but no explosion. Residents rushed off to a warden's post to report it. It was just as well. The delayed action bomb exploded as they were out of sight.

September 11th: Tragedy came to Hartland Way, Shirley, a street of pretty gardened villas when a Spitfire, in combat, fell on the houses numbered 49 and 51. The blazing petrol from the wreck poured down into a garden shelter where a young mother, her two children and another woman had taken cover. They were all killed. The pilot, Sergeant Frederick Shepherd of 611 Squadron baled out, his parachute alight, and fell at Frylands Wood, Farleigh. He is buried at Whyteleafe.

On this night there were a number of alerts and bombs fell right across south London. The anti-aircraft guns were constantly in action and bursting shells produced showers of jagged steel splinters causing damage to a large number of properties. In Wimbledon, the guns were sited on the Common and in the station sidings. "Friendly" shells struck the Horse and Groom pub in Haydon's Road and the girls' school in Merton Hall Road. *continued on page 78*

continued on page 78

German fighter crashes on cricket field

A MESSERSCHMITT 110 attempting to penetrate through to London was shot down by fighters on Monday September 9th and crashed on the Maori Sports Club, Old Malden Lane, Worcester Park at 6 pm. The crew of two were killed and the aircraft was a write-off.

The *Surrey Comet* which was not allowed to publish details of exact locations gave a vivid description of this aerial battle through the eyes of a local householder. "I saw our fighters going over towards the east and then saw them break formation. A moment later there was a tremendous droning sound and I saw the Germans coming up from the south. They were in three wedges, one above the other. Our fighters dived on them from the clouds and they scattered. I saw one Nazi plunging down with white smoke billowing from its tail". The 110 actually crashed onto the cricket pitch, close to the pavilion and impacted into the ground where it remained for many years covered over by new earth.

Some years later members of the London Air Museum dug up the cricket ground and recovered two Daimler-Benz engines, undercarriage legs, oxygen bottles, a parachute and the remains of a compressed airframe.

Farnham received its first and worst incident when a bomb made a direct hit on a house at Firgrove Hill, near the station.

Widespread fighting — and the scent of victory

SEPTEMBER 15th 1940, now celebrated as Battle of Britain Day, was the great turning point in the Luftwaffe's bid to "knock the RAF out of the skies". On that day 21 Squadrons, including 253 and 501 from Kenley and 605, Croydon, were scrambled to meet a solid phalanx of bombers and fighters bound for London.

From the ground it looked like a dense swarm of black insects tearing into each other. The whirling patterns of vapour trails indicated that this was the fiercest, most confused and most widespread fighting of the aerial battle. By nightfall the RAF had shot down 61 German aircraft, 34 of which were bombers, for the loss of 26. It was a day later to be recognised as the last classic intercept of the Luftwaffe by the RAF.

The two Kenley squadrons met the first wave of raiders over Maidstone just before lunch. Two bombers were destroyed and one seriously damaged. Squadron Leader Hogan's Hurricane of 501 was shot in the radiator but the C.O force-landed at Sundridge and escaped unhurt. The charismatic Belgian pilot, Albert Emmanuel Alix Dieudonne Jean Ghislain Van den Hove d'Erstenrijck was not so fortunate. He was hit by an Me 109 over Ashford and bravely wrestled with the controls of his machine. Over Chilham, Kent it exploded and fell into the River Stour.

There were more waves of Messerschmitts, Heinkels and Dorniers on this eventful day and the skies were constantly filled with the curling tracers, smoking aircraft and the crackle of ammunition. One Heinkel fell to a young pilot from Surbiton. Flying Officer Dennis David had already made his mark during the fighting in France in May where he was credited with eleven enemy aircraft destroyed. He was able to increase that score considerably during the Battle of Britain.

Dennis David and his colleagues were helping to swing the balance. The Luftwaffe was not yet beaten but its daylight bombing offensive was drawing to a close.

Hitler postpones his invasion of Britain

IN the fighter-to-fighter duels that took place during those tumultuous days between the raid on Croydon on August 15th and the tense afternoon of September 15th when more aircraft were airborne than at any time in the Battle, the Luftwaffe's losses were always heavier than those of the defenders. The RAF pilots often escaped to fight again and, in many cases, their aircraft could be sent to the repair shop. The Messerschmitts shot down over Britain meant not only a lost aircraft but a lost pilot and the debacle of the 15th confirmed that Fighter Command was gaining the upper hand.

On September 16th, there was a welcome respite for both Kenley and Croydon; the weather in southern England was too poor for large scale fighting. While Dowding's men were relaxing, bitter inquests were being held in the Pas de Calais where Luftwaffe Commanders warned that their force could "bleed to death".

The next day Hitler postponed the invasion "until further notice". The War Diary of German Naval Staff confirmed their fears: "The enemy air force is still by no means defeated — on the contrary it shows increasing activity".

In his lean years Churchill had often been recruited by Lord Beaverbrook to write for the Daily Express. Now it was Churchill's turn to return the favour by appointing the buccaneer publisher Minister for Aircraft Production. Beaverbrook, who lived at Cherkeley, Leatherhead until it was bombed and set on fire in 1942, had a brilliant idea soon after he was recruited to the Cabinet. He appealed to the women of Britain: "Give us your spare pots and pans and we will turn them into Spitfires, Hurricanes, Blenheims and Wellingtons." Beaverbrook knew that the ordinary members of the public would be pleased to contribute towards the war effort even though, in the end, many of the items were not used. The response in Surrey was extraordinary. Hundreds of tons appeared in just a few days including wire coat hangers, cigarette boxes and bathroom fittings. Here children were adding to the pile in the Beaver's home town of Leatherhead.

From 'the cupboard under the stairs'

On September 15th Churchill announced that 1,286 people had been killed in air raids and London and its boroughs had borne the brunt of the casualties. But the Blitz, as it was to become known, was only just beginning. Between September 1940 and May 1941 the capital was to receive a further 19,000 tons of high explosives and incendiaries. Whole streets were about to be devastated and thousands destined to die under the rubble of their own homes.

A letter from Mr Phillippe Willoughby, a violinist of Evelyn Road, Wimbledon to his wife, who was staying with relatives in Cranleigh outlined the fear, the relief at survival and the fatigue which were felt by all those who lived through the opening phase of the Blitz. It was dated August 29th, addressed from "the cupboard under the stairs" and read:

"We've had a terrible week (no danger nor damage) simply incessant raid warnings, continually keeping you on the jump or under cover. I got home from the theatre at 6.30 this morning and I have been 'phoned to go up all day today as one of the violas wants to have the whole day in bed (I could do with it) so I suppose it means the same tonight. We had the warning at 9 o'clock last evening, during the show. We carried on and then afterwards audience and stage had a sort of party all night, dancing, singing etc. All clear went at 4.45 am, then a rush for Tubes etc which all start running. The Tube and Southern cease to run directly the warning goes off, so you are stranded. I'm going to the District tonight; they may run.

"On Saturday after I left you we had another warning. The evening show was not interrupted but it went off as soon as I got home. So Babba (*their daughter*) rushed me over to the shelter at the school (which is very safe, even from direct hits, I should think) and we were there until 3 am. I forget what happened Sunday, there were some short alarms. After the broadcast on Monday I bumped into one coming home. Got to one of those outside shelters at Colyers Wood, but it didn't last long. At 9 o'clock in the evening Dody (*their daughter-in-law*) and I had to go to the school shelter and were there for six hours (perfectly bloody. I'm sick of it. I'd sooner be bombed and what about poor little Dody and her sleep).

"On Tuesday evening at the theatre, UP she went again at 9.30 but we carried on with the show (which is distinctly wrong and risks the whole of the people at the theatre)...

"What are you going to do. Can't you stay at Cranleigh for some weeks until this incessant cursed raiding dies down, as it surely must before long. I don't want you to come back into all this turmoil. I can carry on somehow or other. Love and kisses from Phillippe..."

Bella Willoughby was still at Cranleigh when her husband wrote again to say that the raids had become like "picnics to me when I feel you are relatively safe" He went on: "My apprehensions are entirely outside myself. In this cupboard (and I only go in because I know you wish it) I am perfectly comfortable as though I were watching a show but when I looked down at you and Buffo (*the dog*) sitting there the other night my heart was shrinking with fear. I wish Lily could take you for the duration. Cranleigh must be safer than here.....Don't forget that those bombers which rush over you are mostly OUR bombers returning from Continental raids. Now don't forget that. I know this. Of course, not always but quite a lot."

"We'll find a nice little place after we finish here and perhaps have a few years happiness before the end."

Bella Willoughby did not take her husband's advice, but rejoined him in Wimbledon and tragically "the end" came just a fortnight later. In the early hours of September 16th, the air raid sounded for the umpteenth time and the Willoughbys, who were very tired, declined to go to the school shelter with their daughter Babba and took cover (presumably) in their cupboard under the stairs. They did not stand a chance. Several houses in Evelyn Road were caught in the blast of a bomb that made a direct hit on Number 53. When the rescue parties arrived they found a pile of timber, masonry and debris, a huge crater where the house had stood, mangled flesh among the ruins and an Irish setter, dazed, but otherwise uninjured. Also in the ruins were the two letters from Mrs Willoughby's handbag

J.H.Squire Celeste Octet lost one of their most popular and experienced musicians for Phillippe Willoughby was in his sixties. Ironically, a few days earlier, he had jocularly suggested to his colleagues that should he be killed in an air raid he hoped they would make a donation to the Spitfire Fund rather than buy a wreath. That wish was carried out.

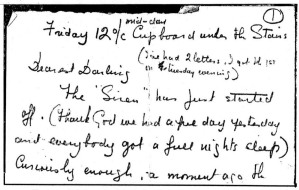

Extract from one of the letters from Phillippe Willoughby to his wife.

Photograph shows firemen and heavy rescue teams searching the wreckage, presumably looking for the bodies of the dead airmen. As on bomb sites in north Surrey, a static water tank, for use by Auxiliary Fire Service trailer pumps, was built after the rubble had been cleared. After the war, new homes were constructed.

Junkers crashes on two houses at Merton

A JUNKERS 88 on a bombing sortie over London suffered a serious loss of control and crashed heavily onto two houses in what had hirtherto been a peaceful estate in Richmond Avenue, Merton. The gunner managed to bale out and was captured, slightly wounded but the other three crew members were killed. In fact the aircraft blew up with such violence that the men were blown to pieces and no appreciable trace of them was ever found. As a result they have no known graves.

The drama occurred at 20 minutes past midnight on September 20th and the aircraft completely demolished two homes, nos 2 and 4. No-one on the ground was killed. The inhabitants of the two houses had responded to the air-raid alert and were seeking refuge in their Anderson shelters.

One woman, who was a resident of Monkbergh Road,

Morden, described the incident in a letter to a friend a few days later. She wrote: "We had a terrifying few minutes last Friday morning when that plane came down by Nelson Hospital. It seemed as though it was coming right on the house and the noise was awful. Then on Saturday there was a bomb which wrecked four houses not far from the back of Fred and Lucy in the next road to us. Our floor came up and our wall bulged. That was another lucky miss".

Her adventures continued during a visit to the dentist. "I've had my temporary set of teeth in", she wrote, "but when I went to fetch them, the dentist had an accident. Just as he was finishing, a bomb exploded. It blew him off his chair and he chipped one of my teeth."

continued from page 73

September 21st: A single German bomber, having broken away from the main force, attempted to destroy the railway line at Earlswood, near Redhill during the afternoon. Bombs fell on the Common and completely severed the main outfall sewer making an enormous crater. In the evening, bombs fell in the Meadvale district and a passing 447 bus was badly damaged.

September 26th: Pilot Officer Wlodzimierz Samolinski of 253 Squadron, Kenley failed to return from combat over the Channel and was posted as missing. His aircraft crashed in the sea. In the same action, Flight Lieutenant Gerald Edge was also shot down in the sea but picked up by motor boat and taken to Ashford Hospital. He was not able to rejoin his Squadron until November.

September 27th: A Hurricane in a sortie over Horsham during the morning was shot down and crashed in Blundel Lane, Stoke D'Abernon. Flying Officer Walerian Zak baled out and was taken to Leatherhead Hospital with burns. He survived the war and was eventually repatriated to Poland. Not so lucky was 20-year-old Pilot Officer Edward Gunter of 501 Squadron. He baled out over Sittingbourne but his parachute failed and he was killed.

September 28th: Pilot Officer Frederick Harrold was in action with 501 Squadron over Kent when he was shot down by Me 109s and plunged to earth watched by villagers at Ulcombe. The Hurricane embedded itself in Strawberry Plantations, College House, Ulcombe and the wreck burned out. Harrold was killed. In 1975, London Air Museum recovered many items including the pilot's gauntlets.

On this day Flying Officer Peter Crofts of 605 Squadron, Croydon fell to his death from his Hurricane which had been shot down over Ticehurst, Sussex. Peter had managed to free himself from his damaged aircraft but tragically fell free of his parachute. He was buried at All Saints Church, Tilford and a memorial was erected on the spot where he fell.

Great suspense in Croydon as landmine fails to explode

THE beleaguered people of Croydon were introduced to a new terrorist weapon on September 28th, 1940 which proved beyond all doubt that the enemy had abandoned all pretence of aiming at a military objective and were now hitting at the morale and the lives of civilians. An aircraft flew over the town and dropped, by parachute, two landmines.

The first fell in Park Hill Recreation Ground — ten minutes walk from the town centre — and made an enormous crater. The vibration and blast damaged all the homes around the Park but there was no loss of life.

The second landmine plunged down within 22 yards of the Town Hall at the junction of Friends' Road and Park Lane and failed to explode. The period of suspense which followed is described by Mr Berwick Sayers who was chief librarian at Croydon during the war years.

"The landmine remained embedded to about five feet of its length until a naval squad came to remove it two days later. All workers in the Town Hall and other offices were sent to safe places, only the Control Room and Report Centre staffs remaining. While the men were waiting to detonate the mine there was an air raid "red" warning but no attack developed.

Suddenly there was a vibrant boom, a sort of lifting of the ground as though by an earthquake; a sudden darkness as all lights went out, a seeping down in showers of dust; a rattling and an overall sense of collapse. Then the emergency light was put on and it was seen that the fabric of the underground rooms in the Town Hall had held although a screen had come away from the wall and the clock face had swung open. Lights were lit in the corridors and the personnel groped around until the normal lights suddenly came on. The cables had not been severed as feared; the shock had thrown over the main switch of the Town Hall. Croydon's first unexploded landmine had been detonated.

"The explosion had blown all the windows of the Town Hall, ceilings came down in the library, locked doors were thrown open and books were littered across the floor. Outside the area of the damage was now cordoned off to keep back the crowds."

More landmines were destined to fall on Croydon and South London in the months before Christmas 1940. Few people were killed but there were many casualties among the courageous men of the Admiralty who had the job of defusing them.

October 2nd: A Messerschmitt 109, shot down by Pilot Officer John Kendal of 66 Squadron, crashed near Swallowfields, Limpsfield Common at 10 am. The pilot Oberleutnant W.Radlick fell to his death into Hookwood Place, owing to parachute failure. Soon after the crash scores of locals gathered at the scene of the crash to pick up souvenirs. Two days later there was more excitement in Limpsfield when a Hurricane of 605 Squadron, Croydon force-landed at Pitchfont Farm.

October 7th: Pilot Officer Kenneth Mackenzie of 501 Squadron, Kenley hit the headlines for a daring feat over the Channel. Picking out a Messerschmitt 109 from a formation of eight, Mackenzie fired, hit its tank of glycol coolant,

saw the aircraft roll and dive towards the coast and then, to his dismay, straighten out and head for home.

Mackenzie pursued his crippled prey and, at just 100 feet above the waves, signalled to the German pilot that he wanted him to 'ditch' in the sea. The German ignored the instructions so the Hurricane pilot manoeuvred his wing into a position above the tailplane of the 109, gave it a great whack and knocked the entire section off.

As the German aircraft plunged into the water and partially sank, two more 109s, intent on revenge, chased Mackenzie at wave-top height across the Channel. The Hurricane, belching oil and smoke, crossed the coast at Folkestone and with its wheels up skidded across a field just 300 yards from the cliff edge. A few days later Mackenzie was awarded the DFC.

Vicar asks Kingston for help in 'David's fight against Goliath'

AWARE that the Home Guard were going to be right in the front line when (and if) the invasion of Britain occurred, the vicar of Kingston Hill, the Rev A Wellesley urged the public of Kingston to supply them with all they needed to defend the community. At a special service in St Paul's Church on Sunday September 15th, he took for his subject the story of David and Goliath and said that many of the men of the local Home Guard had no transport and struggled to fulfil their duty after a heavy day's work. He thought a battalion fund should be raised and, as a gesture to the men, handed to the Captain the collection taken from that service.

It amounted to more than £4.

A Heinkel 111, straying from a mission in the East End on September 24th, was caught in the searchlight beams of 460 Battery of the Royal Artillery based at Weybridge. For the local anti-aircraft gunners the Heinkel was a sitting duck and they scored several direct hits including one that took away the entire tail. The four crewmen quickly dumped their cargo and baled out as the blazing bomber disintegrated. The bombs demolished a house in the village of Bookham, the engines landed in the grounds of the Gordon Boys' Home at Chobham and the fuselage came down on the recreation ground where it burnt out. The press were invited to photograph the wreckage the following day and the picture shows an ATS girl with soldiers examining torn parachute silk. The crew were all captured unhurt and interrogated.

Crew bales out as blazing bomber crashes at Holmwood

THE people of Dorking, and particularly those watching from Box Hill and Newlands Corner, had a grandstand view of the fighting on September 27th, when one raider, a Junkers 88, riddled with machine gun bullets, fell out of the sky in flames. The four German airmen baled out; one came down at Bradley Farm, another at Blackbrook and a third near the Norfolk Arms, Mid-Holmwood. The fourth was the pilot, discovered dead near Leatherhead.

The Junkers buried itself in the ground at Folly Farm, South Holmwood after setting fire to a haystack. The rear gun turret and gun fell in the garden of Mr E.S. Jones, Pilgrims Close, Westhumble and part of the tail came down in Croft Avenue, Dorking. This was later exhibited in a nearby hotel and £3 collected for the Spitfire Fund.

On the afternoon of Saturday September 21st 1940 a single aircraft made an unsuccessful attempt to destroy the railway line at Earlswood. The bomb dropped on the Common and completely severed the Redhill main outfall sewer making a crater 60 feet in diameter. Repairs were quickly underway.

September 30th: It was just like a violent storm

THE last day of September provided the undeniable confirmation that the RAF had virtually won the Battle of Britain. There was more fighting in October and losses on both sides but it was on this historic day that the Luftwaffe lost 32 aircraft including a dozen valuable Junkers 88s. The majority of the bombers failed to reach their targets and numerous German pilots were killed, many of senior rank. The decision was made to withdraw all bombers from daylight attack and never again were those vast V-head formations to be seen over southern England.

In Surrey there was a late harvest of Messerschmitts. Three 109s came down in the countryside and a fifth overturned as it attempted to land near Queen Anne's Gate in Windsor Great Park following combat with fighters over Surrey. The Kenley and Croydon Squadrons were all in action but only one pilot,

Flying Officer N.J.M. Barry of 501, was in trouble — and he force-landed at Pembury, Kent unhurt.

It was in the morning that the first Messerschmitt crashed and burned out at Bell Lane, Nutley with the pilot still inside. Some hours later a 109 crashed at Holmans Grove, Grayswood, near Haslemere and the pilot was captured. Another Me 109 crashed and burned out at Nutfield and, almost simultaneously, a Junkers 88, damaged by AA fire force-landed on Gatwick Race Course, killing one of the four crew.

Thousands of people watched the furious battles overhead and one school boy, Roy Chudley from Guildford described the action in his diary. "There was a terrific dogfight over Onslow Village", he wrote. "The machine gun fire sounded like a violent storm. I saw two planes on fire appear from the clouds."

The Junkers which force-landed at Gatwick Race Course on September 30th went on public display and attracted a steady stream of appreciative onlookers.

This is the Messerschmitt 109 which was shot down over Surrey and attempted to force-land in Windsor Great Park. The pilot, Oberleutnant Karl Fisher somehow crawled out of the wreckage alive and his aircraft was put on display for Windsor's Spitfire Fund.

Blenheim crew killed on routine patrol

REDHILL aerodrome, hitherto little more than a training unit and used only in emergencies, had now entered the front-line with its night-fighting Blenheims and Beaufighters.

On Thursday October 3rd a Redhill Blenheim of 600 Squadron, on routine patrol over Sussex in heavy rain, suddenly suffered engine failure and crashed into a line of trees on high ground at Broadstone Warren, Forest Row at 3.55 am. The crew Pilot Officer Colin Hobson, Sergeant David Hughes, the air gunner and AC2 Charles Cooper, the wireless operator were all killed and the aircraft was a write-off.

Hobson, aged 21 was buried at All Saints churchyard, Banstead, Hughes at Whyteleafe and Cooper at Heath Town, Wolverhampton.

Despite this setback 600 Squadron was able to operate on almost every night of its stay at Redhill but, with the onset of autumn, the appalling conditions deteriorated even more.

The low-lying grass airfield lay in a fog belt and a period of wet weather made the aerodrome surface very soft. The worried pilots appealed for better facilities but instead they were sent north and their place was taken by 219 Squadron who were given more Beaufighters and told that efforts were being made to find an alternative base.

No new airfield was found but slowly the conditions improved, airborne radar was introduced and, by the end of November, all operations from Redhill were carried out in Beaufighters — in which the pilots had been given a hasty conversion course.

Little girl talked cheerfully and then she died

THE village of Brockham, beneath the Downs and just a few miles from Dorking had been slightly bombed and machine-gunned and some villagers had seen a Canadian soldier open fire on a German parachutist as he baled out of his crashing plane.

On October 4th the village was rocked by tragedy when bombs fell on Nutwood Avenue and five were killed. In one house were Mrs Daisy Herrington, her five-year-old daughter June and George Biggs an evacuee. Next door, Mrs Esther Fisher and her two-year-old son William died.

A rescue party worked frantically and courageously through the night and among them was Edith Mercer, a volunteer member of the Dorking General Hospital Mobile First Aid Unit. Here is an extract from her wartime diary which related to that incident.

"At 12.30 when I was just falling asleep, a summons — to Brockham. Four of us went in Mrs Kaye's car while the mobile vans went separately. It was very dark and she seemed to have a great difficulty in driving and seeing even though the searchlights were providing quite a lot of illumination. We lost our way and were redirected. We eventually arrived at Nutwood Avenue, where two houses, little semi-detached ones, had been razed by a couple of high explosive shells. One could just see the outlines in the dark and the rescue party scrambling among the rubbish with torches.

"Someone, a neighbour, was giving an account of the people in the houses. Two had apparently been taken out already with not too serious injuries.

"There were others underneath, a baby, two women, an evacuee boy and a little girl of seven. Dr Bourn-Taylor evidently decided there were enough people in attendance and, without authority, I imagine, ordered the mobile unit back to Dorking. We were hardly back, when we were summoned again to the same place, where we stayed for the rest of the night.

"It was a nightmarish unreal sort of scene; the darkness, the dimly seen collapsed houses, without a wall standing, the rescue party with torches among the ruins, the rest, about 20 people standing in the road waiting to be of assistance, the searchlights overhead, the buzz of planes and the distant anti-aircraft fire. Every now and again torches had to be put out completely until the raiders were past. Two bodies were brought out. A little girl of seven was alive but pinned down by the arm and shoulder. She was able to talk quite cheerfully and did not seem too badly injured.

"It was towards rescuing her that the efforts of the night were directed. Dr Bourn-Taylor got near enough to talk to her and later we prepared a wad on the end of a stick moistened with warm water or tea which could be passed to her lips. At six o'clock it was light enough to see and most of the Mobile Unit went back to the car. J and I stayed with the doctor and nurses. But it was all no good for about seven o'clock the child became unconscious and died.

"People round about were very hospitable with tea and kettles of water. One curious collection of country folk in a kitchen I went into should have been painted. An old fashioned kitchen range, a large cage of birds, a big black dog, assorted large women, crowded furniture, children in grubby pyjamas, a shock-headed boy and a man heating up kettles for us — all at three o'clock in the morning".

This account of the Brockham tragedy is recounted in an excellent book produced for the VE Day celebrations in 1995.

Guildford schoolboy kept "combat" diary

THROUGHOUT September and into October, 1940 London had taken a terrible hammering but the Luftwaffe were still unable to deliver the knockout blow. Civilian morale, in the face of extraordinary adversity, was holding out — and it was the same in the provincial towns and cities as the enemy constantly switched their targets, introducing bigger and even more destructive bombs. Right across Surrey, and the northern boroughs in particular, there were gaping craters in gardens and dispossessed people looking for what could be saved. "We can take it" was the commonly-uttered phrase. The resilience was remarkable.

Guildford, county town of Surrey, had received spasmodic raids. On the day that Croydon airport was bombed, 12 "bandits" passed low over the town and were welcomed by a burst from the Cathedral guns. The raiders replied by machine-gunning the gas works. Guildford was famous for its great factory. Before the war, Dennis Brothers made vans and lorries and fire engines and had now turned their entire production over to the war effort, concentrating on the mighty Churchill tank. The Luftwaffe knew this; their agents had done their homework.

One 13-year-old Guildford boy kept a diary during the Battle of Britain recording the time of all the many air-raid alerts, the all-clear which followed and the incidents (if any) which accompanied them. Roy Chudley described the aerial combats with all the times and dates. He wrote about the ammunition train which blew up at Malden, the raid on Vickers, the enemy aircraft which came down at Newlands Corner, the Luftwaffe pilot who parachuted into Effingham. He told of the bombing of Onslow village on September 25th — "one high explosive burst 15 yards from school. Four bombs on Billings. One killed".

The Luftwaffe, presumably looking for the Dennis factory, came over in some force during the night of October 1st-2nd and dropped 13 high explosives. Roy Chudley noted how they fell between Little Halfpenny Farm and the Tilling Bourne, Burpham and near the Meadway.

The raiders returned again on October 14th at 2.10 am. They may have been looking for Dennis Brothers but the bombs fell on a small housing estate. Three people in Rydes Avenue were killed immediately and one died from her injuries. For Guildford it was the worst incident of the war. The high explosives impacted on two homes, Greenride and Norfolk House and the occupants were trapped beneath the wreckage. Another bomb fell in the front garden of No 107 and a third in the field behind No 101.

The *Surrey Advertiser*, unable at the time to give the exact location, said that two semi-detached houses were hit and three people were found dead, Elizabeth Burgess aged 73, Louisa Moore, 44 and Ronald Mower, 19. Miss Eileen Moore, aged 17, crawled out of the debris and was there when the ARP arrived a few minutes later. Four more were trapped inside.

In October 1940 the Government were urging local authorities to provide more shelters and improve existing ones. Towns throughout Surrey responded. Even in Woking, which had experienced very few meaningful air attacks, a 100-person shelter was built on Wheatsheaf Common to join the five other public shelters in Plough Lane, Oyster Lane, West Byfleet and Kingfield. The Goverment also introduced a new portable shelter named after Herbert Morrison, the Minister of Home Security. This was a box-like structure topped with a steel plate for indoor use. Few were delivered to Surrey homes before Christmas 1940 but the Morrison shelter was to give sterling service later in the war. It was actually capable of withstanding the collapse of a two-story house.

Meanwhile Roy Chudley — destined to join the 1st Airborne Division of the Parachute Battalion before the end of the war — was still writing his diary and on December 8th, 1940 he noted another raid in the vicinity of Rydes Avenue. A high explosive of medium size had fallen and about 50 houses nearby had to be evacuated by the police. Although Roy didn't know it at the time it turned out to be a "friendly" anti-aircraft shell!

Croydon pilot dies in collision with barrage balloon

Flying Officer Ralph Hope, who had rowed in the University Boat Race of 1935, was a second cousin to Neville Chamberlain. He joined 605 Squadron as an auxiliary pilot before the war and came through the Dunkirk campaign, channel convoy patrols and many fierce combats over London. On October 14th he was killed in an incident of tragic irony.

The weather on this day was one of low cloud and drizzle and Hope took off in his Hurricane on a routine patrol above Croydon airfield. He spotted a Heinkel 111, gave chase and inadvertently flew

Flying Officer Ralph Hope.

into the Inner Artillery Zone where his aircraft struck a barrage balloon cable. The Hurricane crashed in Tennison Road South Norwood and 27-year-old Ralph Hope was killed. He was cremated at St John's Crematorium Woking.

It was a bad week for 605 Squadron. On October 7th Pilot Officer C.E.English crashed at Park Farm, Brasted and was killed and a few days later his friend Sergeant P.R.McIntosh was shot down and killed in action off Dungeness. On the 15th Flight Lieutenant I.J.Muirhead lost his life when he came down in flames at Darland near Gillingham.

The Morrison Shelter, introduced in October 1940, had steel mesh bars at the side which could be lifted up into place and protected those inside from flying debris. It had other uses as these two people demonstrate.

Crew killed as bomber crashes in Weybridge

THE barrage balloons had claimed the life of a fighter pilot. A few hours later on the same day, an Armstrong Whitworth Whitley Mark V twin-engined bomber ran into one of the balloon cables which surrounded the Brooklands factory at Weybridge. The wing of the bomber was severed and it plummeted to earth near Weybridge station. Sergeant Wright, the pilot, and his crew of four were killed instantly.

The Whitley, affectionately known as "the flying barn door", of No 10 Squadron RAF Bomber Command had left Leeming in Yorkshire to raid Stettin in the Baltic via Le Havre and it took off

with two other aircraft on the same mission. On his flight south Sergeant Wright strayed off course and was heard in the Brookland area at 8.00 pm, apparently lost.

The pilot fired a correct recognition signal with his Verey pistol but, almost at the same time, struck the balloon cable of Site 21 in the grounds of Brooklands House and severed part of the wing which landed near Weybridge Park. The tail of the bomber also came away and fell on Elgin Lodge.

The aircraft crashed in a wood at Hanger Hill accompanied by a series of explosions.

October 11th: Pilot Officer John Gage Lecky, whose family lived at Farnham, was shot down and killed in combat with Me 109s over Maidstone. Lecky, who attended a preparatory school at Liphook, was commissioned in the RAF and joined 41 Squadron at Hornchurch on October 1st, 1940. He was killed on his third sortie, aged 19 and buried at Tilford Churchyard in the presence of a great number of mourners.

October 12th: A Blenheim of 219 Squadron, Redhill experienced unexpected engine vibration during routine night patrol and stalled at high speed. The aircraft crashed at Court Lodge Farm, Ewhurst. Pilot Officer R.V.Baron baled out but his parachute failed. Sergeant G.M.Mead also baled out and landed unhurt. On the same day a Bristol Beaufighter, also of 219 Squadron, lost and short of fuel, crashed in the village of Send, near Woking. The crew baled out safely.

Thornton Heath High Street was blocked by debris when a bomb demolished a block of shops in the October blitz of 1940. Thornton Heath swimming baths were also damaged.

October 17th: At 4.30 pm 60 aircraft in three waves approached Kenley and Biggin Hill areas and attacked the two aerodromes. No lives were lost and little damage was done.

October 19th: Nine were killed when a bomb exploded at the junction of Portland, Sandown and Enmore Roads, Croydon and caused an enormous crater. Among the dead was a passing motorcyclist. Rescue workers tunnelled perilously for hours under the wreckage to bring out trapped people. Although it was a brilliant moonlit night, lime dust hampererd the rescue operations and an arc light was required. At dawn, more bombing caused the work to stop.

October 22nd: Pilot Officer John Milne, a Canadian of 605 Squadron, Croydon was shot down over Dorking. He forced-landed on the railway bank near the old Westcott sewage works.

October 27th: Ten enemy aircraft dropped bombs on Surrey causing extensive damage to pumping mains in Sutton and fracturing the sewage works at Worcester Park. This was a night of sadness for the small community of Earlswood, near Reigate. A 1,000 lb bomb fell on No 16 Emlyn Road, demolishing five houses and damaging more than 110. Six people were killed and 24 had to be rescued from wrecked buildings. Among those killed were the proprietress of a grocer's shop and a boy of 14. Rescue parties, billeting officers, the mobile medical units and the First Aid squads worked unwearyingly giving aid to the injured and homeless.

October 30th: A Beaufighter of 219 Squadron, Redhill trying to locate base in bad visibility, hit a tree and exploded 150 yards from Balcombe Place. Pilot Officer Ken Wordsell and Sergeant E.C.Gardiner were killed, the only Beaufighter fatalities throughout the Battle of Britain. On the same day Hornchurch also lost two pilots during combat with Me 109s. Alfred Davis came down at Upper Wilting Farm, Crowhurst and Edward Edridge crashed in flames at Longwood Farm, Ewhurst.

The pilots of Redhill and Hornchurch were among nine airmen to die that day — designated as the last day of the Battle of Britain.

Polish patrol lost in Surrey "peasouper"

WHEN a group of pilots from 302 Polish Squadron, Northolt, on a routine patrol on October 18th, became lost over the Surrey Hills because of fog, the leader ordered his men to make forced-landings rather than fly in circles and possibly run out of fuel. As the weather deteriorated even more, Pilot Officer Peter Carter, from Croydon, caught a glimpse of Kempton Park racecourse and attempted to land but then became completely disorientated. He baled out but was less than 100 feet high and crashed to his death on the racecourse, accompanied by his Hurricane.

Within minutes 302 Squadron had also lost three pilots — all Polish. 24-year-old Pilot Officer Stefan Wapniarek died attempting a forced-landing at Nutwood Farm, Thames Ditton and, almost simultaneously, Pilot Officer Aleksiej Zukowski crashed at Boxley, near Detling. He too had lost his bearings but, unlike his colleagues, had run out of fuel. The fourth tragedy also occurred on Kempton Park racecourse when Pilot Officer Jan Borowski plunged into the ground and his Hurricane burned out.

There was one lucky pilot. Pilot Officer Bronislaw Bernas force-landed in the Surrey mist, made his way back to Northolt and went on to survive the war.

The three Poles who died were among hundreds of Polish airmen who fought against the Nazi invader and sacrificed themselves in the cause of freedom and independence. Sometimes on the fuselage of their planes there could be seen the Polish white and red "chessboard" emblem, sometimes red and white stars. On their uniforms there always glistened the Polish pilots' eagles and under those eagles were beating hearts of men whose great effort, heroism and devotion will never be forgotten.

Sergeant Harold Allgood was posted to 253 Squadron at Kenley on September 28th and survived many furious aerial combats. On October 10th the Kenley pilot was on patrol over Maidstone at 20,000 feet when his aircraft, for no apparent reason, went out of control and into a steep dive. Allgood, suffering from oxygen failure, wrestled weakly with the controls as the plane skimmed the rooftops. People below said he was trying to steer his Hurricane towards open ground but it bounced off the roof of a shop and crashed into two houses next door at Albion Place, Maidstone. Petrol spewed over the buildings which burst into flames killing eight people and injuring two. Firemen found the body of Sergeant Allgood in the cellar with his parachute and parts of the engine.

The German High Command Communiqué for October 10th, 1940 which was prepared for Deutschlandsender radio read as follows: "From early morning until dusk waves of reprisal attacks by light and heavy bombers continued uninterruptedly against the British capital. Immediately following these raids, night attacks of heavy bombers started, lasting till the early hours. Very heavy damage was caused in the docks in the bend of the Thames. Bomb explosions also caused extensive destruction to installations and railway tracks in the centre of towns..." The bulletin continued to give more specific details. Among the bombs dropped on that day was one which exploded on the canteen at Kingston Town Hall, killing three people.

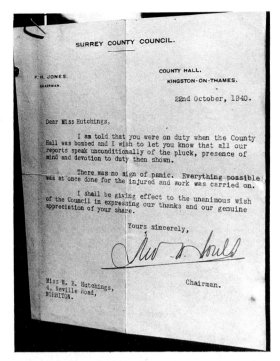

Although it was 7.15 in the evening Miss W.E. Hutchings of Neville Road, Norbiton was among those on duty when County Hall at Kingston was bombed on October 10th, 1940. A few days later she received this letter from the chairman, Mr F.H. Jones outlining the pluck, presence of mind and devotion to duty shown by the staff during the raid. Among the three people killed was Marjorie Newman (left) who was on Civil Defence duty at the time.

Did "Cats Eyes Cunningham" really train on carrots?

NOVEMBER 1940 was the month in which one young, fresh-faced, virtually unknown Addington-born fighter pilot earned a place in aviation history and went on to become a rather reluctant hero.

On the night of November 19th Flight Lieutenant John Cunningham, flying a new Beaufighter from Middle Wallop, shot down a Junkers 88 which limped on for a few miles before crashing in open farmland near East Wittering in Sussex, the crew having abandoned the burning aircraft. It was a few minutes after midnight.

The death-delivering salvo of cannon shells and bullets released by Cunningham that night — and on many more occasions to follow — was so accurate that the pilot was to earn the nickname of "Cats Eyes". Newspapers eagerly followed up reports that he ate carrots to give exceptional night vision and, like a cat, he could see his prey in the dark.

Cunningham, an Old Whitgiftian, tolerated such headlines as "Carrots DFC is Night Blitz Hero" to keep a special secret from the enemy. His night victims were nothing to do with his ability to see in the dark but due entirely to the introduction of Airborne Interception Radar, or simply AI — and it was born on November 19th. On patrol with John Cunningham that night was his crewman Sergeant J.R.Phillipson who was carefully watching the glowing cathode ray tube and waiting for the AI contact, having encountered a number of enemy aircraft streaking towards Birmingham. The contact was made, the crewman steered the Beaufighter onto a single target, Cunningham loosed off his salvo and the legend was born.

The villagers of Addington and the boys of Whitgift were delighted with the feats of their hero who received a public presentation from the Mayor of Croydon in November 1941 when he had 18 victories to his credit. He ended the war a Group Captain and went on to become de Havilland's chief test pilot.

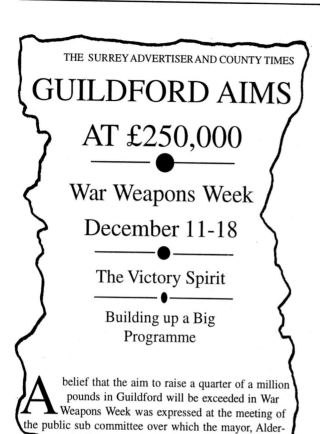

THE SURREY ADVERTISER AND COUNTY TIMES

GUILDFORD AIMS

AT £250,000

●

War Weapons Week

December 11-18

●

The Victory Spirit

●

Building up a Big
Programme

A belief that the aim to raise a quarter of a million pounds in Guildford will be exceeded in War Weapons Week was expressed at the meeting of the public sub committee over which the mayor, Alderman V.G.Wilkinson presided on Wednesday.

Woking is challenged

FOLLOWING the great success of the Fighter Fund a few months earlier, towns in Surrey were quick to respond to the idea of a new appeal for War Weapons. Guildford, ambitiously, promised it would try and raise £250,000 and challenged Woking to meet that sum.

Woking posted its indicator outside the Albion Hotel, achieved its target and watched the Guildford total soar to a mighty £552,000 or more than £12 per head of population in the county town.

Even more impressive was the achievement of Esher who targeted for £150,000 and raised £636,000.

In Dorking there was an exhibition of war souvenirs to raise money for the fund. The exhibits included parts of German fighters, a German airman's helmet and parachute. There was a case containing incendiary bombs and a contraption labelled "Molotoff portmanteau."

Villages also made contributions — East Horsley's contribution, for example, was £7,709.

Chertsey's indicator for War Weapons. The little Surrey town said the fund would help buy bombers and tanks.

Kenley's farewell to the old butcher's shop

BY November 1940, Kenley had been so badly bombed that huge craters and jagged remains of ruined buildings littered the airfield. One hangar remained and that received a visit from a lone raider during the night of November 12th. Bombs hit the corner where a new lookout and searchlight post had been established. Two soldiers were killed.

The butcher's shop in Caterham no longer housed the Operations Centre. The Grange, a large house standing close to St John's Church, Old Coulsdon, had been converted to accommodate Kenley's communications system and the transfer was completed on November 3rd.

Whether or not German Intelligence knew of this move is uncertain but on Sunday December 1st a stick of bombs rained down on Old Coulsdon. At St John's Church a morning service was in progress and, as explosions rocked the building, the congregation threw themselves under the pews. Cottages near the church were damaged and, at The Grange, the blast caused ceilings, doors and windows to collapse.

It was a miracle that no-one was seriously injured. The church congregation included a large party of Guardsmen from Caterham Barracks.

There was a succession of raids on Reigate in the middle of November. On the 7th a 1,000lb bomb exploded to the rear of Barncote, a small hotel on Reigate Hill. Later the same evening a bomb fell inside the bird sanctuary on Colleyhill causing considerable panic among the feathered residents and at 2.30 the next morning another made a direct hit on a house, Culvers, in St Alban's Road (see picture). Two of the three occupants were trapped under the wreckage but not seriously injured.

AS the Blitz on London continued many bombs fell in Surrey causing extensive damage. At Richmond, where enemy bombers flew over the railway network, 100 flats and six houses were damaged on Thursday November 7th. Isolated aircraft, breaking away from the main formations attacked Guildford on November 11th and, four nights later, factory buildings in Bagshot were destroyed. This was the night after the greatest raid of all when one-third of the medieval city of Coventry was ravaged. Towards the end of the month Richmond Town Hall was hit while Croydon, it seemed, was never long out of the firing line.

This is Croydon Town Hall showing the damage caused by the 1,000 lb high explosive which was dropped on the night of Sunday November 24th, 1940. It struck the east side of the building opposite the police station, penetrated the basement and exploded. A second bomb made a direct hit on the Central Croydon Liberal Club in Scarbrook Road which had just opened for the evening and a great crater filled with debris and a pile of ruins was all that was left of the club and a confectioner's shop next door. It was a night of tragedy, for those inside the club had no chance. Twenty-five people were killed including the stewardess and her daughters, three brothers named Bloomfield and an officer, his son and grandson. The heavy rescue squads worked all night, hampered by fire and water from the burst mains. It took 36 hours to recover the victims.

A Junkers 88 lies wrecked in a Surrey field — but where were the crew?

It took years to solve the mystery of Blindley Heath

IN the early hours of November 28th, 1940, the tail unit of a low-flying Junkers 88 was severed by overhead power cables near Redhill. The aircraft plunged to earth at Blindley Heath, South Godstone and, amazingly, remained mainly intact. There were no bodies in the wreckage, no reports of German airmen baling out of a lame aircraft and no prisoners captured in the vicinity.

Air Intelligence were quick to rope off the area and a search revealed various useful documents in the wreckage. Among them was a book with hurriedly-written notes on the cover which gave every indication that the Junkers was in deep trouble. One note read: "I must have a DF bearing". Another read: "Pass round and bale out". The crew had obviously abandoned the Junkers, but where were they?

The solution to this mystery of the Blitz was 130 miles away, although no-one knew it at the time. It was over Northern France that the aircraft developed engine trouble and the crew baled out, all landing safely. As they collected their parachutes and began to make their way back to base, near Reims the troubled, crewless Junkers was flying on over the Channel, across Sussex and into Surrey before it ran out of fuel and came gliding down into a field losing a tail unit on the way.

It was only when German and British records were compared after the war that the mystery of Blindley Heath was finally solved.

Short truce in a desperate Christmas

CHRISTMAS, 1940 was the most desperate that Surrey had ever faced but, as with beleaguered people all over England, the citizens gritted their teeth, took their Horlicks, cleared away the debris and carried on.

The county newspapers were of one accord in noting that this was a very sad Yuletide. The editor of the *Surrey Advertiser* wrote: "While maintaining the formal atmosphere of the festival as fully as possible it has been impossible to forget those who have gone to the wars. Into many homes thousands of men and women on service have been welcomed and thousands of others, driven from their homes by tragic experience or danger, have been remembered."

Looking ahead he said: "As the New Year approaches we welcome the lengthening of the light. We have left the shortest day behind and the sun begins to climb in the heavens. It is a happy augury that the moral blackout is fading, too. The shortest day for the oppressed peoples of Europe is past. Daily, fresh evidence comes that the enslaved nations are stirring in the darkness".

In Surrey the people did their best to observe the traditions of the season. The Kingston Empire was fully booked for its production of Mother Goose with Joe Arthur. The London Philharmonic Orchestra (all 70 of them) were pulling in the customers to The Rembrandt, Ewell. The Hogs Back Hotel was advertising a special Christmas Day lunch for 6/- and a dinner-dance on Christmas Eve for 12/6d.

There was no let-up in money-raising activities and the desire to help touched young and old. A feature of Camberley School's bazaar in the school hall was an attractive display of knitted garments by the girls, the fund to be directed to "the relief of distress caused by enemy action". Ewhurst organised a "delightful Christmas programme of events" including an auction conducted by Richard Gouldon (Mr Penny of BBC fame). Ten pounds was raised in aid of comforts for the village Home Guard.

Many people found the bottle a welcome distraction from the bombs and, during the Christmas week, the newspapers reported several cases of drunkenness. Fourteen people were summoned at Guildford for failing to comply with light regulations and four cyclists for riding without screened and dimmed red rear lights.

One happier story came from Farnham where the little Playhouse Theatre (Now the Redgrave) was almost a year old and was putting on some fine performances. The timber-framed building had been put to many uses in the past as a warehouse, cloth factory, roller-skating rink and a music school. During 1940 it was turned into a small theatre with tip-up seats and a raked auditorium that could hold 167 people at 1s 6d and 3s 6d. By Christmas 1940 it was one of the country's smallest reps, opening with Shaw's *You Never Can Tell*.

As with the 1914-18 war when German and English troops facing each other in the trenches organised a game of football, there was an undeclared amnesty during the Christmas period but this ended with a vengeance on December 29-30th when the enemy attempted to burn down the City of London, and nearly succeeded. Firemen from all over Surrey rushed to help fight the conflagration and probably there had never been such a concentration of fire fighters and equipment brought into action at one time. Certainly Croydon sent a large contingent under Chief Officer Delve.

The fires from London were enormous and visible from scores of miles from all sides; it seemed to the people of Surrey, and particularly to those living on higher ground, that the whole of London was being consumed.

As the great fires of London raged, newspapers were full of pleas for help. Esher was seriously short of wardens. Epsom and Ewell wanted volunteers for stretcher parties and demolition work. Sutton needed women for first-aid posts and auxiliary nursing while every community called for more recruits to the Home Guard. Only Malden, it seemed was satisfied. There, the Civil Defence boasted that all their machinery was in place and ready for maximum operation.

There were many people experiencing an English Christmas for the first time and among them were more than 600 Belgian and Dutch refugees who had found a safe haven in Surrey homes after a "second trek from German barbarism".

The refugees had arrived at Wimbledon station earlier in the year with terrible stories of Nazi atrocities. They were met by the WVS who found them homes in Kingston, Wimbledon, Surbiton and Esher, Hook and other towns in the north of the county.

In these hours of darkness there were some lighter moments as a letter, written in 1940 and discovered in Elmbridge Museum, Weybridge more than 50 years later, clearly shows. It was written by Mr A. Citizen, Flattened Road, Much Blasted, Surrey and was addressed to HM Collector of Taxes. It read: "For the following reasons I am unable to meet your demands for Income Tax. I have been bombed, blasted, burnt, sandbagged, walked upon, sat upon, held up, held down, flattened out and squeezed by Income Tax, Super Tax, Tobacco Tax, Purchase Tax, Beer Tax, Spirit Tax, Motor Tax, Entertainment Tax and every society, organisation and club that the inventive mind of man can conceive to extract what I may or may not have in my possession for the Red Cross, Black Cross, Double Cross and every other cross and hospital in the town".

1941

More rationing, night bombing, Pearl Harbour

January 10th: This day saw Woking's most serious incident of the war when several heavy bombs fell on a housing estate in a nearby village Six people were killed instantly and one died later in hospital. The *Surrey Advertiser* wrote: "Most of the victims were in bed but one family who refused to desert the comparative safety of their Anderson shelter escaped injury. A mother and son sleeping in a downstairs room in a house nearby were not hurt although the house was shattered. They escaped because a plank of wood was over the bunk in which they were sleeping."

January 20th: Men and women aged between 16 and 60 had to register for part-time Civil Defence work. Firewatching became compulsory.

February 4th: Britain's war costs had risen to more than £11 million per day. In April the standard rate of income tax was increased to 50 per cent.

March 8th: The Luftwaffe began its new night bombing assault on London as part of its spring offensive with heavy attacks on other British cities.

March 9th: Ernest Bevin, Minister of Labour , appealed for 100,000 women to come forward and sign up for munitions work.

April 17th: Yugoslavia surrendered.

April 20th: Heavy raids on London and Birmingham with parachute mines.

April 27th: Allied troops evacuated Greece as the German army advanced into Athens.

May 7th: Seven nights' continuous bombing devastated Liverpool.

May 11th: The height of the Blitz. 500 German bombers reduced London to a city of rubble.

Under these flags they fought for you NOW HELP THEM

FORCES DAY · WEDNESDAY APRIL 23RD

SOLDIERS, SAILORS & AIRMENS **HELP SOCIETY**

May 17th: Rudolf Hess was imprisoned in the Tower of London after being brought down by train from Scotland where he had parachuted from his crashing Messerschmitt. He said he had been on a mission of peace.

May 24th: *HMS Hood* was sunk off the coast of Greenland. Only three of the 1,416 crew survived. In revenge the German battleship *Bismarck* was torpedoed in the Atlantic on May 27th.

June 1st: Clothes were now rationed and margarine tokens had to be used until new ration cards were printed.

June 22nd: A German attack on the Soviet Union took the Russians by surprise along an 1,800 mile front from the Baltic to the Black Sea.

July 4th: A new restriction on coal rationing — only one ton per month for domestic use.

September 8th: German and Finnish soldiers surrounded the city of Leningrad, then went on to besiege Kiev.

September 17th: Mashed potato sandwiches and potato pastry were recommended in a campaign to get the British public to eat more root vegetables, of which there was no shortage.

September 19th: Six hundred Morrison shelters were received for distribution in Dorking. They were issued free to householders whose income did not exceed £350 per year. For other homes the charge was £7 per shelter.

September 23rd: Charles de Gaulle formed his national committee in London as France's government in exile.

October 12th-13th: RAF bombers made their first large-scale raid on Nuremburg.

October 31st: The Army Catering Corps was formed, enlisting professional caterers to advise on feeding the troops.

November 7th-8th: RAF bombers attacked Cologne, Berlin and Mannheim in heavy night-time raids.

November 14th: *The Ark Royal* was sunk by a U-Boat off the coast of Gibraltar.

December 4th: Unmarried women between the ages of 20 and 30 were called up to serve in the police, fire service and armed forces.

December 8th: Japanese air force attacked Pearl Harbour and the following day President Roosevelt signed America's declaration of war on Japan.

December 25th: Hong Kong surrendered to the Japanese.

Following the raids on London by fire bombs in December 1940 Herbert Morrison, the Home Secretary, told the Cabinet that there were "gaps in the rank that were dangerous in Blitz conditions". He suggested that Fire Guards be enlisted. One month later the order was given that all men between the ages of 16 and 60 were liable to enlistment and should be trained to deal with incendiary bombs and the use of stirrup pumps.

The maximum amount of duty required was 48 hours per month. The photograph shows the Bishop of Croydon the Rt Rev Maurice Harland with a group of parishioners on fire watching duty in the vestry of the parish church. They had been trained by the chief of the Croydon Fire Brigade. The church suffered no damage until 1944 when the windows were blown out by a flying bomb, which fell in Cranmer Road on July 27th.

Amy Johnson — the darling of Croydon — drowns in the Thames

AMY Johnson, the Englishwoman who made aviation history with her 10,000-mile solo flight from Croydon to Darwin, Australia in 1931 was killed on January 5th, 1941 when the aircraft she was flying ditched into the Thames estuary.

Miss Johnson, aged 38, had been working for Air Transport Auxiliary — ferrying new aircraft from various factories including Brooklands to front-line fighter squadrons. There was no enemy activity at the time and it was believed she lost her way in bad weather or ran out of fuel.

Her friends in Croydon to whom she was known as "Johnnie" and all those who had seen her take off on her epic voyage in May 1931, were devastated by the news. Eyewitnesses from the mainland said the aircraft's engine appeared to cut out before it crashed into the water.

The captain of a naval trawler, Lieutenant Commander W.E.Fletcher saw her bale out. He dived in the sea, reached her but despite valiant efforts could not support her. He died later in hospital from hypothermia.

The Spitfires of 485 Squadron on the grass runway at Redhill.

Redhill ready to welcome the heroes

GREAT news for the little satellite airfield at Redhill. In February 1941 it was raised in status to RAF Redhill and the decision was made to move Kenley Wing's third squadron (No 1) there from Croydon. By this time the aerodrome had a new perimeter track, army mesh runways, a communal complex, dispersal areas and hangars. Number 1 Squadron arrived on May 10th and were immediately in action, destroying eight German bombers on the last night of the Blitz.

Redhill was now ready to welcome and accommodate the heroes of the Battle of Britain including many pilots of the Dominions. No 258 Squadron led by Squadron Leader Wilfred Clouston, a New Zealander who had already a dozen or so "kills" to his name, arrived in late February. The squadron was the most cosmopolitan of Fighter Command and included in its ranks, British, French, Czechs, Polish and American pilots who liked nothing better than to wander through the beautiful countryside around Redhill on fine summer evenings. They also helped on the local farms, not for practical reasons but merely to lend moral support to the land girls.

In the summer a complete New Zealand Squadron arrived, No 485, led by Squadron Leader Michael Knight. The pilots had little battle experience but were to learn the hard way, flying on three or four operations a day as they strove to dominate the skies. There were many losses which led to a visit from the New Zealand Prime Minister, Mr W. Fraser to express his admiration and condolences.

In July 1941 the airfield's refuelling and re-arming facilities were completed and many squadrons involved in the fighter sweeps over France refuelled at Redhill. In August 485 Squadron was re-equipped with Spitfire Vs and was involved in a bizarre incident that is described by Geoffrey Tait in his informative little book *Redhill at War*. "One morning while training flights were in operation", he wrote "two Spitfires were observed circling over an area to the south of the aerodrome and were soon joined by a third. Those watching from the airfield feared that one of their aircraft had crashed. Soon more aircraft arrived and joined in the general melée to the utter bewilderment of the onlookers. It transpired that one of the pilots had spotted a number of lady nudists basking in the morning sunshine." It appeared that the ladies either didn't care or were totally oblivious to the aerial interest!

In November 1941 the New Zealanders moved to Kenley and were replaced by fellow Antipodeans No 452 (Australian) Squadron who had suffered very heavy losses while flying from Kenley. Among their numbers was Irishman Paddy Finucane, one of the best-known pilots of the day who was interviewed by the BBC and said: "Our chaps sometimes find they can't sleep. You come back from a show and find it very hard to remember what happened. Maybe you have a clear impression of three or four incidents which stand out like an illuminated lantern slide in the mind's eye. Perhaps a picture of two Me 109s belting down on your tail from out of the sun and already within firing range. Perhaps another picture of your cannon shells striking the belly of an Me and the aircraft spraying debris all around. But for the life of you, you can't remember what you did."

At the height of the Blitz, the ARP section known as the Rescue, Shoring and Demolition Department was renamed. It became the Heavy Rescue Squad and was the responsibility of town and city engineers. The gangs consisted of eight men and a leader and were equipped with old lorries which proved ideal for demolition work. They carried steel cables, wheelbarrows, timber joists, adjustable metal supports and all the tools necessary for rescue and worked in shifts of 24 hours on duty and 24 hours off.
The photograph shows the Heavy Rescue Squad of Coulsdon and Purley who at the time had probably little idea of what they had let themselves in for. But it was not long before they were working side by side with firemen as office blocks and warehouses blazed and shouts went up to "watch that wall" as timber and masonry crashed. Long before the fires became damp smouldering piles of rubble, the Rescue Squad would be beavering away for several hours at a time looking for possible survivors and carrying out the dead. It was dangerous, unpleasant but necessary work.

Weybridge girl wins military medal

JANUARY 18th, 1941 was a red letter day for 19-year-old Miss Youle of Weybridge — she was awarded the Military Medal for bravery. The citation explained how Miss Youle, a WAAF sergeant was on duty in the telephone exchange at the RAF fighter station, Detling in Kent on August 13th, 1940 when it was bombed. The Operations Room next door received a fatal hit and several men were killed and two seriously injured. Dust and fumes filled the air and debris and splinters rained down but Sergeant Youle maintained that vital link between exchange and Command headquarters "with coolness and most complete efficiency at a dangerous time for all". Corporal Josephine Robins, a non-commissioned officer who went to the assistance of the wounded also received the Military Medal.

Miss Youle, daughter of Captain and Mrs Youle of Clydebank, Oatlands Park, Weybridge was well-known in the town as a member of the St George's Hill Lawn Tennis Club. She had earlier attended the Ingomar School, Walton. Only six Military Medals were won by WAAFs during the war.

Love, sex and war on the Surrey farms!

BY the spring of 1941 the Land Girls of Surrey had long forgotten their glamorous pre-war life in the towns and cities and were well established in farming and forestry all over the county. Wearing green jerseys, brown corduroy breeches and slouch hats they had watched the Battle of Britain rage over their heads, dodged the bombs and the shrapnel, put up with the lack of comforts and had proved to themselves and their critics that they were as useful as many men in the fields.

In August 1940 the Women's Land Army had only 7,000 members. By 1941 more than 25,000 had registered and completed their initial training and many thousands of them had been dispersed to farms in rural Surrey. One of the problems that concerned the Surrey Agricultural Committee was the "gossips and goings-on" between the Land Girls and the Canadian soldiers billeted in their hundreds throughout the county. A strict 9 o'clock curfew was urged to keep the girls out of mischief during the blackout hours. That wasn't popular with either sex.

The committee was also worried about "the wisdom of casting on one side, even temporarily, the whole elaborate system of agricultural education, for the purpose of training a few thousand Land Girls".

Before the war the girls had such jobs as dress designers, artists, hairdressers, waitresses, factory girls and domestic servants. By the spring of 1941 their hair was untidy and their pretty frocks were packed away and long forgotten. During their 48-hour week they drove tractors, brought in the harvest, milked the cows and cared for the livestock. A minimum wage for a man doing such a job was £3 a week; for the women it was 32s, or 18s after they had paid for board and lodgings.

The girls chose to exchange the shops and factories for the rolling farmland of Surrey for all sorts of reasons. One had worked at the Woolwich Arsenal, producing munitions but she suffered from skin problems and volunteered for a healthier life. On her farm near Ewhurst she learnt to milk, hoe, hedge, ditch, dig drainage trenches and bring in the harvest.

Another young girl lived in an Army Girls' Hostel in Queen's Road, Hersham, near Hanger Hill and worked for one farmer in Esher and another in Walton. According to Mr Neil White manager of the Elmbridge Museum who met the lady (now Mrs Hussey), she moved on to Thorpe Park Farm, near Staines putting in tomato plants for one shilling a row, milking cows from 6 am and haymaking at dusk. On another occasion she worked at Rivernook Farm, Walton alongside many German PoWs.

Her sister, now Mrs Blackmore, worked on a farm at Dorking where she just had one day's holiday a year — on Christmas Day. She wore bib and brace overalls with hobnailed or Wellington boots.

By 1943 no more volunteers were being accepted into the Land Army or the womens' uniformed services. It was then more important for the girls to go into the aircraft factories. Brooklands and Kingston were to take hundreds of new female recruits.

Bess Pendry from Chertsey volunteered to work as a Land Girl and was posted from Croydon to work at George Crawley and Sons who were tree surgeons. Later she became a farm hand at Mr Glennie's arable farm at Lyne. She remembers the "uniform" and was grateful on occasions to be wearing gaiters. "I was on top of the stack", she recalled, "pitchforking sheaves to the men on the thresher and suddenly saw lots of mice. One of the girls didn't have her gaiters on and you can guess what happened — a mouse ran up her trouser leg and there was mayhem!"

Margaret Bray and Naomi Smith, Land Army girls on Netley Farm at Shere. The ladies, still live in the village today.

The Land Army girls at Rivernook Farm, Walton-on-Thames

Land girl Daphne Snow poses with an estate worker by a grain elevator at Long Grove Farm (now Horton Park Farm), Epsom. The farm had been mechanised and updated before the war. At nearby Woodcote Park, 110 acres had been ordered by the Surrey Agricultural Committee to be brought under cultivation.

The rhyming couplet on the banner across the High Street (below) shows Egham's determination to raise as much as possible for War Weapons Week and try to forget the devastating attack on the town that had taken place in November. In that raid a bomb had fallen on Arkell's drapery store, killing three young people — two boys who had been evacuated to Strode's School from Stepney and the younger daughter of Mrs Arkell. Egham, by Runnymede, was attempting to raise £100,000 for War Weapons Week and had placed an indicator on the town's 54-foot hose drying tower showing the progress towards the target with the words "every copper helps to arrest Hitler". A feature of the week was a long procession through the town in which members of all the fighting forces took part. Among them were the Calgary Highlanders, complete with pipe band.

ARP wardens stand nonchantly next to an unexploded parachute mine knowing the sting had been taken out and that no damage had been caused to the nearby homes in The Meadway, Shirley. The residents had been lucky. The mine was found to have 36 1 kg incendiaries in the tail and had been packed with the tails towards the nose of the mine so on explosion they would have been thrown out over a wide area starting many fires. No-one knows why it failed to explode. The parachute (draped over the wall on the right) may have been caught up (by tree branches) as it floated to earth, lessening the impact. Officially the existence of parachute (or land mines as they were known in England) was not disclosed to the public until 1944 but scenes such as this one in Shirley were not unusual during the Blitz. It is believed that the detached cone on the right of the mine was part of the parachute compartment.

Frozen siren failed to sound as raiders approached

The residents of Shirley were not the only people to experience a little bit of luck in those trying days. On the bitterly cold evening of January 19th, 1941 the air raid siren on top of the Co-op stores in London Road, Redhill failed to sound because of frost when many raiders were on their way. The police attempted to come to the rescue by sounding the bell on the police car but by this time the bombers had droned harmlessly overhead towards their more important target in London. Two days later the siren again failed to sound as a lone "hit and run" raider approached the town. On this occasion an 11-year-old schoolboy was killed as he walked along Colley Lane, Redhill. Four soldiers in a nearby camp were injured.

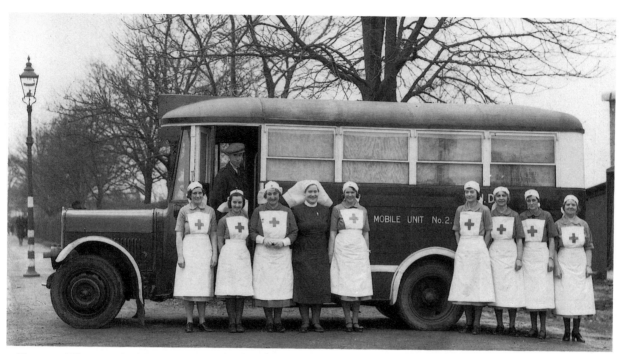

Nurses at Westway, Guildford with their Mobile First Aid Unit which was part of the Auxiliary Ambulance Service.

The ambulance service in Croydon began with a nucleus of young women trained by the Red Cross and St John Ambulance Brigade. As the bombing began it expanded rapidly and trade vehicles were commandeered and depots established. Whenever a bomb fell in the neighbourhood a stretcher party squad located the incident and sent for an ambulance. Sometimes the crew would return with badly wounded casualties through dark streets, obstructed with debris and accompanied by gunfire. It was a hazardous business. The headquarters for the ambulance service was at Wellesley Road and they controlled 12 depots and dealt with hundreds of casualties. August 1940 was a great test of endurance for the girls, two of whom were commended for gallant conduct in dangerous situations. Here are the girls from the 9th Croydon making time to pose with their mascots and a commandeered vehicle.

Air Transport Auxiliary pilots in their flying kit. Their job was to ferry aeroplanes from factories such as Brooklands to the airfields where they were needed.

Women at War

IN April 1941 many women were officially registered to fill positions normally undertaken by men. They took jobs in munitions and shell-filling factories, delivered milk, became butchers, printers and postal workers.

Other women volunteered for the services. Most of them were recruited into the Auxiliary Territorial Service (ATS), although the WRNs and the WAAFs were considered more glamorous because of their association with the sea and the air.

In Surrey many ATS were trained to operate the aiming mechanism of anti-aircraft guns but not allowed to fire them. They were, however, allowed to train as drivers and mechanics but cooking, cleaning and clerical work were the most common jobs.

The WAAFs at Croydon, Kenley, Redhill and other RAF bases had become mechanics, photographers, radio operators and bomb plotters.

But these were not the only girls in uniform. Popular in most Surrey towns was the London Passenger Transport Board's women conductors easily recognisable in their pale grey jackets and slacks with blue piping.

Aircraftswoman June Buddle was the popular postmistress at Kenley.

The women of Surrey were the great deliverers. A customer of Job's Dairies — there were branches all over the county — receives her daily bottle from the milk lady on her rounds in Primrose Road, Hersham. Notice the gas mask in its case, still ready for possible use.

Epsom Fire Brigade in 1941. Notice the requisitioned vehicle still bearing the name Thomas Pocock.

A victim of the Atlantic Battle

THE Battle of the Atlantic was now in full cry. Between February and May 1941 Allied shipping losses from attacks by destroyers and mines ran into hundreds of thousands of tons but as the war at sea escalated there was a greater hazard for the sailors — German U-Boats which, in February alone, accounted for 58 Allied ships.

Among the thousands of brave sailors on the sea during this hazardous month was Bill Mutimer of Chessington, a Merchant Navy navigation officer on a cargo ship bound for Newfoundland. He and his crew were aware of the dangers from above, below and either side. They could only be vigilant and pray.

Bill's story of the events of Saturday February 22nd, 1941 appeared in the *Surrey Comet* after the war. He explained that he had taken a nap after his duty on watch and was awoken by a shattering explosion in the sea. He quickly discovered that the assailant was neither U-Boat, destroyer or mine but an aircraft which was making another swoop towards the ship. Bombs were dropped, accompanied by machine-gun fire and among those injured was the second mate, a great friend of Bill's.

He wrote: "As I dragged the mate towards the wheelhouse what appeared to be an iron bar hit me with almighty force in the right upper arm and I staggered below to seek help. The cook managed to get a splint on my arm and stem the flow of blood and the steward gave me mor-phine and mercifully the excruciating pain left me...

"We were 500 miles east of Newfoundland and all I could do was wait and hope that help would come. At 9 pm I heard several boom. boom sounds from a direction to starboard and a gunner said to me 'this is it mate, f.....g shells'. Seconds later a crashing sound like 150 dustbins all flying around and hitting one another was accompanied by deep, thundering noises. They appeared to go on for ever.

"On deck I saw the ship's funnel had disappeared and deck houses were burning fiercely. The ship was sinking and the lifeboats were being lowered... Despite my condition I ran towards the port lifeboat, clambered on and shouted to the bosun to take the tiller and ordered all who could to start rowing. We picked up several men on a raft and knew from shouts in the darkness that there were others all around us in the water...

"Our ship was almost on its beam ends but then appeared to right itself, the stern rose in the air and it plunged swiftly below the waves, bow first. It was an awesome and sad sight. It was not only my ship but my home which had disappeared beneath the waves of the Atlantic Ocean."

Bill and his colleagues were captured by the Germans and he was taken to a military hospital where his right arm was amputated. He was then transferred to a German PoW camp.

There was a good muster for the Farnham Home Guard Church Parade on a Sunday morning early in 1941 — an event held in most towns throughout the county. Here they are in Castle Street, a military picture of smartness.

Six killed in Purley as UXB explodes

THE highly exacting responsibility of defusing unexploded missiles was divided between the three services. The Royal Navy was responsible for parachute mines and bombs which fell on Admiralty property, the Air Force dealt with those which fell on Air Ministry property and the Army took charge of the rest of the mainland. "The suicide squads" as these brave men were known, spent day after day in water and mud attempting to remove the "sting". Many were killed.

One of the worst tragedies to befall these brave men occurred on February 5th, 1941 when a bomb fell in Bynes Road outside Purley Oaks School and failed to explode. The bomb disposal section of the Royal Engineers sent a crew of seven to deal with the missile but as they were working on it the bomb exploded, six were killed and the seventh was badly injured.

The explosion was enormous and could be heard for miles around. Part of the school collapsed and damage was caused to several homes in Bynes Road which had already suffered from previous action.

There were heroes and there were heroines and among them were the members of the British Red Cross who dealt with many mutilated bodies both in Surrey and in German occupied territory where they were allowed into PoW camps to report on conditions. Here are a few volunteers who worked with the Red Cross Unit at Pelham House, Harestone Valley, Caterham. They worked eight-hour rotas. In Weybridge many ladies spent time on the Red Cross trains which ran from Walton to Southampton to pick up the injured who came home on the liners.

9,000 members in Surrey Red Cross

FROM THE SURREY ADVERTISER: FEB 1, 1941

The Surrey branch of the British Red Cross Society was told at a meeting last week in the Guildhall, Guildford that the county strength stood at more than 9,000 and detachments numbered 172.

Sir Alan Broadway was in the chair and was supported by Lord Ashcombe (patron), the Duchess of Northumberland (President) and Lady Lawrence (deputy President).

The secretary gave details of the work of the Red Cross in Surrey during the year mentioning in particular the comforts scheme which had provided wireless sets, games and clothing for air raid casualties in over 100 hospitals in the county.

He reported on the immediate relief scheme which had provided timely help in cash and kind to casualties, the prisoners of war packing centre where 200 voluntary workers had despatched some 70,000 parcels in just seven months.

The branch was reminded of the difficulties in finding houses for additional convalescent homes and accommodation for more than 300 beds was still wanted.

North Downs like a candlelit Christmas tree

GERMAN aircraft retreating from raids on London with incendiary bombs to spare were dropping them indiscriminately on the Surrey towns and villages during the early months of 1941. In Leatherhead between Hawks Hill and Ashstead hundreds were jettisoned, lighting up the surrounding hills. Edwina Vardey, in her history of Leatherhead, wrote that Fetcham Downs one night was likened to a huge candlelit Christmas tree and some properties were set alight but, due to the vigilance of the firewatchers, successfully extinguished.

Four bombs fell on Charterhouse School, near Godalming and another hit a sewer in Hurtmore Road and failed to explode. An army officer and NCO detailed to make it safe were killed when the missile detonated prematurely.

At Puttenham, under the Hogs Back, incendiary bombs fell on the Priory Gardens. They looked like stars in the sky as they fell. At the time Lady Harcourt was dining but, holding an umbrella as protection against any more missiles, she went outside in evening dress to see the cause of such an infuriating disturbance. Fires were still burning in the trees so she ordered her butler to put them out. He needed help and the Home Guard were the best bet. He found most of them in the Good Intent pub.

Between January and March there were serious incidents in Chobham, Bletchingly, Banstead and Oxted and all along the valleys of the Tillingbourne, Mole and Wey. Searchlights were in place along the North Downs and a particularly powerful one was installed on the Memorial Sports Ground at Redhill. Its powerful, probing light was one of dozens piercing the dark skies on those blitzy nights of 1941.

My last night as a serving airman

WHEN a formation of Heinkel bombers, detailed to attack Liverpool on the night of March 12-13th, 1941, encountered the Defiants of 264 Squadron, one of them caught fire in the air and began to spiral earthwards. Two of the crew were killed in the inferno and a third died when his parachute (if he had one) failed to open. The fourth was Karl Bruning, the pilot, who landed near his burning aircraft at Ockley, Surrey and was taken prisoner. This is an extract from Karl Bruning's story of that grim night. It was written in 1978.

"We left our airfield at Avord, south of Chartres at 2100 hours and crossed the English coast at 5,000 metres. The target was Birkenhead and the weather was perfect for nightfighter operations — no flak and no searchlights. I felt we could expect fighters so I put my crew on alert then all hell was let loose.

"We were surprised with many direct hits and the aeroplane caught fire. Both engines were hit and stopped at once. The oil temperatures shot up and the speed fell. Through the intercom I could hear the groaning and screaming of Steiger, my wireless operator and Weisse, the flight mechanic, both of whom seemed to be seriously wounded. My left hand and left ankle were injured but I felt no real pain. Dussel, my observer seemed unhurt so I told him to go back and throw Steiger and Weisse out after preparing their parachutes. The situation was desperate.

"Dussel came back and said he could not reach them as the gangway was ablaze. They would have to take des-

Karl Bruning's Heinkel was hit by several bursts from a Boulton Defiant flown by Flying Officer F. Hughes and his gunner Sergeant Freddie Gash of 264 Squadron, Tangmere. In their combat report they said "the bandit crashed at Oakwood Park, south of Dorking".

tiny into their own hands. I shouted to everyone to jump but found that Dussel had already gone. I think he jumped without a parachute. Perhaps his pack was in the fire and maybe he preferred to die that way rather than be burnt or die in the crash. Poor Alexander.

"I jumped, opened the parachute and below me saw the aeroplane spiralling earthwards in flames. I saw it impact and explode. I landed in a clump of bushes in a daze and shouted for help. I saw two people approaching and one of them called "hands up". I soon realised they were kindly disposed towards me and gave them my pistol and holster. In exchange they gave me cigarettes. I was handed over to a Home Guard post and then interrogated.

"It was a dreadful night. Sometimes the interrogators went beyond the limits of what was permitted. They told me I was the only survivor and kept me awake all night. Next morning I was taken to the Horsham Hospital and found that my Iron Cross had been stolen from my tunic which made me sad, but I was alive. This was my last day as a serving airman and my thoughts turned to Steiger, Weisse and Dussel. I had some luck; theirs ran out on March 12th, 1941."

By April 1941 the once much-maligned Defiant was a successful night fighter and 264 Squadron, based at Biggin Hill, was achieving many of the "kills". On the night of Wednesday April 9th, a Heinkel was shot down by Sergeants Ted Thorn and Fred Barker over Surrey. It crashed at Shepards Hangar, Busbridge, near Godalming just before midnight and three of the four crew were killed and one taken prisoner. This photograph of the two pilots surrounded by their colleagues in 264 Squadron was taken on the following day. The Heinkel had taken their score to 13 and they were now the top-scoring Defiant pair in the RAF.

Lord Haw Haw reveals his identity

IN April 1941 the announcer of the English language news programme *Germany Calling*, in one of his famous propaganda broadcasts, boasted that "for every microscopic part of enamel England rubs off a German tooth, England will lose a complete set of her own". The statement was heard by thousands who regularly switched on the wireless to hear the programme which was beamed from Hamburg via the powerful Hilversum transmitter in Holland.

Among those who listened regularly to the German announcer with the superior English drawl was Leslie Pratt who worked at the radio monitoring station in Cherkley, Surrey. He described the well-spoken into-

nation to Sidney Smith, who was in charge of the radio reporting team as a "proper Haw Haw voice". The description stuck. The *Daily Express* dubbed the announcer as Lord Haw Haw, the name quickly became a household word and newspapers speculated as to who the well-spoken newsreader could be.

They soon found out. In a later broadcast the announcer said: "I, William Joyce left England because I would not fight for Jewry against Adolf Hitler and National Socialism. I thought victory which would preserve existing conditions would be more damaging to Britain than defeat."

All Saints Church, Merstham was so badly damaged that it could not be used again for worship. See pages 146-147

Ten killed in Merstham's landmine disaster

LAND MINES continued to be dropped in Surrey. On March 19th 1941 two fell in Leatherhead, killing one person and injuring 27. One exploded on St Andrew's Convent School injuring five nuns and destroying many of its buildings. The blast was so great that a gymnasium at St John's School, half a mile away also collapsed.

Exactly one month later, on April 19th, the borough of Reigate experienced its worst night of the war when two parachute (or land mines) were dropped on Merstham. The first came down in Wells Nursery and failed to explode and the next morning it was rendered harmless by the Admiralty Mine Squad.

The second buried itself some 12 feet on waste ground to the west of the junction of Battleridge Lane and Nutfield Road and exploded with such a devastating effect that ten people, living in the vicinity were killed, more than a dozen injured and 300 buildings badly damaged.

In his book about Reigate, *The Borough in War Time*, Charles W. Preston writes: "Some of those who lost their lives were waiting for a bus at the nearby stopping place, another was driving a car which came to a stop about two yards from the edge of the 15-foot crater. One boy was on his way to the Wardens' Post to report for duty as a messenger when he met his death. All Saints Church suffered heavy damage, rendering it unfit for Divine Services, as did the vicarage. The vicar, the Rev H.G.Baker was injured and his 90-year-old sister killed.

"A Canadian unit stationed nearby sent an officer and 15 men and rendered invaluable service in search and rescue work. The Merstham Wardens, the Fire Brigade, the stretcher party and rescue squads worked in a way which brought them the highest praise and the gratitude of all the sufferers."

All that remained of the Crystal Palace after the great fire of 1936 were the two towers, visible for many miles around and, presumably, helpful landmarks to enemy raiders as they approached the centre of London. Because of this fear the decision was made to demolish them and the South Tower, adjacent to Anerley Hill was taken down gradually. On April 16th, the North Tower — sufficiently far from any houses — was demolished by explosives just after mid-day. That night with no Palace towers to guide them, German bombers launched their greatest raid on Croydon and the London boroughs.

A HIGH explosive bomb which fell on Addison Road, Guildford on May 12th, 1941 killed one person, seriously injured four and caused extensive damage to more than 100 homes. The bomb impacted in the centre of the carriageway at the bottom of a footpath leading to Pewly Way and made a crater that was 32 feet in diameter and 10 feet deep.

Tea and sympathy in a Guildford suburb

The *Surrey Advertiser,* reporting at the time, was not allowed to mention the town but said that "rescue parties were quickly at work and the cool, courageous behaviour of the bombed people evoked warm praise. A rest centre was established in a church hall and neighbours hastened to ascertain the circumstances of people less fortunate than themselves and give shelter until daylight to those in need. One man with a car brought a large quantity of tea and went home for more after the supply was exhausted".

The smiles of these survivors in Wimbledon show their relief at escaping death. They emerged unscathed from the shelter after their home was demolished.

Bombers crash in Surrey during the heaviest raid yet

ON April 16th, 1941 in the heaviest raid of the war to date, 728 long-range bombers, 11 light bombers and 20 long-range night fighters set off from their bases in France to attack London. Bombing was indiscriminate and widespread. Residential, industrial and commercial premises in 66 boroughs suffered extensive damage and by the end of the raid 1,179 people had been killed, 18 hospitals and 13 churches were destroyed and more than 2,000 fires raged.

The Beaufighters of 219 Squadron were among the 164 aircraft of Fighter Command in action that night and they patrolled the skies above Surrey with considerable success.

At 1.15 am, Wing Commander T.G.Pike and Sergeant W.T.Clark shot down a Junkers 88 which dived into the ground at Thorns Flush, Cranleigh. The crew were killed and the aircraft destroyed. An hour later in their second combat of the night the Beaufighter pair destroyed a Heinkel 111 which broke up in the air over Petworth Road, Wormley. One of the German crew baled out and was taken prisoner. The others died.

The most famous incident occurred at 9.30 in the morning when a Junkers 88 crashed into the garden of a private house, 15 Denmark Hill, Wimbledon after an attack by Flight Lieut. Dotteridge and Sergeant Williams of 219 Squadron. Three of the German crew were taken prisoner and the fourth died when his parachute failed.

The postlady and the parachutist

This story of the discovery of a dead German pilot was published in a book entitled *Surrey Within Living Memory* which included wartime accounts by members of the Women's Institute throughout the county. Four German airmen were killed in the crash at Cranleigh on April 17th and the postmistress stumbled across the body of one of them the next day. Parts of the Junkers, which had taken off that night from its base in Beaumont-le-Roger, are now in the Tangmere Military Aviation Museum in Sussex.

"IN the spring of 1941, my husband was in the Army and I was the local postlady at Hascombe, south of Godalming. The postal area was spread out over lonely places and the only way to get to some of the houses was over the fields and through the woods, on foot.

On the morning of April 18th, 1941 I was on my way to a large house called "Nore", when I noticed something pure white hidden by the undergrowth, down in a valley. I knew a plane had crashed locally and most of the wreckage and one body had been found along the Guildford Road area of Cranleigh but I wondered what this could be and decided to investigate. Fighting my way through the bushes I came upon a parachute. "Oh good", I thought, "lovely white silk to make some clothes".

As I stood looking at this I noticed a heap of greenish-khaki coloured straps and things, then I suddenly saw a leg with a black flying boot caught in a blackberry bush. The "heap" was a body! I was so frightened I couldn't move. It dawned on me that it was the German airman the Home Guard were looking for. I rushed back to the village policeman who had to send for the police to come from Godalming, then I had to take them to the place.

One didn't know at that time of the war what the Germans would do to you, it was frightening. I wondered if the young man was still alive, but it was not so — he had baled out of the plane which was flying too low. I was only 22 and so scared that that was the end of my postlady job. No-one would take it on then to deliver to those lonely places. Later it was taken over by a postal van service which had to go around the lanes from Cranleigh."

The London Transport Bus Garage, Brighton Road, Croydon which was destroyed on May 10-11th, 1941 (see story opposite).

Stretcher bearer was hero of tragic night

NO-ONE who lived in the borough of Croydon and the surrounding villages and survived the night of April 16th-17th will ever forget it. The Fire Service alone received 4,655 messages as dive bombers, machine gun fire, parachute mines and incendiaries rained on the town in wave after wave of enemy attacks. By morning 230 fires were raging, gas, water and electricity services had been cut off, hospitals, churches, residential houses and offices were smouldering ruins and scores of people were killed or badly injured.

The worst incident occurred at 10.25 pm when a parachute mine fell in the grounds of the Queens Road Homes, a hospital for the old and chronic sick. A fire watcher saw the monster on its ugly descent and attempted to raise the alarm but he was blown across the grounds by the explosion.

The hospital building containing the wards was badly wrecked; so were the staff quarters and offices. The rescue squads, in circumstances of great danger, worked all night in the debris to free the injured including nine old men buried under the rubble. So heavy was the debris that the search continued for four days when the last of the 17 dead patients was recovered.

A second mine fell on Limes Avenue, Waddon and the blast wrecked or damaged every house in Lodge Avenue, Wandle Side, Waddon Court Road, Mill Lane and many of those along the Purley Way.

The people of Croydon braced themselves for further attacks but there was an uncanny, uncomfortable respite until May 10th-11th when raiders again came in waves and this time it was South Croydon's turn to suffer when eight high explosives fell in two sticks with a four-minute interval between them. One exploded on an Anderson Shelter killing four, another fell on the polishing store of Carrington Manufacturing and two on the bus garage of the London Passenger Transport Board. Mr Berwick Sayers who was chief librarian at Croydon during the war recalled this dramatic and tragic night:

"It had been customary to disperse the buses round roads during raids but owing to the fear of the residents that the lights in them during cleaning would attract raiders, they had been returned to the garage. That night many had been filled with petrol.

"The whole garage seemed to go up in a roaring conflagration and there were men inside, some of whom, when the first bomb fell, had dived into one of the examination pits under the buses. Heroic attempts were made to get out these unfortunate busmen but a bus on top of the pit

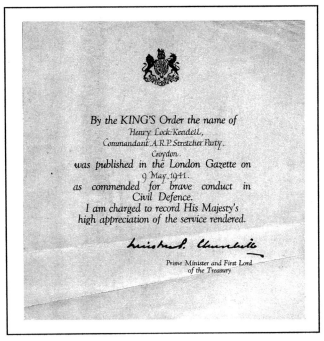

Mr Henry Lock-Kendall was Commandant of the ARP stretcher party (St Augustine's Hall depot) and led the rescue services when the Croydon bus garage was hit on the night of May 10th-11th, 1941. He crawled into an inspection pit under the blazing bus, rescued three busmen and returned four times while the fire brigade played water which scalded when it splashed him, such was the heat. Mr Lock-Kendall who was later Mayor of Croydon received a Royal Commendation for his bravery on that night. The date on the certificate above is incorrect.

was on fire. Other men had been blown under buses and were unconscious and one, not unconscious, was hysterical."

The garage was completely destroyed and with it 65 buses. The casualties of the night were 14 dead, many badly injured while others were given assistance at various first aid posts. On this night too an aircraft fell in flames at Farnborough Crescent and the pilot was killed.

This was to be the last big raid on Croydon for three years for the Blitz was almost over. In less than 12 months 362 people had been killed, 672 sent to hospitals and 813 treated at first aid posts. The damage was beyond anything experienced outside London and a few big cities. More than 1,000 houses had been totally destroyed and 26,000 damaged with 3,954 homeless, leaving the Borough with the formidable task of initiating a re-housing project. There was also the important work of emergency feeding and clothing.

Many Croydonians had lost everything.

Frenchmen, Aussies and bags of bull

AS the great RAF sweeps or offensives over France continued, many squadrons of Fighter Command operated from aerodromes closer to the Channel and the enemy coast and Croydon's importance as a front-line station began to fade although it was still used for brief periods as a squadron base.

Redhill, on the other hand, was growing in size and importance. In regular use by visiting Wings operating over France, the main runway was lengthened to 1,300 yards while the large original hangar was taken over by a Vickers team repairing Spitfire wings.

Kenley, too, had visitors. During the early part of 1941 the station was besieged by journalists, photographers and script writers. Actor friends of the pilots came, so did politicians and prime ministers — these official visits requiring "bags of bull".

One of the most popular pilots at Redhill was Squadron Leader Peter Brothers who had been given the command of 457 (Australian) Squadron which had not flown over enemy territory but was soon to be pitched into some of the heaviest fighting known, losing a number of pilots. They were joined, briefly, by the first Free French squadron to form, No 340 commanded by Squadron Leader de Scitivaux, who were desperate to make their flying debut over enemy territory.

The Australians' flying discipline was high and they found that of the French somewhat less conventional, aircraft frequently appearing from nowhere to taxi across the aerodrome. On one occasion a Frenchman took a short cut and his aircraft was in collision with another.

Flight Lieutenant Peter Brothers, pictured here with his future wife Annette and her mother Eve Wilson, lived in Westerham close to the Surrey border. He served with 32 Squadron from 1936 to 1940 and in 1941 formed 457 Squadron with Australian pilots and RAF ground crew. In June 1942 he took command of 602 Squadron at Redhill.

Wartime welder in Walton

"DURING the war, as a young man, I was employed as an Air Ministry approved welder in a small aircraft factory at Walton-on-Thames and by April 1941 the bombing raids had become a familiar part of my life and gave me and my colleagues an extra urgency to the job in hand.

It must have been harder for some of the women who were, by now, doing a full-time job and running a home and contending with the rationing and the shortages. It seemed strange though to find a new kind of humour develop and class distinction almost disappear.

As production in the factory got into top gear and increased so did the number of employees, and in our section alone there were 10 welders. Two of these — Jack Hubbard from Norfolk and Bob Pearson from Coventry — were to become good friends. They both kept their accents and we called them "foreigners".

Bob had worked at the famous Triumph factory before being transferred to Walton.

He was a piece work welder, paid on results. He did not wear the usual goggles with dark green glasses but his own spectacles perched on the end of his nose.

One of our welders was a young woman and she was an expert at aluminium welding which was required for the Halifax bomber. We were still turning out the Airspeed Oxford and Miles Master engine frame mountings or nacelles as they were called.

As the months passed I became more proficient in my welding but some of my colleagues found the constant repetition very boring. The molten pool that you kept chasing with the torch and filler rod became second nature and I found that my mind would wander to what Peggy might be concocting for my evening meal. I hoped it would not be whalemeat or horseflesh. I preferred spam, that great tinned meat brought over from America by our merchant seamen — S.Burville, Hersham, Walton-on-Thames."

As the Blitz intensified so did the vigilance of the men of the Observer Corps especially those whose posts were situated below the path of the raiders. Their job was to identify, plot and then report the aircraft. The posts were set about 10 miles apart and linked by a telephone line to the various operation centres. Here the many reports were numbered and assigned to an RAF sector and the "bandits" plotted across a gridded map table with coloured counters, bearing track, designation, height, number and aircraft type. In recognition of the fine work by the Observer Corps the King added the title "Royal" and said they were no longer the unsung heroes of the war. Photograph shows an Observer Post, spotting and tracking.

The staff of the Control Centre beneath Soper Hall, Caterham. Left to right (standing): A.G. Crowdy (deputy clerk), P.E.Dimmock (clerk). Bates (Scout 1st Caterham), E.D.Holburn (treasurer). Seated: Mrs Hay, Miss Baverstock, Miss Mary Elsey, Miss Molly Fearis.

This is all that was left of No 36 Waterloo Road, Epsom. Two people died in the raid.

The night that London almost died

THE night of May 10th, 1941 was one of the coldest May nights on record. By midnight the temperature had dropped to below freezing and, on the Thames, the ebb tide was low. There was also a full moon, a "bomber's moon". People in every town and village in Surrey were gripped with tension and it was almost a relief when the sirens sounded in nerve-tingling harmony across the peaceful countryside.

It was not peaceful for long for the greatest concentration of enemy aircraft ever seen crossed the coast and droned on towards the capital. By dawn London was burning. More than 550 planes had dropped hundreds of thousands of high explosives and incendiaries. They came in continuous waves throughout the night, returning to their French bases to refuel and re-arm. The fires stretched across almost every borough and south as far as Epsom.

This raid was to be the last of the Blitz and it was almost the end of London. More than 5,000 houses were destroyed and the provisional figures for casualties indicated that 1,400 were dead and 1,800 badly injured. Much

of historic London had suffered. The chamber of the House of Commons was a heap of rubble. The roof of Westminster Hall was ablaze and the tower of Westminster Abbey had fallen in. The British Museum had been hit and so had St Paul's Cathedral. People were seen to be weeping in the streets.

Fire appliances from all over Surrey were called to help with the 2,200 fires which were sweeping across the capital. By the early hours of the morning 700 acres of London were burning, nearly twice the area damaged by the Great Fire in 1666. Among those to die in the Surrey boroughs on that devastating night were 14 in Croydon (as told on page 113), two in Epsom and four in Wimbledon. Here the Gap Road/Plough Lane area was saturated with incendiaries and high explosives fell in the car park of the All England Lawn Tennis Club.

It really marked the end of the Blitz for the Germans were now committed to the invasion of Russia and, confident that London had been damaged beyond repair, the bulk of the Luftwaffe were on their way east.

The 59th Surrey Battalion of the Home Guard who manned the 4.5 inch anti-aircraft guns at Shirley Park Golf Club.

The Cobham hot shots bring down a Junkers

THE accuracy of the men on the anti-aircraft guns throughout the county was improving all the time, a fact confirmed by the gunners at Fairmile Common, Cobham who were operating the heavy 3.7 inch guns.

On the night of May 2nd-3rd they shot down a Junkers 88 on a bombing mission to Liverpool which crashed on the Common about a quarter of a mile from the gun site. All four crew members baled out and were taken prisoner. Today the actual site of the Common is obliterated by the A3 Esher by-pass.

Boy sailors go down with the Hood

FOR seven traumatic days, families in nine Surrey homes waited for news of their sailor sons or husbands who were serving on the world's biggest battle cruiser HMS *Hood*. The ship had been attacked on May 24th by the German vessel *Bismarck* with the loss, it was feared, of most of the crew.

The telegrams giving the grim news eventually arrived from Admiralty headquarters a week later. All of them were "missing, presumed killed, on war service". They were among 1,413 sailors who went down with the *Hood* in the icy waters off the coast of Greenland. Only three survived.

The *Hood* with her sister ship, the *Prince of Wales* had been stalking the *Bismarck* but it was the German vessel which fired first — with devastating effect. There was an explosion of incredible violence and flames leapt up from the depth of the ship. It sank within minutes.

Among the Surrey sailors to drown were Able Seaman Stephen Smith of Barrack Road, Stoughton, aged 20, already a holder of the Palestine Medal; Able Seaman Eric Weldon, 20, of Alpha Road, Chobham; Leading Signalman Charles Gibbs, 20, of Springfield Cottages, West End, Chobham who had been married earlier in the year; Boy Seaman Percy Collyer, 17, of High Street, Horsell; Boy Seaman First Class Stanley Jelley, 17, of Gloster Road, Old Woking and Acting Leading Seaman Stanley Cox, 21, of Farm Road, Woking.

Two men from Addlestone went down with the *Hood*. Mrs Heath of 15 Station Road was notified that her husband, Ordinary Seaman David Heath was "missing, presumed killed". Mr Heath, 30, was on the Naval Reserve and had volunteered for service in August 1940. He left a widow and three children. Mr and Mrs Boon of Liberty Lane, Addlestone were told that their son Michael was also missing. Michael was educated at St Paul's School, Addlestone and had worked at Shanks Garage before the war.

Leading Cook Edward Harvey, 28, of Foxhills Road, Ottershaw also lost his life in the *Hood*. His mother had only just received a letter from him saying he had passed his exams and was now a qualified Petty Officer.

Esher saddened by the loss of the Cossack

THE Surrey newspapers were full of news about the disasters at sea during 1941, frequently giving details of the boys who were missing. It was not all bad news. When the destroyer HMS *Greyhound* was sunk at Crete there was considerable anxiety about the fate of Leading Signalman E.Shepherd who had worked for the *Surrey Advertiser* before the war. The expected telegram arrived at the sailor's home in Woking Road, Guildford. He had survived the sinking and was safe and sound on a Mediterranean island.

Some weeks later the people of Esher heard that HMS *Cossack*, the Tribal Class destroyer, had been torpedoed. This was a tragedy. The ship's captain, Edward Lyon Berthon, lived in the town and his family were desperate for more news.

The story unfolded gradually. HMS *Cossack* had been torpedoed on October 23rd and as fires raged around the bridge Captain Bethon had given orders to abandon ship but, sadly, he and 158 officers and ratings were lost. In the early hours of October 24th a party was put back aboard the stricken ship which was still afloat and the fires were extinguished. Steam was raised in the undamaged engine room and a rescue tug arrived from Gibraltar. Unfortu-

HMS Cossack, Tribal Class Destroyer in her prime.

nately weather conditions worsened and the salvage attempt was abandoned, HMS *Cossack* finally sank on October 27th.

During Warship Week in 1942 (see page 126), the people of Esher raised more than £1million and said they would like it to fund another HMS *Cossack*. The new destroyer was built, launched and enthusiastically adopted by Esher Urban Council.

A plaque in Portsmouth Cathedral is dedicated to this achievement by the Surrey town.

The last moments in the life of a proud ship. October 27th, 1941. The salvage attempt was abandoned and the Cossack sank.

When Pilot Officer John Archibald Milne of 605 Squadron, Croydon was shot down over Dorking during the closing stages of the Battle of Britain, he force-landed on a railway bank, dislocated his hip and was taken to Dorking County Hospital cursing his bad luck. But not for long. The young Canadian pilot fell in love with pretty Staff Nurse Nan Jones and began to date her as soon as he was released from hospital. A year later (October 1941) they were married. The couple are pictured here. Nan is wearing the uniform of Queen Alexandra's Imperial Military Nursing Service Reserve.

Rabbit for a pint in a Hindhead pub

THE scarcity of food and the restrictions caused by rationing were biting deeply into the average family's way of life. Many Surrey housewives were receiving food parcels from the Dominions, others were self-sufficient thanks to their skills in the garden and allotment; recipes for such things as carrot jam and nettle tea became more popular. The less popular dried eggs encouraged people to keep chickens.

The Guildford Food Control Committee, meeting in the summer of 1941, said that seven tons of fruit had been given away by the Food Office in 1940 but now the growers were allowing fruit to remain on the trees until it dropped — and that was criminal. The committee decided to establish a jam making centre and said they would seek the support of the WI movement.

The women responded immediately. Throughout Surrey they set up a network of Preservation Centres and made a register of all those who owned steam pans. Lord Wootton, Minister of Food visited Egham to see how the WI had extended its scheme to include other women's organisations and set up branches at Hatchford and Stoke D'Abernon. He watched with growing admiration as villagers brought huge bundles of rhubarb and gooseberries to the centre and received wholesale market prices for them. He then tried his hand at topping and tailing, boiling, bottling and labelling.

Another innovation in most Surrey towns was the introduction of a British Restaurant. Here the price of a meal was 1/-, or even less, with soup for 1d and tea at the same price. In Leatherhead the new British Restaurant was a tremendous success. On June 28th 1941, The *Surrey Advertiser* wrote: "Over 300 cheap lunches are being served there daily and the peak figure is 429. All classes of people are patronising the venture and the takings have more than covered expenses. It has now been decided to open a similar restaurant in Ashstead."

One of the staple foods of which there was no shortage in Surrey was the potato. There were also plenty of carrots and swedes but for many other foodstuffs there was so much shortage that long queues formed every day outside the shops.

Pamela Wackrill of Thames Ditton recalls that food rationing was strictly observed but very few people went hungry. "My mother queued for three hours outside Walter's", she said, "but the last piece of fish was sold in front of her and she came home in tears. I spent Saturday mornings in Kingston market place queueing for horse-flesh labelled 'unfit for human consumption'. It was for our dog and it smelled horrid."

There was much "swapping" particularly in the countryside. In the Surrey WI book *Within Living Memory,* a lady from Hindhead explained how her father would regularly go to the pub and exchange a pint of beer for a rabbit, shot by one of the locals. He would then buy another pint for one of the Canadian soldiers stationed in the area and receive in return a packet of sweets sent from Canada.

In the same book a member from Kingston recalls eating rabbit stew and Irish stew washed down with rose hip syrup followed by cod liver oil.

On June 1st 1941 clothes were also rationed, joining food and petrol. It was agreed that every man, woman and child should be given 66 coupons to last for a year. The coupons varied according to the size of the garment; a woman needed 14 coupons for an overcoat while men required 13 for a jacket and eight for trousers. The new regulations paved the way for second-hand clothing shops to be established.

One month later on July 4th coal was rationed, principally because of the call-up of young miners.

A British Restaurant in Wallington where the price of a meal was a shilling.

There were queues everywhere during the war but none were longer than those outside shops. Here, the people of Shere patiently queue outside the fish shop and, among them, with the muffler, is one of the village's more distinguished residents, Lord Pethick-Lawrence, Secretary of State for India and Burma. Lord Pethick-Lawrence liked to do the weekend shopping which he regarded as a happy relaxation from his work in politics — but he had to take his turn in the queue.

Milkmen defy 'enemy' at Hampton Court bridge

THERE was a brave attempt by "the enemy" in August to capture one of the most vital supply lines over the River Thames — Hampton Court bridge and then perhaps take over the great house itself. But this was a military training exercise carried out by the Home Guard and the famous bridge was chosen for a large-scale mock battle, the organisers hoping the various platoons might get an idea of their duties if the invasion ever occurred.

Defending the river crossing were a platoon of Home Guardsmen formed among members of the staff of the Milk Marketing Board at Thames Ditton. The action that ensued was described by the *Surrey Comet*: "Bags of sawdust, representing hand grenades, came whizzing over a parapet. There was a sharp rifle engagement and after 10 minutes half a dozen 'Nazis' crept along the side of one of the blockhouses and tried to gain possession by a hand-to-hand scrap".

The platoon commander, Captain R.A.Pepperall said:

"A tank painted with the German Eagle and swastika machine-gunned one of the blockhouses. I led the attacking party and, to make it more realistic, I used a genuine German revolver, helmet and firestick". Actually, he said, they were his souvenirs from the last war!

THE *Caterham Home Guard Gazette*, published quarterly, contained this note about No 4 Platoon: "There are now not more than 10 men left of our original strength but one cannot think of those volunteers without mentioning our "young man". "Would that we all had the enthusiasm, endurance and stamina of L/c Dunn of section one — 74 years old and never a duty or parade missed.

"We were born in an open shed at the rear of an inn, spent our early childhood in a sandbagged air-raid shelter and graduated to garage, coach house and now Transport Hall where we are arranging a musketry class for recruits."

'We sang songs and joked as the Ark Royal went down'

THE Royal Navy avenged the loss of HMS *Hood* by sinking the much-feared German battleship *Bismarck* after a thrilling chase across the Atlantic by more than 100 ships. Her pursuers included the *Ark Royal* and it was Swordfish "stringbags" from the great aircraft carrier which struck the crucial blow.

A few months later, on November 14th, the *Ark Royal* was also at the bottom of the sea. She was hit amidships by a torpedo, 25 miles from Gibraltar and began to list at once losing all power and light. It seemed for a while that, under tow, she might reach Gibraltar but a fire broke out in her port boiler room, the list increased and the great aircraft carrier sank with the loss of one crew member.

Among those who were rescued was First Class Stoker Leonard Redding, 22-year-old son of Mr and Mrs C.Redding of College Road, Ash. He reached his village home dressed only in his overalls to give his worried mother "a lovely surprise".

Also safe and sound was Charles Henman of High Street, Old Woking, a sailmaker's mate who had joined the *Ark Royal* only in April. Recalling his last voyage he told the *Surrey Advertiser*: "I was down below getting a cup of tea when the ship was torpedoed. After orders had been given to abandon, the main concern of the crew was to get as many of their possessions off as possible. Everything that could float was pushed overboard but there was complete order all the time. The sailors joked with each other and sang songs as they prepared the lifeboats".

As the men of the Ark Royal were fighting for survival, with or without their possessions, the good ladies of Wimbledon were busy knitting garments for sailors in distress. Here is the team, hard at it, needles clicking in unison as scarves, socks, jerseys and all types of woollies flowed off the production line.

1942

Singapore, Dieppe and El Alamein

January 6th: President Roosevelt announced that American forces would be sent to Britain.

January 10th: The Germans were forced to retreat as the Red Army launched a counter attack against the Nazis 'winter line' that ran from Bryansk to Rzhev.

January 20th: The first Japanese air raid on Singapore killed 50 people.

January 21st: The British 1st Armoured Division were in full retreat in North Africa to escape being trapped by Rommel's panzers.

February 3rd: The Prime Minister of Eire, Eamon de Valera appealed for 250,000 more soldiers to help defend the country's neutrality.

February 9th: Soap rationing came into force with an allowance of 4oz of household soap or 2oz of toilet soap per person per month.

February 19th: Singapore surrendered to the Japanese, claimed to be the greatest military defeat in the history of the British Empire.

February 22nd: Air Marshal Arthur Harris, aged 49, took over as commander-in-chief of Bomber Command. He impressed Churchill with his views of 'strategic' bombing to attack German civilian morale.

April 15th: The island of Malta was awarded the George Cross in recognition of its people's bravery in the face of repeated bombing by the Axis.

On the same day a new death camp in Poland was ready to receive its first transports of Polish Jews and gipsies.

April 26th: Princess Elizabeth, aged 16, registered for war service.

April 26th: Hitler assumed the position of "Supreme Judge" of the Reich and gave himself powers to act independently of the law.

April 28th: Pay and prices were frozen in America and rationing of petrol and sugar was introduced.

May 14th: Women were asked not to wear stockings in the summer so as to conserve supplies for winter. This started a fashion for dying legs with onion skins and drawing-in seams with eyebrow pencil.

May 20th: The Japanese completed their capture of Burma.

May 31st: RAF bombers devastated Cologne in the largest raid in the history of aerial warfare. Rommel launched his new offensive in the Western Desert.

June 1st: Firemen from all over Surrey were called to Canterbury to help put out hundreds of fires in the ancient city. 43 people were killed.

June 21st: Rommel captured Tobruk.

June 24th: Allied PoWs were put to work by the Japanese to extend the 294-mile Singapore to Bangkok railway line north through the jungle to Rangoon.

June 25th: Dwight David Eisenhower was appointed commander of US forces in Europe.

June 26th: Sweets and chocolates were rationed. It was now ½ lb per person every four weeks.

August 12th: Montgomery took over command of the British Eighth Army in North Africa.

August 15th: The first summit meeting between Stalin and Churchill took place.

August 20th: Allied forces suffered defeat in Dieppe with more than 4,000 killed, mostly Canadians.

October 24th: Montgomery launched attack at El Alamein.

October 26th: Cakes in shops were limited to only one layer of jam or chocolate with a maximum price of 1s 6d per pound.

November 3rd: Rommel, the "desert fox", ordered a retreat and "good old Monty" was hailed as a hero.

November 15th: Church bells, silent since June 1940, rang out to celebrate the victory at El Alamein.

November 22nd: Herbert Morrison, Home Secretary, replaced Sir Stafford Cripps in the war cabinet.

December 31st: The Red Army celebrated the defeat of the Germans at Stalingrad but Leningrad was still under siege.

Surreys lose 185 men as Singapore falls

APART from one or two isolated raids, the gift of 1942 to the people of Surrey was immunity from bombing. The tragedy of war was now unfolding many miles from home and the stories that came back were both sad and glorious.

Following the debacle at Dunkirk, two battalions of the East Surrey Regiment were in England, a third was languishing behind a high wire fence and arc lights in Germany and a fourth was in Malaya defending the Peninsular against the Japanese who had entered the war following their attack on Pearl Harbour a month earlier.

The Japanese advance was awesome. On January 11th the oil-rich Dutch East Indies fell and the next day Kuala Lumpur, the capital of Malaya, followed making the consequences for Singapore very grave. The 2nd Surreys, having amalgamated with the 1st Leicesters, became the 'British Battalion' fielding a side of 760 of all ranks. They defended their position north of Kampar with outstanding heroism but soon found themselves surrounded and withdrew to Singapore. Their arrival brought the strength of the fighting troops, under the army commander Lieutenant-General Arthur Percival, to 70,000.

The enemy, however, had control of sea and air and on the evening of February 8th troops landed on the northwest shore of the island and were so invincible that the British Battalion stumbled from one disaster to another. A week later Percival surrendered. Arms were stacked. and troops were told to stay where they were. Churchill, who had sent a telegram saying that "the battle must be fought to the bitter end; Commander and senior officers should die with their troops", now described the surrender as "the largest capitulation in British history".

Scores of families in Surrey were soon to receive the dreaded telegram. Of the 760 men who had formed the British Battalion only 265 remained to surrender to the Japanese. The Surreys' death toll alone amounted to 13 officers, three warrant officers and 169 NCOs and men. The dishevelled remnants were marched to Changi jail — a hell hole where 50,000 men were squeezed into just four barracks — followed by years of captivity in Thailand and Burma constructing the infamous railway line. *See page 190.*

It looks like a garage and workshop but, in fact, it's a dispersal depot in Birwood Road, Hersham. There were many such sites and all deliberately inconspicuous. Just a watchman at the gate, a defence point and all reference to the location removed.

Food for civilians in a bogus Red Cross truck

THERE were many conspicuous acts of gallantry during the heroic defence of Malaya and the hectic days preceding the capitulation of Singapore, but one stood out and did not come to light until many months after the event.

Soon after Percival surrendered, four soldiers, including Private William Slade and Private Arthur Crowhurst of the East Surrey Regiment, somehow obtained an ammunition truck, draped it with Red Cross flags and pretended it was an ambulance. For several days the truck made repeated journeys to and from the civilian Internment Camp with food and necessities obtained from various sources in the town. They also conveyed elderly, stray Europeans to the Camp who were stranded, homeless in Singapore.

In their journeys with food and comforts in a bogus Red Cross truck the soldiers were repeatedly interrogated by Japanese sentries but carried on at strong personal risk.

The people of Croydon were grateful that the bombs were no longer falling. They followed the sweeping advance of the Japanese, the fall of Singapore and then the terrible battle of the Java Sea in which every single Allied ship was destroyed by the Japs. They were particularly interested in the fortunes of an Old Whitgiftian and an Honourary Freeman of the town. Air Marshal Sir Arthur Tedder was commanding the air operations in North Africa where the Eighth Army had returned to see if they could throw back Rommel. The sirens still sounded in Croydon and although very little happened the town continued to be vigilant, reorganising the Civil Defence services, reinforcing surface shelters and continuing with tests in first aid, fire fighting and the use of stirrup pumps. The photograph shows the fire wardens of Park View and The Mount, New Malden, outside No. 12 The Mount.

The Immortal Prisoner

THE people of Walton could hardly believe the news. Their most famous son, fighter pilot Robert Stanford Tuck, was not going to make his usual fleeting visit to his parents at Garrick Close for some time. The man they called "The Immortal Tuck" was in enemy hands.

In less than 18 months Flight Lieutenant Tuck had managed to abandon his blazing aircraft over Kent, glided 15 miles before landing on a dead engine and had been shot down in the Channel. His latest and last escapade occurred during a mission to Le Touquet when he found himself trapped by crossfire, made a forced-landing and was immediately arrested.

His adventures, however, were not quite over. Tuck was destined to escape from his prison camp and then fight alongside the Russians.

Subscribers 'felt the call of the sea'

FUND raising for the war effort continued to be given high priority. The Spitfire Fund, in 1940, raised enough money for scores of communities in Surrey, big and small, to buy the much-needed fighters. Then there was War Weapons Week in 1941 which was another great success considering the demands that were being placed on individuals from other charitable appeals such as Aid to China, Aid to Russia, the Red Cross, Salvation Army, War Bonds, Prisoner of War Fund and many more.

In February 1942, towns, villages and even small hamlets in Surrey ambitiously named their targets and the dates for the next effort — Warship Week. No-one was under any illusion as to the seriousness of the appeal. The Royal Navy were reeling from a series of heavy blows in the Battle of the Atlantic and news had just been announced of the loss of four cruisers and 16 destroyers in the Mediterranean. The Admiralty was desperate for replacements.

In Egham, for example, the town set out to raise £135,000 for the provision of a first class minesweeper. By the end of the week the total was in excess of £200,000 and in a congratulatory telegram the First Lord of the Admiralty said "the response to Warship Week had been greater than that to any other appeal for deep down in the heart and blood of every Britisher there was a feeling of the call of the sea".

Godalming welcomed a most distinguished guest to the inauguration of its Warship Week which was reported by the *Surrey Advertiser*. "Admiral of the Fleet, Sir Roger Keyes, his breast aglow with six rows of ribbons and other decorations was present to hear the town adopt the corvette HMS *Vega*. 'I hope you will be a very good parent', he told Godalming and not only pay for the *Vega* but for more *Vegas*'".

Dorking aimed at £200,000 and reached the objective by Thursday. Thanking them was Admiral Sir Edward Evans who gave an address at the Embassy Cinema. Woking beat its £400,000 Warship Week aim by almost £150,000 and announced that the money would go towards the cost of HMS *Southdown*, the Hunt Class destroyer which the town had adopted. A committee was immediately formed to maintain contact between the ship and the town.

It was not only the larger towns which responded to the appeal. Byfleeet raised £116,000 and small villages such as Busbridge £11,000, Chiddingford £12,000, Whiteley, Enton and Wormley, £5,000, made generous donations.

Pride of Chertsey

IN February 1942 Chertsey Urban District adopted HMS Dianthus during Warship Week and the townsolk followed the progress of the corvette with a great sense of pride.

A few weeks later came the news that Dianthus had been involved in a midnight battle in the Atlantic during which she spent three hours chasing a German U-Boat. Dianthus eventually caught up with her prey, rammed it four times and then blazed away through the night with every gun, rifle and revolver that she could muster. The U-Boat's bow reared up, crashed onto the deck of the corvette and then sank.

The crew of the Dianthus picked up a number of German survivors and rejoined her convoy in time to rescue survivors from a torpedoed merchant ship.

Farnham's "warship" was HMS Chiddingford, a Type 11 Hunt Class Escort Destroyer which was allocated to the Mediterranean Fleet in 1943 and joined the 59th Division in Malta.

Some of the children of Shere School who wrote to and made presents for the crew of the Stornest from 1938 until 1942 when the vessel was "lost". The letters are not lost; they are preserved in a special album in Shere Museum.

Children of Shere adopted a merchant ship

IT was not only the warships that were vulnerable. Air attacks, mines, surface raiders and submarines had accounted for the loss of millions of tons of Allied merchant shipping and the lives of many sailors.

Through the British Ship Adoption Society, many schoolchildren throughout Surrey wrote letters, sent presents and made it known to the beleaguered merchant seamen that there were people back home praying for their safety.

Among those to adopt a ship was Shere School whose headmaster Mr Claude Blogg urged his senior pupils to keep writing constructively with all the news about the village and the wonderful morale of the people.

In Christmas 1941 he gave his students a few suggestions for presents for the sailors. "From the girls", he wrote "how about long woolly scarves for the cold winter watches and socks about the same size as dad's. Make handkerchiefs embroidered with his initials if you know them and bookmarkers, for sailors love to read.

"From the boys", he suggested, "ashtrays are useful

when you get untidy people from ashore and you can make piperacks, bookends and bookmarkers."

He added a special note: "You will have noticed that the name of 'your' ship is omitted from the letters they send you. You, too, must be guarded. In no letter mention the name of 'your' ship".

The secret now is out. Shere's ship was *Stornest* and she plied the Atlantic, dodging mines and U-Boats, her sailors replying to letters from the children until early 1942 when the letters suddenly dried up. *"Stornest the brave"* had lost her final battle. She and her crew lay at the bottom of the ocean.

After the war, in 1948, Mr Blogg, then headmaster at Cranleigh School wrote to the British Ship Adoption Society asking what became of "Shere's ship". The reply was thus: "It is inspiring that you should retain such happy and proud memories of your old friends of the *Stornest* and I deeply regret that they are remembered among those who made the great sacrifice".

The men of Caterham show no signs of the horrors to which they had been exposed.

Two firemen about to enter a smoke-filled building.

Firemen moved to tears by the horrors of the Blitz

BY the start of 1942 the Auxiliary Service had been re-named the National Fire Service, the Blitz was over and the men had time at last to pose for pictures and reflect on the most hectic months the service had ever known.

For the firemen of Caterham (above opposite) there had been many local bombing blazes to deal with but in addition they and their pumps had been required to help quell the fires in Croydon and in London during the height of the Blitz between December 1940 and May 1941. At times they had worked alongside 9,000 firemen with 2,000 pumps and seen the City and docks in danger of becoming a huge conflagration. These men had admitted that they were moved to tears on occasions as they gazed at the unimaginable scenes of destruction, with flames and smoke rising together from the capital.

The firemen (opposite below) are putting on their self-contained breathing apparatus which was used for entering smoke-filled buildings. One Surrey fireman, Bob Velde from Guildford recalled how his station at the top of the High Street was called to Shalford Station where a train-load of tankers carrying more than 100,000 gallons of high octane aviation fuel had been derailed. "When I arrived", he said, "the petrol was still streaming and spectators on the road bridge, which was too near for comfort, were told not to smoke. I was caught in one of the many explosions and spent some days in hospital badly burned."

Members of the Upper Thames Patrol on duty in 1942.

It was not the world news, but the morning post, which held such terrible fears

IN the greater field of war, events were moving fast. The British 1st Armoured Division in North Africa was in full retreat, the Japanese Pacific offensive was threatening Australia's northern doorstep, convoy patrols in the North Sea, the Mediterranean and the Atlantic were still dodging U-Boats and mines, fighter pilots were now over enemy territory and British bomber crews were probing deep into the heart of Germany. But for the families back in Surrey it was not the world news, but the morning post, which held such terrible fears.

Take the month of March 1942 for example. Inspector and Mrs Armstrong of Woodham Lane, Weybridge received a telegram informing them that their eldest son, Captain S.G.Armstrong of the Queen's Royal Regiment had been captured in Syria. A further communication told them that he had been released but, sadly, killed in action in Tobruk.

Mrs L.Hart of By-pass Road, Leatherhead heard from the Air Ministry that her son, Sergeant Frank Axe was missing following an offensive patrol. Days later came the news that the 21-year-old pilot, who had so excelled in Leatherhead at cricket and swimming, had been killed.

Widowed mother, Mrs Ralph Carver of Shortheath, Farnham was informed that her son, Squadron Leader J.C.Carver had been shot down over the Channel and was missing, presumed killed. A few days later the intrepid pilot walked into the house. After his Spitfire had hit the water he drifted

| POST OFFICE TELEGRAM |

for 57 hours in a rubber dinghy uncertain whether he would be picked up by friend or foe. His only injury was a frostbitten foot caused by the loss of a boot when his parachute opened.

There was triple bad news for Mrs Marrable of Beckingham Road, Guildford. Her husband Donald, aged 30 — an old boy of Guildford Grammar School — who was in the submarine service, was missing and no word had been received as to the whereabouts of her brother and father who were in Hong Kong. She feared the worst, for her father was chief engineer to the Kowloon-Canton railway.

News came through on March 28th that Wing Commander Victor Beamish, one of that small band of near-legendary figures in the RAF, was also missing. Beamish, from 485 Squadron, Kenley was on a sweep over the French coast when he was attacked by Focke-Wulfs. His damaged Spitfire was last seen heading out to sea emitting a trail of smoke. The pilots at Kenley waited for more news but it never came. Beamish was dead.

Mr and Mrs Knight of Mount Hermon Road, Woking received the news that the MBE had been awarded to their son, Third Officer Harry Knight. Days later came the confirmation in the *London Gazette* which stated that Knight's ship had been struck by a torpedo

which wrecked the bridge and accommodation amidships. All the senior officers were killed and the vessel was ablaze. "Knight", said the *Gazette*, "took charge of the after part of the ship, collected all the survivors and got away the aft lifeboat." Third Officer Knight, aged 21, knew nothing about the award at the time. His lifeboat drifted in the Atlantic for 13 hours before being rescued, and it was several weeks before he arrived home in Woking.

While the Knight family was rejoicing, Mr B.A.Sayer was mourning the death of his daughter Betty Eileen Sayer of Vincent Road, Stoke D'Abernon. She was one of three officers who lost their lives when an Air Transport Auxiliary plane which was ferrying them to their respective ATA airfields, crashed onto a bungalow. Miss Sayer was 24 and had been flying with the ATA for 10 months.

The parents of Lieutenant Ian Brettell heard that their son was a prisoner of war in Libya. Days later they learned he had escaped and a third communication informed them that the young Royal Artillery officer had been awarded the Military Cross for gallantry. Before the war Lieutenant Brettell worked as a solicitor in the office of his father, head of the firm of Messrs Paine and Brettell of Guildford Road, Chertsey.

The news, good and bad, continued to be received by Surrey families. Every day a husband or son was killed in action, or lost, or believed to be a prisoner of war. Every day came news of miraculous escapes and acts of gallantry.

The heavily sandbagged ARP Report Centre at Bagshot. Warden Leon Chapman (left) prepares the instructions for the day while one of the men stands ready for patrol armed with all the necessary equipment including tin helmet, gas mask and stirrup pump.

IN 1942 the Royal Naval School — then the oldest girls' public school in continuous existence — was established at Stoatley Hall, Haslemere. The school had spent more than 100 years at Twickenham but had been bombed in 1940 and it was necessary to find new premises for the daughters of naval and maritime officers. President of the school was Princess Elizabeth.

THE SUTTON DISTRICT WATER COMPANY.

WATER SUPPLY IN AIR RAIDS.

In the event of an air raid, damage may be caused to water mains, supply pipes and fittings, and while every effort will be made to isolate and repair the damage to mains as quickly as possible, there may be considerable waste of water and some interference with supplies. Consumers are reminded that the water supply system from the main is the responsibility of the owner or occupier of the premises. The Company's responsibility is limited to the mains in the street.

In order to avoid waste of water and damage to property, consumers are advised to make themselves familiar with the position of the stopcocks on the service pipe inside their own premises and at the entrance to their premises, so that they can shut off the supply to prevent flooding should internal pipes and fittings be damaged. All premises should be equipped with a storage cistern of adequate capacity, which should be covered, as a protection against frost and contamination. In the event of the temporary suspension of the water supply, the water in this cistern should be sufficient for the careful use of the occupiers of the premises, so long as the cistern is kept in a clean condition. As regards hot water systems, if the supply of water fails, and a fire is burning, it is advisable to put out the fire as soon as possible to avoid the danger of a burst boiler.

It is of the greatest importance that consumers should do their utmost to economise in the use of water as large quantities will probably be required for fire fighting, essential supplies, and decontamination purposes.

G. R. WITHERS,
Secretary.

41, Carshalton Road West,
Sutton, Surrey.

Most of the senior boys boys of the famous Strode's School in Egham joined one of the local organisations linked to the ARP, a few enrolled in the local Home Guard and all seniors were expected to join the roster of Strode's fire guards which, with masters — and after 1941 mistresses — kept watch in the school every night. The photographs show two young, efficient 14-year-old roof spotters (above), and fire drill (below). As with most schools in the county, winter holidays were extended and school hours altered from November until late January to economise on fuel and lighting. The Strode's school canteen was also open to the public from November 1942.

Acting Squadron Leader Keith "Bluey" Truscott with his colleagues of 452 Squadron. In February 1942 the red-headed Australian helped to sink an enemy destroyer and a German float plane and was awarded a bar to his DFC. He also took possession of a new Spitfire called "Ginger Bread" which had been presented to their hero by red-headed women in Australia. See page 136.

Busy days in Surrey for George VI

KING George VI visited Kenley on April 29th, 1942. He was taken to The Grange, Caterham where he watched on the plotting board the progress of the entire Wing on a sweep. He then waited for the pilots to return to congratulate them all personally on their achievements over France. Nos 485 and 602 Squadrons landed at Kenley and then waited for 457 Squadron to arrive by bus from Redhill.

One pilot who the King was anxious to meet was "Ginger" Lacey of 602 Squadron. During the Battle of Britain Lacey was credited with the destruction of a Heinkel which had bombed Buckingham Palace and His Majesty was rather keen to learn a little more about his exploits.

Sadly, the King was unable to meet another legendary pilot, Flight Lieutenant Al Deere who had led 602 Squadron since July but was briefly in America lecturing on fighter tactics. Deere, who had used his parachute more times than any other Spitfire pilot, already had 22 confirmed victories and a great number of adventures. His place as CO of 602 was to be taken by the charismatic Irishman Brendan "Paddy" Finucane.

A week after his visit to Kenley, King George VI was back in Surrey, this time on a sports field at Pixham to inspect the soldiers of a tank unit who were in full battledress. From there the Royal procession moved on to Wotton House where more troops were billeted followed by a further inspection at Brockham Green. The King must have been impressed; he returned on May 22nd to watch a unit of an infantry division take part in a mock battle using live ammunition near Betchworth Lime Works.

The military exercises were getting tougher and the King saw khaki-clad figures attempt to scale the steep slopes of the chalkpit on the Surrey hills accompanied by rifle and machine gunfire and grenades. Two were actually injured during the battle but it was considered to be good practice for any future invasion of occupied Europe.

Children from Caterham take scrap metal and waste paper to the lorries waiting outside the Capitol Cinema.

Controversy in Westcott as iron railings disappear

BY the summer of 1942 Surrey was being ransacked for every piece of waste metal that could be found. The Goverment impressed on everyone that even scrap metal could be turned into guns, tanks, ships and bombs.

The strangest donations were handed in to the scrap metal centres. Youngsters at Ripley borrowed a horse and cart to search the neighbourhood for junk, a farmer near Milford gave the remains of an oil bomb, a publican from Dormansland offered an old treadle sewing machine.

In July it was announced that the removal of all railings would commence at Caterham and Warlingham. That was followed by a similar, rather controversial, ruling in Dorking district which prompted this letter to the *Advertiser*. "The removal of railings and gates has been effected with little discrimination. Recently, houses facing a busy main road have lost their gates despite the fact that this endangers the lives of their small children, while in some cul-de-sacs with light traffic and no children, gates, railings and chains have been left. We should like to know who made the selection and on whose authority the exceptions were allowed. (Signed) M.Tite, Deaconess, Westcott."

A minute from Chertsey Urban District Council meeting of June, 1942 stated: "Iron railings around the recreation grounds, under the jurisdiction of Chertsey UDC, except those which form the war memorial at Victory Park, Addlestone, are to be removed for scrap and chestnut palings erected in their place".

No Cathedral yet so Guildford is spared

THE new chief of Bomber Command, Air Marshal Arthur Harris believed in strategic bombing in a bid to break German morale and, on Saturday May 30th, more than 1,000 aircraft crewed by 6,500 young men dropped 1,455 tons of bombs on Cologne. In 90 minutes the beautiful historic city was transformed into a shattered skeleton as 3,000 buildings were destroyed and the great Cathedral badly damaged.

The Luftwaffe retaliated by stepping up their "Baedeker" raids — English Cathedral cities picked from the famous guide book of that name.

Guildford, county town of Surrey, had abandoned work on the building of its Cathedral and so escaped the attention of the Luftwaffe but in Kent, Lord Haw Haw's pronouncement that Canterbury would be next chilled the residents of that city to the bone.

On June 1st, Canterbury was devastated and hundreds of firemen from Surrey joined colleagues from Kent in trying to contain the fires which blazed across six acres of the city.

More than 100 high explosive and 6,000 incendiaries had been dropped, 50 people were killed and 400 ancient buildings destroyed. Vast craters and grievous scars surrounded the Cathedral which miraculously survived the onslaught.

Work on the building of Guildford Cathedral was controversially abandoned on the outbreak of war.

In 1942 the ladies of Surrey continued to be fashion conscious despite the fact that clothes made from utility cloth were now on sale in the shops. There were now fewer styles available, hemlines rose and pleats were limited. Photograph shows a "utility" wedding. The bride is Betty Taylor and she is with her bridesmaid outside the family home in Cobham. Both dresses were made using clothing coupons.

Flight Lieutenant Brendan "Paddy" Finucane who won the DSO, DFC and two Bars by the time he was 22 is pictured here at Kenley flanked by two of his best friends, Australian Keith "Bluey" Truscott on the left and Ray Thorold-Smith. Finucane is using a stick as a result of an accident after he left The Greyhound pub in Croydon. The photograph is an nostalgic one. Some months later Finucane, then in command of 602 Squadron, was returning from a low-level sortie over France with his Wing when his glycol tank was hit by anti-aircraft fire from the French coast. As his Spitfire glided to the water he continued to give instructions to his colleagues who were devastated to see Paddy still trapped in his cockpit. By then Bluey had returned home to Australia to help his countrymen fight off the Japanese invasion threat and he too was killed while flying a Kittyhawk off the coast of Western Australia. Pilot Officer Thorold-Smith also lost his life in 1942.

Explosive nights at Puttenham, Abinger and Leith Hill

NO town in Surrey was worth the attention of the "Baedeker" bombers but that did not prevent isolated "hit and run" attacks across the county.

In July 1942 German raiders tried to demolish the searchlights at Cutt Mill. They missed and the bombs fell on Puttenham Common which blazed for two days. Fire crews from Guildford and Farnham dealt with the blaze, some working for 36 hours without a break.

Abinger Common was also set on fire and burned so furiously and spread so fast that the whole village was evacuated. Greatest fear was that the ammunition store on the corner of the Common might blow up. The fire reached the rifle range and huge explosions damaged most of the houses in the village.

An ammunition dump between Friday Street and Leylands also caught fire in the summer of 1942, although there are no records to say the enemy were to blame. But it was a dramatic night with monster explosions scattering ammunition all over Leith Hill.

The area was sealed off and it was not until January 1955 that the Royal Engineers decided to take their detectors to Leith Hill to clear the area of any unexploded devices. They found 250 mines and bombs — all relics of the "big fire".

For three nights beginning on July 27th the Luftwaffe mounted raids and the gunners across the county were in action with little to show for their efforts. But in other parts of the country they had more success. Sixteen raiders were shot down and the Luftwaffe's latest initiatve ended.

The "Dig For Victory" campaign, launched by the Government in 1940 was accelerating fast in 1942. Lawns, flower beds and any suitable ground was turned over for vegetable production. Cauliflowers, potatoes and cabbages grew on the platform of Norbury Station, carrot plants adorned the former grass verges of the A30 near Bagshot and scores of window boxes in the village of Tandridge contained tomatoes. Many people in the country grew root crops, greens and fruit and kept pigs, rabbits, chickens and goats to supplement the meagre meat ration. Farmers and growers were short of labour and children would spend summer holidays picking beans, peas and sprouts, cutting cabbages, weeding spinach and picking fruit. In Purley the 70 acres of playing fields which were not required for a gun site or military camp were turned over to growing wheat and potatoes. The produce was sold to hospitals, British Restaurants and welfare organisations. Photograph (above) shows green crops growing in a fire break between the wheat on the Purley Way playing fields. Local housewives and boys from Whitgift School helped with the harvest.

Also Digging for Victory were the nurses at Botley's Park War Hospital, near Chertsey. The hospital had more than 1,000 beds including 620 in huts and played an important part in the treatment of casualties. It was also one of the country's main orthopaedic units. (From the album of Nurse Marie Clarke).

Squadron Leader Peter Wickham, leader of 111 Squadron, standing beside a Spitfire Mark V which had been presented to his Squadron by the town of Sao Paulo, Brazil. During the Dieppe raid, Wickham was "loaned" to the 308th Fighter Squadron USAAF. His operational experience was to prove invaluable to the Yankies who were providing cover for Flying Fortresses.

Kenley Wing gives cover at Dieppe

IN mid-summer 1942, black and white stripes were painted on the aircraft at Kenley and Redhill and, under a cloak of secrecy, the crews were briefed on the roles they would play for Operation Jubilee. On August 20th, the Allied attempt to seize the French port of Dieppe and destroy its German defences took place with the Surrey squadrons providing vital air cover.

The raid was a disaster and, of the 6,100-strong force of British and Canadian commandos, more than 4,000 were reported killed, wounded or missing. On that day the RAF lost 106 aircraft including many from the Kenley wing.

By the summer of 1942, the Canadian flag waved proudly over dispersal huts and parade grounds all over Surrey. The county, it seemed, had been taken over by the English and French-speaking, poker playing, good natured men from such places as New Brunswick, Alberta and Vancouver. The Kenley Sector was certainly dominated by the Canadian squadrons who were to remain until the build-up of the D-Day landings in 1944. These squadrons were to play important roles as escorts to the ever-increasing bomber offensive over German towns and cities.

There were few raids on Surrey during this period although Camberley suffered when a bomb was dropped on the town from 40,000 feet by the new Junkers 86 which specialised in high-altitude daylight attacks.

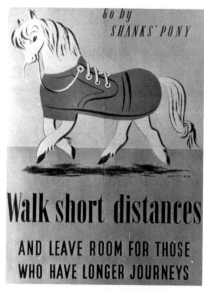

Issued by the Ministry of War Transport, a propaganda poster designed by two Poles — George Him and Jan de Wiff.

Members of the Royal British Legion hand out food parcels in Morden Hall. Tinned food such as the Natco Corned Beef and Aussie jam were a welcome addition to family store cupboards. The lady 2nd right has 2 large blackout buttons (luminous discs) attached to her coat.

Bells ring again as Monty drives on

THE threat of being invaded by the enemy was now fading and towns, which a few months earlier had feared being cut off by enemy action, began to enjoy some normality. Open-air dances were held twice a week in Brightwells, Farnham, concerts were organised at the Crescent Cinema in Leatherhead with songs by Isobel Baillie, Anne Ziegler and Webster Booth, and aquatic sports were held in most towns; in fact during one such event at Guildford more than 1,000 spectators packed into the baths. All over Surrey the British Restaurants were full to capacity and even the food tasted better.

'Make do and mend' became the phrase most closely associated with the wartime drive for self-sufficiency. In the absence of stockings women painted their legs with a commercially produced lotion, they made their own jewellery from beer bottle tops and corks and they helped enthusiastically with the salvage drive.

The gloom was certainly lifting and, as the fourth Christmas of the war approached, Surrey reflected on the good tidings that recent events overseas had brought. The greatest talking point was Montgomery's victory at Alamein and the part the 1st East Surreys had played in the Torch landings. For gallantry during fierce fighting in Tunis, Major T.A. Buchanan commanding B Company won the MC and RSM.

The Surrey newspapers, notably the *Mirror, Advertiser* and *Comet,* gave every indication that "victory was in the air". The bells rang in every church in the county to mark the turning point and Churchill said: "Alamein, if not the beginning of the end, is at least the end of the beginning".

At Brooklands, Vickers devoted their production line to improved versions of the Wellington bomber and the Warwick which was to play an important role as a transport and air/sea rescue aircraft.

Before Christmas, Weybridge said goodbye to the Hawker team. Fighter production was transferred to Langley so the assembly shed at Brooklands could be used by scientists working on a new bomb.

The mastermind behind its development was Dr Barnes Wallis who was working on a 'crazy' notion that he could make a bomb which would hit water and then bounce. Work on this theory continued in the utmost secrecy.

On the afternoon of December 16th, 1942 the people of Reigate heard aerial cannon fire to the west of the station as a train was passing. A Focke-Wulf had turned south and machine-gunned the train. The bullets bounced off the roofs of houses in the High Street, West Street, Broadhurst Gardens and South Park. A bus, travelling from Horley, along the Hookwood Road, was also fired at but no-one was injured. The bus stopped, passengers scrambled for cover, the train continued on its journey and the Focke-Wulf vanished into the clouds. Minutes later, at Bramley, near Guildford, another train was attacked. This time the aircraft was a Dornier, three passengers were killed and a further four seriously injured.
A few days later this report appeared in the Surrey newspapers:

SURREY WEEKLY PRESS   **DECEMBER 19, 1942**

DAY RAIDERS IN HOME COUNTIES

ATTACK ON RAILWAY TRAIN

DEATH ROLL OF SEVEN INCLUDING DRIVER AND GUARD

Taking advantage of low clouds, enemy aircraft crossed the Channel coast on Wednesday in the early afternoon and two of them penetrated to the Home Counties. Bombs were dropped at a number of places causing some casualties.

The most serious attack was on a train near a village station in the Home Counties. A stick of bombs was dropped and while the train did not receive a direct hit, there were some casualties among the passengers, three of whom were killed outright and four died later.

The nuisance raid was not without cost to the enemy. Two of the raiders were destroyed, one a FW 190 fighter and the other a Dornier 217, the latest type of German twin-engine bomber. The plane which attacked the train was thought to be the Dornier.

The train in question was a small one conveying, for the most part, shoppers and business people from a neighbouring town (Guildford) to a number of villages (among them Bramley and Cranleigh). Unfortunately it happened that more people than usual were travelling.

The damage to the train arose largely by blast from a bomb which exploded on a railway bank at the same time as the train was passing. There was damage to the carriages and glass was blown out of the windows. The fact that the train kept the metals reduced the number of casualties. The ordeal of the passengers was one which few could pass through without being shocked.

According to one of the passengers, Miss Ashford of Mount Road, Cranleigh who is employed at Messrs Whites, the well-known drapers, the train was unaware that a public warning had been sounded. She was travelling in the same compartment as Miss Sevenoaks, one of the three people killed outright. When the bomb exploded they were lifted up from their seats and one of the passengers in the compartment was blown out of the window onto the railway line. Miss Ashford assisted to remove Miss Sevenoaks from the compartment. Assistance was speedily forthcoming. Doctors and ARP services were quickly summoned and magnificent work was rendered by a Canadian medical unit.

A fleet of ambulances conveyed the injured to a major hospital (in Guildford). The clearance of the line was rendered more difficult than otherwise might have been by the fact that it was thought there were two unexploded bombs in the vicinity. Troops were drafted into the vicinity to help clear up the debris.

The bomb which was the cause of the main damage behaved in a freakish manner. It was seen by villagers (of Bramley) to have been released from the plane when it was flying about the height of some trees. The bomb went clean through the two front bedrooms of a pair of cottages, wrecking the furniture in transit and then ricochetting off the ground and onto the railway bank.

Those who died immediately were Donald Melville Clyde, a Canadian soldier, Miss A.M.Sevenoaks from Horsham and Mrs Ada Newham from Devizes. Those who died later were George Budd, driver of the train, George Jeal, guard, George Marshall of Sevenoaks and Michael Evans, a schoolboy.

1943

Stalingrad, Dambusters and Surrey's Canadians

January 14th: President Roosevelt and Mr Churchill met for talks in Casablanca.

January 23rd: Unemployment figures dropped to their lowest levels in British history.
British troops entered Tripoli.

January 31st: Germans surrendered in Stalingrad.

March 3rd: Tragedy at Bethnal Green tube station when people hurrying to shelter after an air raid warning were crushed when someone fell and others fell on top. 173 died of suffocation.

March 5th: Britain's first jet fighter aircraft, the Gloster Meteor made its maiden flight.

March 7th: A "Wings for Victory" campaign was launched by National Savings. People were asked to stick savings stamps on to 500-lb bombs positioned in the streets to raise £150 million for building bombers.

April 12th: War costs for 1943 were estimated at £5,756 million. Purchase tax on luxury items was raised once more — on some goods to 100 per cent.

May 7th: Allied troops captured Tunis and Bizerta.

May 8th: Part time work became compulsory for women between the ages of 18 and 45, except for mothers looking after their own children under 14.

May 13th: General Alexander, Commander-in-Chief, reported that the Allies were now masters of all North African shores.

May 14th: Operation Mincemeat was confirmed a success by the Intelligence Service. This involved depositing a corpse off the coast of Spain, complete

with briefcase and papers leading the Germans to think that the Allies intended to invade Greece.

May 16th: The Warsaw ghetto was finally destroyed by the Germans.

May 17th: The 617 "Dambuster" Squadron led by Guy Gibson dropped the bouncing bombs designed by Dr Barnes Wallis on the Möhne and Éder dams. Gibson was subsequently awarded the Victoria Cross. He died a year later.

June 25th: RAF and USAAF bombers continued to bombard towns in the Ruhr valley; 870 acres of Wuppertal lay in ruins.

June 30th: An announcement was made that signposts were to be re-erected in rural areas of Britain now that the danger of invasion had receded.
Factory workers responded positively to *Music while you work* and production increased by 15 per cent for the hour following the broadcast.

July 8th: French Resistance leader Jean Moulin known as "Max" died after being tortured by the Germans.

July 12th: The UK birthrate reached its highest level for 17 years in the first quarter of 1943 despite the fact that most men were away from home!

July 25th: Mussolini was dismissed from his post and arrested. Italy was in political chaos with strikes and riots.

July 31st: The city of Hamburg was razed to the ground by RAF bombers. 40,000 people were believed to have been killed; more than in the entire London blitz.

August 18th: RAF bombers attacked the top-secret rocket and flying bomb site at Peenemunde on the Baltic coast.

September 3rd: Allied troops landed in Italy and the country surrendered.

October 13th: Italy declared war on Germany. Five weeks previously they had been allies.

November 6th: The Russians recaptured Kiev.

November 20th: Amid much protest from the general public, Sir Oswald Mosley was released from Holloway prison for health reasons.

December 2nd: It was announced by Ernest Bevin, Minister of Labour, that men would be conscripted to serve in the coal mines for reasons of "urgent national necessity".

December 24th: General Dwight Eisenhower was appointed supreme commander of the Allied Expeditionary Force being prepared for the cross-Channel invasion of France.

December 25th: It was estimated that only one family in ten would be able to enjoy a traditional Christmas dinner of turkey or goose. One butcher said he had only received 15 birds for 800 customers.

Major C.F.Jacottet MBE, an Officer in Charge of the Home Guard at Addlestone, and his wife a stalwart member of the local WVS, were the proudest parents in Surrey. Their three attractive daughters were all serving their country. Pamela (left) had joined the FANY's, Joan (centre) was a WAAF and Suzanne was in the WRNs and about to embark on another of her eight trips to America on the Queen Mary. Joan Nicholson (née Jacottet), who sent this photograph and that on page 36, would be delighted to hear from anyone who knew her and her sisters. Please contact the publishers.

'Grand' hat-trick for Beaufighter aces

WHEN the Luftwaffe launched a surprise night attack against London on the night of January 17th-18th 1943 it did so in two waves separated by eight hours. For the second wave the Beaufighters of 29 Squadron stationed at West Malling, Kent were scrambled and one of them, flown by Wing Commander C.M.Wright-Boycott and his A1 operator, Flying Officer E.A. Sanders achieved the miraculous feat of shooting down two Junkers 88s and a Dornier 217. The entire crew of the first two enemy aircraft were killed and all but one died in the third. He baled out and was taken prisoner in nearby Limpsfield.

Wing Commander Wight-Boycott who was awarded an immediate DSO for his achievements that night was interviewed by the BBC the following day. He said: "Our last Hun of the night was a Junkers 88 which caught fire in both engines. The fire spread along the wings and back along the fuselage and it lit up the sky so clearly that we could see the black crosses on the aircraft. We watched four members of the crew bale out one after another. The aircraft went down exploding with a brilliant flash. It was a grand night for night fighting, for the moon and the cloud made conditions almost ideal".

The third aircraft actually crashed on the Town End recreation ground, Caterham at 5.30 am and the bodies of the three dead crew members were found in adjacent gardens. Their parachutes were ablaze as they jumped.

The raid, considered to be a reprisal for the RAF attack on Berlin, caused little damage but it was sufficient for the Reigate anti-aircraft guns to burst into life and create mayhem. One of the "friendly" shells dropped in Church Street close to a bus queue in the Market Square. One man was killed and six badly injured in the explosion. Other AA shells fell at various spots including Chaldon and Chipstead that evening.

Grandad was a brave man, but he chose not to fight

SINCE 1939, men from Surrey had been regularly appearing before tribunals to explain why they preferred to be registered as conscientious objectors. In 1943 a Kingston youth declared that conscription was as objectionable as German totalitarianism and a man from Cheam said he saw no distinction between killing in war and murder. Another, from Knaphill, said it was not Britain's quarrel so he saw no reason why he should fight. All of them were registered.

An eight-year-old child from Farnham who was asked in 1995 to explain what his grandad did in the war, gave this reply which was featured in the town's VE Day exhibition at the museum:

My grandad, he wrote,was a very brave man. He did not believe that killing was right and he was against any kind of violence because God told us to love our neighbour.

My grandad did not want to be a soldier. This did not mean he was afraid. He had to face a lot of bullying from people who thought he should fight. My grandad hated what Hitler and the Nazis were doing but he could not kill. He said it would make him no better than them.

Grandad had to go in front of a tribunal who believed he was truly against killing and said he would not have to fight. They asked him what he would do for England and he chose to drive ambulances to rescue people from burning buildings. My grandad was a conscientious objector.

"La guerre est fini pour moi," says captured German pilot

TWO nights after the Beaufighter triumph a Focke-Wulf 190 crash-landed in a ploughed field in Capel. It actually hit the ground, ran into a hedge and the pilot was thrown clear. He destroyed the aircraft before giving himself up.

The *Dorking Advertiser* described the event: "The plane caught fire and burnt fiercely. To villagers who were running towards it the German made a sign that they should stop and crouch down, a warning that was given just in time because explosions of the petrol tank and ammunition quickly made what an eye witness described as a fine display of fireworks. Some of the people who went towards the plane were blown over by the force of explosion.

"In the meantime the German pilot had been taken into custody. He walked away from the plane, across a field into a garden where he was first met by two brothers Messrs P.F. and W.A. Teasdale, grocers who were delivering goods to nearby houses.

"He spoke in French to Mr Teasdale who recalled the French he had learned during the last war. The pilot said he was 'tout seul' and continued 'la guerre est fini pour moi'. Mr Teasdale agreed and handed him over to PC Cooper who was hurrying from his home to the scene of the crash."

Meanwhile women were still doing a man-size job and, judging by the smiles, really enjoying it.

10,000 Canadians in Surrey: nothing like it since the Roman Occupation

THE soldiers of Surrey who were not following Rommel's retreating Afrika Corps, or preparing for the invasion of Sicily, or on the Burma Road, or languishing in PoW camps in Eastern Europe or Asia, or among the countless other fighting men all over the world were deployed in various parts of England on the many diverse military aspects of defence. Some were stationed in Surrey but generally the county was defended by the guests from another country. Canada looked after Surrey and Canadians remained until the Normandy landings on D-Day when the war was almost won.

The first contingent of the Canadian active service force arrived in 1939. Without a mishap or the loss of a man, this vast army was conveyed across the Atlantic and given tented accommodation in the Surrey countryside.

The whole span of Canada was represented — lumbermen from New Brunswick, wheat farmers from Alberta, trappers from the North-West, fruit growers from British Columbia, Canadians who spoke only French, coloured Canadians and Red Indians. There had been nothing like it in Surrey since the days of the Roman Occupation.

Among the Canadian Regiments who settled in quickly were the Nova Scotians and they saw themselves as settlers in the Roman tradition. They built camps, mapped long straight roads and courted the local girls.

The Novas were attached to the Canadian First Division and they arrived at a time when the war was ominously quiet. Life wasn't quiet. It was filled with parades, instruction squads, route marches over the Surrey hills, lectures, drills, tank demonstrations, rifle shoots at the ranges, gas training and so on.

But when British forces were making their desperate but successful escape from Dunkirk, leaving all guns and equipment in enemy hands, the Canadians remained the only troops in England fully equipped to meet the invader. During the summer of 1940 the Regiment was encamped near East Horsley in a position of readiness. Here they had seats in the stalls during the Battle of Britain which was distracting as far as training was concerned, for the boys found it hard to put proper zest into sham fights with a real one going on overhead.

One German pilot who baled out found himself surrounded by several hundred armed Nova Scotians. He was the Regiment's first prisoner and the first German prisoner taken by the Canadians overseas.

The men moved around the county. They loved Woldingham but found an irritating drawback — the nearest pub was three miles away at Warlingham.

In June 1941 the Novas had the honour of providing a guard for the Prime Minister at Chartwell, near the Kent/Surrey border. Here they felt at home for Westerham was the birthplace of General Wolfe and Quebec House had been his home.

Canadian historian Thomas H. Randall said there was something more important to his countrymen than playing ice hockey at Purley, boxing at Caterham against the Guards, assault courses in the Surrey countryside or darts in the Mess at Kenley and Biggin Hill.

"To the Bluenoses (as the Regiment was called) most important of all was their everyday association with English people in their homes. The first impression of the troops was that of an old country, fallen far behind the pace of the world. They compared the size of trains and cars, they wondered at the absence of central heating in a climate as bleak as that of Nova Scotia. But if they could not admire British plumbing they appreciated the hospitality they received from the people of Surrey. They also admired their courage and the troops had a word for it. 'Guts'. The English had guts and that is all that mattered."

The army from across the Atlantic were encamped at Surrey Heath, Albury Heath, Abinger Forest. They were at Chatley Heath, Painshill Park and Epsom racecourse. Canadian Highlanders, complete with kilts and bagpipes, were stationed around Newdigate. The Royal Canadian Engineers and the Royal Canadian Artillery were billeted in Banstead Park. The 1st Battalion of the Hastings and Prince Edward Regiment, Ontario were in Reigate, Betchworth and Dorking. Cape Britain Islanders were in Farnham district where a unit occupied Willmer House, now the Museum of Farnham while others were encamped on the hockey field at Barfield School, Runfold.

Tangible gifts from the soldiers of Canada are still to be seen right across Surrey. In the village of Mickleham they built a New Road with a Bailey Bridge spanning the river. In Leatherhead where they were stationed from 1940, the YMCA established a Red Triangle Services Club in North Street. The Canadians returned the favour by building a new road, Young Street, which bridged the River Mole — for the town's streets were too narrow for tanks and other armoured vehicles. It is believed that the street was named after Yonge Street in Toronto which is 300 miles long.

One of the most remarkable gifts was at Merstham where the All Saints Church had been devastated by a landmine. Serving in the district as Chaplain to the First Canadian

The West Nova contingent of the Third Canadian Regiment on the march in Surrey.

Corps was the Rev George Hedley Wolfendale who offered to get a temporary church erected. Canadian sappers responded to his plea for help and a new church was built from the stones and timbers of the destroyed edifice and dedicated on Easter Day 1943. Later the Rev Wolfendale went to Italy and was wounded by rifle fire. He died in a prison hospital.

Memories of Canadian soldiers in Surrey are still very vivid. Queenie Collins of Farnham recalls how they were billetted at Pierrepont, a large house near Rowledge in the ownership of the Watney family. The secret of their presence there was eventually lifted. The Rev J.Dance wrote in the parish magazine at the time: "It does seem ridiculous that the BBC should broadcast for all the world to hear that thousands of Canadian troops have been quartered in our county but that we, in our little parish, must preserve a hush-hush over the fact that a few soldiers are stationed amongst us for fear of giving vital information to the enemy".

Another lady from Farnham remembers how hundreds of Canadians would walk down the Portsmouth Road from Witley to Thursley camps through Milford on their way to Godalming for their weekend entertainment. She also recalls how children from Milford and Whitley were collected in various army trucks and taken to the camp for a Christmas party each year.

In the Surrey villages which hosted the Canadian soldiers, children were advised not to play (or go blackberrying) too near to the camps for fear of hearing them swear but many of them still managed to learn new words. The Canadians' brash way of life intrigued, annoyed and, in most cases, absolutely thrilled the locals.

There were romances of course and, as with the American GIs, several Canadian soldiers married their English sweethearts and took them back home. One of them, Walter Moir who was stationed at Round Down, Gomshall with the Royal Canadian Engineers met Peggy at a local dance, married her and, after the war, the couple made their home in New Brunswick. Walter was among the Canadian troops who met Montgomery at Albury Heath.

(See page 171).

Johnnie Johnson (second from left) with Canadian colleagues of the Kenley Wing.

Top-scoring Englishman takes command of Canadian Wing

THERE were Canadians on the ground and in the air. By the summer of 1943 the Canadian Wing was well established at Kenley and Redhill under the command of a small, charismatic tiger of a fellow called Squadron Leader Johnnie Johnson who immediately instilled a bit of discipline and introduced his pilots to the new Mark IX Spitfire which he felt was a good match for the Focke-Wulf fighter. He then set out to prove it.

By day there was a lot of hard flying. The Wing provided escorts for the heavy bombers of the USSAF and continued with their sweeps over France. By night there was lively entertainment in the Officers Mess, the NAAFI and the pubs in and around both stations. One of the favourite venues for dances was Nutfield Priory, then the home of a ATS unit where there was plenty of beer and no shortage of females. On occasions the pilots would go to the Kimmul Club in London or join the boys from Biggin Hill at the White Hart, Brasted.

Between April 3rd and September 4th, 1943 Johnnie Johnson was constantly in the headlines. In this period he destroyed ten Focke-Wulf 190s, four Messerschmitt 109s and shared in the destruction of five others. He was awarded the DSO, a bar to his DFC and then a bar to the DSO. His extraordinary success continued. By the end of the war he was the top-scoring Allied pilot with 38 confirmed victories.

Wings for Victory — an appeal with hope

DESPITE the astonishing success of the big appeals (Fighters in 1940, War Weapons in 1941 and Warships in 1942) which had raised millions of pounds for the war effort, Surrey was asked to contribute in a big way once more. And this time there was a note of hope in the chosen title — Wings for Victory Week

In every locality six-figure targets were ambitiously announced, the week was set for early summer and the events were advertised. Costume cricket matches, flower shows, fancy dress parades, whist drives, beetle drives, auction sales, street collections, victory dances.

Up on the fountains and statues, fire stations and town halls went the big indicators while vans with loud speakers toured the streets of Surrey: "Hello, hello, please go to your bank and arrange the maximum investment. Remember, we are now raising funds for Victory".

Some weeks later towns and villages proudly announced the results. We've won our Wings, they said.

The Wings for Victory parade in Dorking on Sunday May 16th, 1943. The week ahead was to bring extraordinary news from the war front, including the destruction of the Ruhr dams and the withdrawal of all U-boats from the North Atlantic. This was also the week that ULTRA was born — a device that could break the German Enigma enciphering machines. Headquarters of the Government's code and cipher school was Bletchley Park in Buckinghamshire where work was continuing in utmost secret.

Fighter bombers on a 'secret' airfield

FOR the people who lived in the villages south of Godalming, a distinctive new silhouette was seen in the skies during August. It was a North American bomber — the B-25 Mitchell Mk II — and it landed at Dunsfold where Royal Canadian Engineers had converted a stretch of pasture land to the east of the village into a runway. Dunsfold, in fact, was more than an advanced landing ground. By the summer of 1943 this area of Surrey countryside housed a three-runway fighter station with the standards of an 'A' class bomber airfield.

It was an extraordinary transformation. In May 1942 it was a beautiful, heavily-wooded site almost hidden among the rolling hills. A few

A B-25 Mitchell Mark II (FW 172) of 180 Squadron taking off from Dunsfold Aerodrome in 1944.

months later, even before the necessary land purchases had been completed, trees were being bulldozed, stumps blasted by explosives and giant earth-movers were everywhere. In his book on *Surrey's Most Secret Airfield*, Paul McCue wrote: "A local dairy farmer never quite recovered from the shock of finally shutting the door on his home and then seeing it bulldozed into an adjacent pond before he had even reached the bottom of his garden path. At the same time, Major Rowcliffe of neighbouring Hall Place was dismayed when one of his favourite views disappeared. His custom was to stand in his bathroom and admire a row of ten magnificent oak trees. He was doing exactly that when the Canadians bulldozed all ten to the ground within minutes."

By October of that year Dunsfold boasted a runway over a mile long, a control tower, two large T2 hangars, squadron offices, workshops and dispersal areas. Beyond the northern boundary and stretching as far as the Cranleigh to Godalming Road were administrative and communal sites, WAAF and general accommodation sites, sick quarters and sewage disposal works. It was a full-scale Army Co-operation Aerodrome.

Mustang, Mosquito and Tomahawk squadrons of the Royal Canadian Air Force were briefly at Dunsfold but it was the arrival of the Mitchells of Nos 98 and 180 Squadrons which caused the greatest stir. Property was requisitioned at Hall Place and Stovolds Hill Farm for the crews and activity at the station increased rapidly as Bomber Command diversions became common.

The Southern Railway staff at Cranleigh and Witley were the first to suspect that Dunsfold's role was a vital one when ammunition trains loaded with 1,000 and 500lb bombs rolled into their station. A large maintenance unit also moved in and set up camp in the grounds of Satchel Court, an extensive country house nearby.

The Dunsfold Mitchells were quickly in action. They bombed St Omer railway-marshalling yards on August 23rd, 1943 and were crucially involved in the *Operation Starkey* attack on Boulogne docks. Equally important was the attack on pilotless aircraft launching sites in northern France and a large installation near Mimoyecques, south-west of Calais.

For the Mitchell aircrew the mode of operations at this time was daylight formation bombing so, off duty, the airmen would often visit the Three Compasses while ground crews of both 180 and 98 Squadrons preferred the Leather Bottle on the Guildford Road. It was not until October 1943 that night-flying practice began for the Mitchell crews.

It was also during October that Cranleigh railway station was evacuated and RAF detachments cordoned off the village centre. Worried residents saw airmen arrive with waterproof capes and gas masks and watched fire engines line up as a mysterious cargo was unloaded from a train and then taken to the aerodrome. The secrecy was soon made clear. It was Mustard Gas, a weapon banned by international convention but likely, or so it was thought by Allied High Command, to be used by the Germans in desperate situation like the invasion of Europe.

From December 1943 to February 1944 the Dunsfold Squadrons were even more involved in bombing Crossbow targets — the name given to sites in Pas de Calais where, it was suspected, Hitler might be storing and preparing to use his much-vaunted secret weapons. There was a switch in the spring to attacks on marshalling yards and other railway targets and then vital orders concerning the invasion. Only one question regarding D-Day remained for the Dunsfold Squadrons — WHEN?

Sappers of the 2nd Battalion Royal Canadian Engineers enjoy a break from the arduous task of creating an airfield out of a pastoral piece of English countryside at Dunsfold. The men worked an 18-hour day in two shifts and even in the remaining six hours at night, movement never ceased. Lorries brought cement from Shoreham, sand and gravel from Farnham and Ewhurst and, for many months, a stream of vehicles rumbled around the countryside lanes of Surrey. Sadly there was one accident when a postwoman from Cranleigh was killed by a lorry.

Rural pies, mock steaks and life-savers

MANY Surrey villages, led by the enthusiastic and eager ladies of the WI introduced a 'pie day' for agricultural workers. For the consumers it was the highlight of their week for the pies were huge, extra to rations and cost only 5d each.

In their book *Within Living Memory*, WI members recall helping their mothers to make the pies and other "scratch meals". One favourite was Marmite spread on bread dipped in milk and fried. It was known as a mock steak.

One WI member wrote: " I never went short of sweets as the Canadian soldiers stationed in the area would go to The Legion (Hindhead) and for the price of a drink willingly gave away a packet of sweets sent from home. How I remember those fruity sweets with the hole in the middle, known as Life-Savers'. The coal ration was supplemented by going to the woods to gather twigs and fir cones and dragging home fallen branches. The cat was fed the same as we ate except in very dire times when he might have to have a slice of bread soaked in gravy. In addition to our regular weekend meat order there was always 'two-pennyworth of lights' for the cat."

Hundreds of people in Hindhead bought their produce from a tiny shop opposite the Pride of the Valley Inn between Churt and Hindhead. The local farmer was none other than David Lloyd George, Prime Minister during the 1914-18 war who had built a house nearby called Brom-y-de. On Lloyd George's death later in the war the shop was converted into a restaurant and Brom-y-de eventually burnt down.

There was rationing for everyone but extra provisions for priority groups such as free school meals for the children of poorer families, free cod-liver oil and orange juice for the under-twos and extra eggs and milk for expectant mothers.

Bouncing Bomb — made at Brooklands

AS the bombing of German cities and reprisal raids on England continued to dominate the news one man was working in utmost secrecy on a plan that he believed could devastate the heart of German industry. Brooklands-based inventor, Dr Barnes Wallis considered the Ruhr Dams were military targets and their destruction would deprive the Germans of water and electrical power and cause widespread damage to industrial plants and railways.

In a small office at the back of the Vickers factory Dr Wallis remembered from history that naval gunners in the eighteenth and nineteenth centuries had deliberately bounced cannon balls off the sea to extend the range of their guns. Why not, he thought, a bomb that could do exactly the same. He converted his thoughts to the drawing board unaware at the time that his ideas and sketches were to be the forerunner of the most legendary air attack in British history.

The scientist who lived at White Hill House, Effingham built a large water tank in his garden and began to experiment by borrowing a set of marbles from his daughter Elizabeth and acquiring a catapult. Marbles projected from his catapult ricocheted into the tank, some missed and whizzed into the garden, never to be found again. But Dr Wallis, on this scale, perfected the bounce technique and made more drawings in his upstairs study.

Barnes Wallis, already famous for his Wellington bomber, knew the dams were protected by a dual screen of torpedo netting suspended from large steel buoys. An underwater attack by any torpedo-like projectile was out of the question but the possibility of a bouncing or skipping bomb could be feasible. As his Brooklands' team made models of the dams, experiments in the garden and the drawing office were transferred to the Teddington water tanks. Wallis was attempting to establish a scientifically predictable pattern of bounces and back spin.

The first tests proper were made at Chesil Beach, near Weymouth using a Wellington bomber with Barnes himself acting as bomb aimer. They were a disappointment. The casing broke off. It was back to the drawing board. The tests were transferred to Reculver Bay in Kent, Churchill became interested in the project and tagged it *Churchill Priority*. The Lancaster bomber which had entered service in 1942 was chosen for the new tests and Wing Commander Guy Gibson of 617 Squadron was asked if he would lead a proposed raid on Germany, but not given any details of the possible operation.

That was on March 15th, 1943. For the next 42 days and nights crews were hand-picked, trained and assigned to 617 Squadron while Gibson was fully briefed and told to attend more trials at Reculver with Dr Wallis. Here he

Not a marble but the real bouncing bomb, 50 inches in diameter, fitted with a 90 second time fuse and set to detonate 30 feet below the water.

was given a flavour of what to expect at Möhne, one of the Ruhr Dams, for the twin towers of Reculver were chosen as the release point for the experiments.

Wallis was still not happy with the results. With his engineers he worked in a guarded hangar to strengthen again the outside casing of the bomb. He also decided to reduce the drop height and then devise a method of spinning the bomb as it left the aircraft. The final trial took place on April 29th, two weeks before the planned raid and this time the bomb dropped on its target, bounced on and on and then slid through the special marker buoys representing the base of the dam. As the pilot banked and turned he could see Barnes Wallis below also bouncing in the dunes, waving his hat in the air.

On the night of May 16th 1943, 19 Lancasters led by Gibson set off from Scampton in Lincolnshire to attack the heavily reinforced Möhne and Eder concrete dams while Dr Wallis followed the raid in the operations room. It was an enormous success. The dams were breached and 300 million tons of water swept into the Ruhr valleys. The floods drowned 1,294 people, destroyed or damaged 125 factories, ruined nearly 3,000 hectares of arable land, destroyed 25 bridges and flooded many coalmines.

Eight of the 19 specially-adapted Lancasters were lost and 53 of the 133 crew died. Gibson remained in the target area throughout and survived — but only for a year. He died leading an attack against a factory, near the Ruhr.

An aerial photograph of the Möhne Dam in the Ruhr valley just after it was breached by Barnes Wallis' bouncing bomb. This photograph has been signed by Guy Gibson and other members of the bombing mission to the Ruhr.

'Hoppy's' bomb destroyed the Möhne powerhouse

AMONG those who flew with Guy Gibson on this famous raid was a young pilot from the Surrey village of Shere. Flight Lieutenant John Hopgood, with his colleagues was fully briefed, while his bombed and fuelled-up Lancaster stood ready to go from its base at Scampton. Neither his family nor friends knew anything about his mission on the night of May 16th, 1943.

Hopgood, affectionately known as "Hoppy", took off with Gibson and two other Lancasters at 9.39 pm, crossed the coast and was immediately in trouble. His aircraft was picked out by searchlights and then damaged by AA fire. Hopgood and two of his crew were wounded but the pilot pressed on and reached the Möhne dam just after midnight where they again came under intense flak fire.

Two Lancasters, in turn, dropped their bombs on the water; they bounced three times and slammed into the dam. Each time there were huge gushes of water but no apparent breach. The badly bleeding Hopgood in his damaged Lancaster was called by Gibson to take his turn. With his spotlights gleaming on the water he approached the Möhne and his bomb aimer let go of Wallis' masterpiece. It was a fraction too late. The bomb hit the water, bounced over the wall of the dam and hit the power house on the other side which immediately exploded.

Hoppy's aircraft had flown through the thickest of the flak and was blazing. Two of the crew baled out and were taken prisoner but Flight Lieutenant Hopgood and his fourth crew member were killed. They never saw the dam breached.

The village of Shere mourned his loss.

Dr Barnes Wallis, who in later years played bowls for the British Aircraft Corporation, shows his colleagues a new bowling technique he had devised. He bounced the bowl along the green and watched it 'breach' the jack!

Leslie Howard, of Westcott, shot down and killed by raiders

HOLLYWOOD actor, Leslie Howard, best-known for his portrayal of Ashley Wilkes in the epic film *Gone With the Wind*, was one of 13 passengers killed when a civil aircraft was attacked by enemy raiders over the Bay of Biscay on June 4th, 1943. Cinema devotees throughout the world were shocked by the news but the grief was greater in Dorking because Howard was a neighbour and friend. For many years he lived with his wife and family at Stowe Maries, a picturesque house on the outskirts of Westcott.

Mr Howard (real name Leslie Stainer) had been in Spain and Portugal to deliver lectures urging those countries to show British documentary films. He stayed in Lisbon to be present at the showing of the film *The First of The Few* in which he portrayed the designer of the Spitfire, R.J.Mitchell.

Mr Howard's aircraft left Lisbon on June 4th and an hour and a half later the wireless operator signalled "enemy aircraft attacking us". No more was heard.

The *Dorking Advertiser*, in its obituary, said that Mr Howard's film work often took him away from Westcott but he returned there whenever he could to spend quiet, happy days with his polo ponies and in country pursuits. He often opened fetes, spoke at local gatherings and was as charming at these affairs as he was on the screen.

Leslie Howard was passionately fond of the countryside around Dorking and, on one occasion, when he was addressing the Dorking Rotary Club he said the town should become a centre of culture and the arts — an ideal place for film work.

His film *The Lamp Still Burns* was left unfinished.

Lady Stella Reading, who had helped to form the Women's Land Army, was also the founder of the Women's Voluntary Service (WVS) Civil Defence units . The membership was middle class and the members wore green-grey tweed suits, red jumpers and felt hats. The ranks were filled with highly motivated ladies who achieved miracles. They provided meals for bomb victims, set up incident posts, helped with the evacuation, drove mobile canteens, acted as messengers and provided comfort for millions of people. They were best known for their emergency clothing store and, in 1940 alone, distributed £1.5 million worth of clothing to those in need. In Farnham, WVS organiser Audrey Foss and her team sorted out 52,866 books given by local people for soldiers overseas. The photograph shows Lady Reading (centre) on one of her many visits to local units.

Guns are fitted to a Churchill tank.

700 Churchill tanks made and tested in Guildford

THE men who led the infantry across the battlefields of North Africa and Europe in their massive 38-ton Churchill tanks would have had no idea that their slow-moving, heavily-armoured, mechanised monsters had been tested and approved by a 'slip of a girl' who worked for Dennis Brothers at Guildford.

The 800-plus Dennis girls had a wide variety of jobs but this was the most surprising of all, for the young lady was not employed as a Churchill 'pilot' but actually handled the controls to see if they would stand up to battlefield conditions!

Dennis Brothers — famous throughout the country for its Dennis vehicles — had employed 1,400 people during normal peacetime conditions but with the stress of war this was doubled and divided between an increased day shift and a night shift. Many of them lived in Dennisville, a company housing estate for 121 families.

The company gave over its entire production to the war effort. It made subsidy vehicles — vans and lorries available for food transportation — ARP pumps, bomb cases and trailer fire pumps, of which several thousand were ordered by the Home Office through the Minister of Works.

Dennis, however, was best-known for constructing the giant Churchill Tank. More than 700 were built and when they left by train from a special siding in the works they were ready for gunnery tests, having completed trials by road, in deep water tanks and on the testing ground adjoining the Bagshot Road. The ears of many Guildfordians and Stoughtonians had suffered from the roar and rumble of the Churchill engines and then the clash and clatter of their steel tracks.

One former employee, Winnifred Hayes recalls that she couldn't be called up because of the important work she was doing at Dennis. "I remember travelling in a Churchill tank with a test driver", she said. "We went up the A3 as far as the Milford crossroads. One tank was inscribed *Winnie* and they kidded that it was named after me. It went to the front like this."

Those privileged to visit the works during the war, and it was a 'protected place' throughout, saw some astonishing sights. One would have been a team of girls engaged on the manufacture of bomb tails, a series of operations mainly concerned with spot welding. The gang started with an output of 150 a day and by the end of the war it had risen to more than 1,100.

Surrey at work — in the summer of '43

ALL over Surrey, heavy and light manufacturing industries switched their activities to war work — the majority ordered to do so by the Government. There were firms which specialised in telecommunications, cipher machines and radar components. Others made anti-aircraft fuses, bomb sights, predictors and shells of various sizes. Some turned out aeroplane and tank parts, rifle and gun sights and even submarine locaters.

The factories were mostly well organised from the way the workforce initiated teamwork and massive productivity to welfare. Most firms had canteens, first-aid rooms, shelters and arranged lunchtime concerts. They had Home Guard battalions, ARP workers, fire watchers, aeroplane spotters and the bosses encouraged all to listen, when they could, to the wireless on the factory floor where the greatest favourite was *Music While You Work.*

In 1943 Britain had the fullest employment in its history. Of the 17 million in civilian jobs, which included seven million women, less than 100,000 were out of work. Those in the armed forces (men and women) totalled 4.7 million, almost equalled by the 4.3 million in the munition industries. By May 1943 war work for women was compulsory, only those with children aged under 14 being exempt.

It is not possible to mention the contribution to the war made by all the factories and industries of Surrey but to take the Borough of Reigate as an example here are some statistics. The **Redhill Tile Company** made 3,444,000 4.2 inch mortar bombs, **Universal Cleaners and Polishers Ltd** of Holmthorpe made 40 million square yards of steel wool for camouflage, **Wray Park Engineering** rebuilt 1,699 W.D.vehicles, **Monotype Corporation** made 73,000 Bren Guns and 1,000 machine guns and **Redhill and Reigate Aero Supplies Ltd** made sleeping bags, oxygen cases and flags in the basement of the old Reigate Town Hall. There was also an ENSA office in Redhill which supplied artists for troop concerts.

The huge Lagonda works at Egham contributed heavily to the war effort. The company made rocket tails, flame throwers, anti-tank gun carriages, parts for Crusader tanks, engines for patrol boats, RAF trailer equipment, shells, depth charges and aircraft equipment including fuel tanks. Our picture shows a fuel tank for a Tempest under construction.

The troops abroad were well catered for but one unusual need for their leisure hours was darts, a popular game in most billets and the reason for many illegal late nights. The only dart factory in the world during the war was at Alexandra Road, Addlestone where girls, mostly teenagers, made the lead banded darts with turkey feathers. Phyllis Barnes of The Ridings, Addlestone recalls her days with Eldant Darts and how they would be frequently visited by officials who explained the importance of their work for the morale of the troops.

Doreen Bridger at work in the Metropolitan Gas Company in London Road, Camberley. Her machine was probably in the former White's Garage which was taken over as war broke out. She is wearing red, white and blue ribbons in her hair to indicate that victory was in sight.

The toolroom staff of the Hawker Aircraft Company at Kingston in 1943. The toolroom was then housed at the Old Skating Rink. Among the men in the front row are Fred Croft, Harry Vincent, Wally Lightfoot and Reg Payne (second from right) who loaned us the photograph.

A British armoured car, fast and well-armed is seen on a scouting expedition in the desert. The air filter by the left front wheel was made by Vokes of Epsom.

Pint of mild a day for the Crosby girls

BEFORE the war the building firm of Crosby's in Farnham was the largest manufacturer of doors in Europe but, like all big companies, they transferred to war work, constructing radio trailers, packing boxes and pontoon bridges.

The company, under the chairmanship of Basil Crosby, employed many local girls who were mainly involved in making ammunition boxes. The fumes in the factory were terrible and the girls were given a pint of mild a day, as the management thought this would help with sore throats. Throughout the war the women worked from 7.30 am to 6.0 pm, Monday to Friday with just two breaks of 10 minutes each. They had a half day on Saturdays and a half day on Christmas Day.

The painting of the Crosby women at work on a radio trailer, reproduced here, is fascinating. It was painted by John Hutton, an internationally famous glass engraver who became friendly with Basil Crosby and often visited the factory. Hutton immortalised the wartime workforce in four large paintings which now hang in the library at Farnham.

Hutton was one of the artists who helped to set up a large camouflage development unit at Farnham Castle where various patterns helped to confuse the enemy into thinking it was worth the attention of their bombers.

Hurricane production continues at Kingston. By 1943 the Brooklands factory at Weybridge had been moved to Langley in Bucks.

Young people worked hard for the war effort and among those to the fore were the Scouts and Guides throughout the county. Here Scouts are busy recycling waste paper at the Cheam Parochial Rooms in the autumn of 1943.

Headmaster of Selhurst Grammar School, Mr Bill Turner, watches as the school gardener and some of the boys dig up the lawns fronting the school in The Crescent. It was part of a new campaign to encourage schoolchildren and housewives to help the Dig For Victory campaign. The boys must have wondered, somewhat anxiously, if they would soon be eating their own cabbages!

Bomber crashes near Bletchingley after horror raid on two towns

ON the murky, extremely cloudy afternoon of Friday July 9th, 1943 a small formation of enemy aircraft crossed the coast on a hit-and-run bombing mission to London. Because of the weather conditions the RAF was grounded and the raiders actually reached England before they were picked up by radar.

Of the ten aircraft, two reached Croydon. Another hovered above the Surrey/Sussex border and then homed in on East Grinstead where the pilot saw below an Army convoy of 20 to 30 trucks which had drawn up in the car park near Caffyns Garage. He dropped his deadly cargo.

At the Whitehall Cinema in London Road, East Grinstead, an air raid warning was flashed on the screen, but it was too late. A bomb went through the roof with a loud whistling sound and exploded in the auditorium. The raider circled round for a while then began to machine gun the road below which was quickly reduced to a battlefield. Bodies and rubble littered the street. Cars and vans were alight and, from inside the cinema, came the groans and cries of the injured and dying. The death toll amounted to 108.

Among those in the building was relief projectionist, Mr Roy Henn. "I heard a crunch as the bomb went through the roof", he said. "The next second the blast had blown the door in my face and tumbled me down the stairs into the rewind room. I was completely blinded by dust but could hear screams coming from the audience. I groped my way out into the street just as the bomber began to machine-gun and threw myself to the floor in a hairdresser's shop. When the raider left I found half a dozen bodies lying in the road. People were already forming a chain and passing the injured and dead out of the cinema. Inside the cinema there were terrible sights to see. The bomb had actually exploded among the women, children and soldiers."

The other bombers turned their sights on Croydon not knowing that two RAF Mosquitoes, flying blind and relying on radar, had taken off to intercept them. The air raid siren went off in Croydon at 5.14 pm and a few minutes later the first bombs came whistling down on a line from Park Hill to Aurelia Road.

Nine people died in Croydon that evening. They included three at Powers Works — a factory policeman, a gatekeeper and a draughtsman. A housewife in Aurelia Road, two men and a baby in Thornton Heath and two young women who were in the town were also killed.

Severe damage was caused to houses in Aurelia Road, Limpsfield Road and Fairlands Avenue.

As the German bombers headed back to their base flying at less than 500 feet they passed over Kenley where the station's anti-aircraft battery opened up and hit one of the Dorniers. Fire broke out and the crew found themselves in a blazing coffin, which they were unable to leave because they were flying so low. As the plane flew over Caterham the engines began to splutter and eventually cut out. The Dornier banked in its death throes and nose dived to the ground at an angle of 45 degrees crashing at White Hill between Caterham and Bletchingley. It burnt out leaving the remains of the airmen almost unidentifiable.

Mr B.R. Osmond of Farningham Road, Caterham was walking home from work when he heard an aircraft which he could not see because it was so cloudy. "It circled once and then headed south still above the cloud", he said. "About a minute later the engines seemed to cut out. I heard no more sound of the aircraft. Two days later I went to see if the bomber had crashed but I could not get to the actual spot. I believe that troops were keeping the public away."

A week later the Rector of Bletchingley, the Rev. Albury Crawshaw buried the remains of the crew in the parish cemetery. The bodies were badly mutilated and, despite many efforts to identify them, only a brief report of the incident appeared in the parish records.

After the war the men were removed to a German war cemetery at Staffordshire and identified as Lt Hans Dunzelt, pilot, Obergerf Karl Dubiak, observer, Obergerf Ludwig Reichl, wireless operator and Obergerf Willy Hoffmann, air gunner.

One person who was pleased that the crew had been identified was Mrs Eva Dobson of Bletchingley who had lost a son while he was on a bombing mission over Antwerp. Once a week she had put flowers on the grave of the German airmen at the local cemetery and was eventually able to contact the mother of Karl Dubiak in East Germany who sent a photograph of her son.

The other German bomber which had attacked Croydon didn't get back to its base in Holland. It collided head-on with one of the Mosquitoes and both crashed at Detling, killing the two crews.

The mission on that terribly murky July day resulted in the deaths of 117 civilians and soldiers and the entire crews of three aircraft.

Construction workers at Messrs Gale's of Kingston busy putting the finishing touches to landing barges. This was taken in 1943.

The recovery of the Bletchingly Dornier (Do 217 E4) took place many years later (above) when the dig revealed that there were several unexploded bombs buried with the wreckage. This immediately caused doubt among those who were linking this particular aircraft with the bombing of Croydon. A bomb disposal unit was called immediately to the scene and the cargo rendered safe. Top photograph shows the recovery team hauling the main landing wheel away from its grave of nearly 30 years. In the background is the house which stands at White Hill, overlooking the village of Bletchingley.

Christmas letter from a village that can love and hope

The well-known writer Grace Herbert lived in Shere and wrote regularly for the national press. During Christmas Week 1943 an account of life in her village appeared in the Daily Express. We reproduce part of it here.

This is a Christmas letter from home to the men who have gone away. In spirit it might be from any part of the country, or from any country that can still love and hope. But it is written from Shere, Surrey, one of the prettiest villages in England. Shere has 1,000 inhabitants, a church with eight bells, two pubs, a village school, an old prison, recently converted for use as a first-aid station, a police station, a bank, a memorial, a telephone exchange, an antique shop, a yew-flanked smuggler's lane, a swimming pool and the hamlet Gomshall and the village Shere share the same railway station.

I walked down Middle Street last Saturday night at half past nine. There was no-one in the street. There was no light. The only sound was the trickling of the fountain opposite Forrest's Stores. The grapevine ironwork around the front has not been taken for scrap. It still, ostensibly, prevents little children from falling in. Shere men may remember, as boys, that they did fall in.

They said I was to tell you that nothing has changed in Shere. Jack Grover still serves fish and vegetables in his red-painted wooden store opposite the elms in Middle Street. Old Mr Vaughan, the baker, still bakes hand-made loaves and refuses to have anything to do with form filling. Photos of himself and friends in firemen's uniforms and flowing whiskers are still to be seen in the parlour. Nothing's changed.

Now Shere is mostly inhabited by the young and the old. According to Alfred Clumper's British Legion records 146 men left Shere right at the beginning of the war. The girls left, too, to go into the services and the factories.

Fourteen of the men will never come back. One, John Hopgood (Flight Lieutenant) flew with Wing Commander Guy Gibson on the famous Möhne and Eder Dam raids. Gibson affectionately called him Hoppy.

Flight Lieutenant Leslie Sanderson was mentioned in despatches. He was killed in a plane that crashed on his home field. He left a fine daughter aged two. He married Bunty, daughter of Mr Forrest, owner of Forrest's Stores. Mrs Sanderson has had a sad war. Her brother, Squadron Leader Neville Forrest is missing. He was a Bonfire Boy.

There is a new master at the village school, Mr Dobbin, young, fair and rather shy of grown-ups. He's taken on a tough role following Mr Blogg but one of the first things he did was start a youth club. Those old football stars, George Killich, Arthur Killich, Roger Minns and John Oldman had better look out because Mr Dobbin's boys are good at soccer and are getting into shape. The football pitch is in good order. And the last dance at the village hall was in aid of the cricket pitch.

I went to the village dance on Saturday night, Jack Grover came along to look after me. He introduced me to a few of the boys on leave. We did the foxtrot. There were one or two Paul Jones, rather straggly affairs with the boys and girls making up their minds beforehand with whom they were going to dance. And there was some rather nonchalant jitter-bugging, not up to the American variety, but quite good.

Orchard Cottage is still headquaters of the ARP. But the first aid post has been moved from the old smugglers prison to the White Horse. Mrs Isherwood (daughter of the previous rector, Frederick Hill) gives all her time to the parish. "She'll even go up and collect fish for me from the station", says Jack Grover. "She mothers everyone."

Mr Askew, at the White Horse, still has as his motto, "temperance in all things". Mr Parsford, the postman, has been laid up since last July. Lizzie Hooker delivers most of your letters. Before she goes to the post-office at six each morning she prays the day may bring nothing but good news.

Mrs Theobalds runs a communal dining-room for children and grown-ups and nearly everyone uses it. The men's club is going strong. Miss Margaret Bray is doing land work up at Cotterells Farm (see page 98) and Mr R.A Bray JP is living in two rooms of the Manor House.

I went to Matins on Sunday. Crumper's daughter Mavis (she works in Jack Grover's shop) is learning to drive the lorry. She sings in the choir, so do Stanley, Roy and Phyllis Harding. There is a boom in weddings. St James averaged about seven a year before the war but that has almost trebled. Youngest bride — Patricia Chapman, 17.

I sat in Ted Summers' barber's shop on Friday night and watched him at work. He still does a good trade for he doesn't close until 7 o'clock. Old Harry Jelley (87) still gets his weekly shave and Harry Ketcher still gets his daily pint. The stout and bitter has improved, they tell me, at the Prince of Wales.

Well, that's about all I have room to tell you here. There's no cinema yet, no theatre and as I said, at 9 o'clock the village is quiet. It waits for the "Bonfire Boys" to come home to let off the fireworks again. To all the boys at the front who have ever burned a squib, or lit a bonfire, or burned a Guy Fawkes for liberty, Alf Weller, Jack Grover, Lizzie Hopper, Grace Herbert and all send you a message of good luck. Good hunting and a happy return. May you all come back long before old man's beard in Shere is replaced by honeysuckle once again.

The first-aid post was in the old prison at Shere before they moved it to the White Horse.

Led by Basil Crosby (right) are the men of the Farnham Home Guard at Farnham Park with a giant SC 1000 bomb, or Hermann, as they were known. The relaxed atmosphere and the presence of lighted cigarettes gives this away as a training exercise. The men who had the real task of defusing unexploded bombs were the bomb disposal units of the Royal Engineers — or "suicide squads" as they were known in the early days of the war. They spent day after day in many feet of water and mud, in danger every minute. According to Churchill most of them had "haggard faces with a bluish look and bright gleaming eyes". They certainly didn't smoke cigarettes!

Rudolf Hess held in prison camp on Surrey Heath

GERMAN prisoners of war were held in camps right across Surrey. They included many officers but the most infamous of all was Rudolf Hess, once Hitler's trusted deputy and devoted Nazi Party member. Hess, who parachuted from a crashing Messerschmitt, near Glasgow in May 1941 and claimed he was on a peace mission, became a long-term PoW and moved around the British prison camps. At one time he was held at Mytchett Place Camp, Frimley, Surrey Heath.

Kingwood House, Sandhills, Wormley, Godalming was a PoW camp for captured German officers and among the prisoners was Heinz Möllenbrok who had been shot down in August 1940 and badly wounded. In 1993 Herr Möllenbrok made a sketch of the house and sent it to the police in Godalming asking if anyone knew of its whereabouts. The sketch was published in *The Messenger*, the house was indentified and the former German airman made a nostalgic return visit to the scene of his long detention a few weeks later.

There were German camps right across Surrey and one of the best known was at Wimbledon Common, close to Chester House, where the prisoners were employed on the land and in local factories. There were also scores of camps for the Italians captured in North Africa. In fact 130,000 were shipped to Britain and dispersed to hutted accommodation throughout Surrey, one of the largest prisons being at Banstead Wood.

When Abinger Church was hit by a V1 flying bomb in 1944 (see page 177), the Italians nearby willingly cleared up the debris under the direction of the Rector.

1944

D-Day, Doodlebugs and Arnhem

*Fast Scouts tanks of the 2nd Northants Yeomanry near Albury Heath.
Military activity in Surrey increased as D-Day neared.*

January 4th: American and British bombers began to drop supplies to the resistance movements of Europe to arm them for the forthcoming invasion. It was called *Operation Carpetbagger.*

January 27th: The Red Army freed Leningrad after a German siege lasting 872 days. Over a million people died.

February 5th: Michel Hollard, the French resistance leader who spied for the British on the development of the launching sites for the V1 flying bomb, was arrested by the Gestapo.

February 12th: Residents of the Channel Islands were near to starvation, existing on a diet mostly of root vegetables.

March 8th: A faster Spitfire, the Mark XIV, came into service. It was able to compete more easily with the German Focke-Wulf 190.

March 19th: Hungary was occupied by the Germans.

March 24th-15th: A total of 76 Allied PoWs escaped through a tunnel from Stalag Luft III after two years of preparation and digging. Only three, two Norwegians and a Dutchman, reached England; the rest were recaptured and many of them were shot.

March 31st: The Battle of Berlin was finally called to a halt. Since November 18th, 1943 a total of 1,117 bombers had been lost.

April 27th: As part of the preparations for *Operation Overlord*, all foreign travel from Britain was banned and civilians prohibited from coastal areas.

April 30th: The first pre-fab house was erected in three days in London. The two-bedroom, single-storey factory-made house cost £550.

May 18th: Monte Cassino in Italy fell to the Allies after a long battle. The East Surreys played a major role in opening the road to Rome.

June 6th: The D-Day landings took place on the beaches of Normandy. This was the beginning of the end of the war.

June 13th: Hitler's secret weapons made their appearance in England. The first flying bombs in Surrey fell in Croydon and Worcester Park.

June 16th: Sutton and Cheam launched an appeal to raise £550,000 to maintain two battalions of the East Surrey Regiment for a year.

August 25th: Paris was liberated by the Allies.

September 8th: The first V2 rocket fell in Chiswick, killing three people. The first in Surrey was at Coulsdon on September 17th.

September 27th: Allied troops failed in their attempt to capture Arnhem.

September 29th: Scores of repatriated prisoners-of-war came home to Surrey. Among them was Gunner Albert Seymour of Collingwood Road, Sutton who was given a hero's welcome. Gunner Seymour was captured in Libya and spent two years in an Austrian PoW camp.

November 12th: The last remaining German battleship, the *Tirpitz* was sunk.

December 3rd: The last parade of the Home Guard was held in London. The stand down in Surrey had been a few weeks earlier.

December 22nd: The Battle of the Bulge raged in the Ardennes between German and Allied troops.

Christmas Day: Churches were allowed to light their stained glass windows and a few days later car headlight masks were abolished.

Bomber crew taken to Wotton Hatch hotel

OPERATION *Steinbok,* known to the British as The *Baby Blitz,* began on January 21st, 1944 and lasted until the end of March. It was a last-ditch offensive by the Luftwaffe who completely re-equipped its bomber force, trained new pilots and, for the first time in months, was able to to retaliate in some strength.

The *Baby Blitz* lasted nine weeks and in that time 15 large-scale operations were carried out. A few Surrey towns were damaged by random bombing but it was the attackers who suffered the most grievous setbacks — 300 aircraft lost and as many crew members killed as civilians in London. In fact the Luftwaffe was so badly mauled and morale so completely shattered that all manned bomber operations over Britain virtually ceased.

On the first night of the *Steinbock* raids every available bomber in the West was pressed into service. It was appalling weather and 21 failed to return including a Heinkel 177A which was intercepted by Warrant Officer H.K.Kemp and Flight Sergeant J.R. Maidment in a Mosquito of 151 Squadron. The badly damaged Heinkel attempted a forced landing but the aircraft hit rising ground and broke up at Whitmore Vale, Hindhead at 9.20 pm. Two were killed and four taken prisoner.

Despite the appalling losses the raids continued and it was no surprise that Croydon suffered badly again, bombs falling in the borough almost every day for a month. The worst incident was a direct hit on the Davis Theatre in which an audience of some 1,500 were watching a Sonja Henie film. The bomb fell into the front stalls, its great weight and impetus flinging a score of seats aside, killing seven people and injuring 31.

The heaviest attack came during the night of February 20th-21st when 120 aircraft were plotted over England, a number of them in the Croydon area where the AA gunners had been working overtime. This time a Junkers was shot down and fell into the back gardens of Nos 64-66 Bagnall Park, Selhurst. Of the crew of four, one was killed and the others taken prisoner having baled out.

Four nights later 90 bombers were launched against London and the Mosquitos of 29 Squadron were among those scrambled to meet them. There were several successes, among them Squadron Leader C. Kirkland and Flying Officer Raspin who shot down a Dornier over Dorking. It came spinning down out of control, struck a tree and landed in the garden of a house at Parsonage Lane, Westcott with one of its wings actually touching the wall of the house.

The *Dorking Advertiser* wrote: "The plane had a crew of four, two of these baled out and landed in a village about two miles away and after firing pistol lights to attract attention to themselves, were captured by a special constable living nearby and taken to a well-known inn in the locality. The other two members of the crew were found dead with their plane. Many people in the village and surrounding districts saw the bomber spinning to its doom".

The " well-known inn" was in fact the Wotton Hatch hotel which was full of locals and soldiers at the time (9.56 pm). Bomb disposal squads arrived to take the sting out of the Dornier's bombs after evacuating some of the residents in nearby homes.

On this night (February 24th-25th) the Luftwaffe lost nine aircraft and took a breather to regroup. But the raids continued in earnest and on March 14th an attacking force of 140 bombers actually reached London, released their bombs and turned for home. Flight Lieutenant N.S. Head and Flying Officer A.C.Andrews in a Mosquito of 96 Squadron singled out a Junkers and shot it down at Blackbrook, Holmwood Common, again near Dorking.

The *Advertiser* reporters were hot on the scene. "A German twin-engine plane crashed in flames in a wood near a Home Counties town. It caused no damage excepting by smashing the trees among which it fell and the only casualties were among the plane's crew. Almost certainly the plane was brought down by a British fighter. Cannon fire was heard immediately before it crashed."

As the summer of 1944 arrived the bomber offensive gradually fell away. With talk of a possible Allied invasion and absolutely no sign of the "secret weapons" which Hitler had claimed he would soon be using, there was cautious optimism in the air. The war would soon be over.

Flying Officer Raspin inspects the remains of the Dornier which he helped to shoot down on February 24th, 1944.

Nine killed as bomb destroys four houses in village

THE villages below the North Downs, especially those between Guildford and Dorking, had suffered their share of random bombing and had seen scores of aircraft and airmen come tumbling out of the sky. By January 1944 the end of the war seemed closer than ever but, sadly, it was not the end of the bombing. On the 7th, in the early hours of a Wednesday morning, four houses in Watson Road, Westcott were destroyed by a single bomb and nine people were killed.

For the small community it was their biggest single tragedy of the war. The demolished homes stood at the end of a long street and beyond them were open fields. If the bomb had fallen just 20 yards to the west or north all would have been well.

Among those who died were Mrs Nellie Wakeford and her two daughters Barbara and Ann. Her husband had been fire watching in Dorking and he was called home with the news that only his third daughter Mildred had been saved. Among the other fatalities was a woman aged 92, a two-year-old child and two evacuees from London.

Canadian soldiers helped Civil Defence workers release all the victims in less than four hours and neighbours provided shelter and comfort for the homeless.

One of the worst of the Steinbock raids was on February 22nd-23rd when a great cluster of bombers dropped flares over the Thames which drifted towards Weybridge. The flares were followed by 15 high explosives which killed 15 people and injured many more in Vale Road, Baker Street, Old Palace Road and also at Cobham and Hersham. A number of homes in Queens Road, Weybridge were also destroyed and the picture shows members of the Home Guard taking a break from the salvage work.

The searchlight batteries, situated liberally across Surrey, contributed significantly to the destruction of many German bombers. The men, aided by many ATS girls, plotted the course of the quarry with skill and accuracy and then handed over to the fighters or gunners on the anti-aircraft batteries. Photograph shows the men of a searchlight unit near Guildford welcoming a travelling library. Off duty, on their lonely outposts, these men needed something to help pass the time and the library service was most popular.

Life on the ocean waves — no, you must go to the pit face

BY March 1944 the first batch of young recruits to the mines had started work. These were known as "Bevin Boys", after the Labour Minister Ernest Bevin and their names were picked by ballot. They spent a few weeks training under experienced miners and were paid a weekly wage of £2 10s 6d.

Surrey lads who had volunteered for the Services were rather stunned to be picked out of the "Bevin hat". Among them was Walter John Barley of Bishopsford Road, St Heller who for years had looked forward to the time when he could join the navy. He volunteered but was dismayed to be told he was a Bevin Boy and must work in the mines.

Walter, aged 18, went to Pontefract where he was directed to the pit face as an underground trainee but after three days returned to the Employment Exchange at Sutton and said he did not intend to return to Yorkshire. The coal mines made him ill. He preferred the open seas.

Walter appeared at Wallington court summoned for failing to perform service as directed by a National Service officer on underground work at the Prince of Wales Colliery, Pontefract. The chairman was unable to induce a satisfactory explanation but Walter, still hankering for the Royal Navy, reluctantly agreed to go back to the mines. There were many such cases in 1944.

New Malden boy wins VC for gallantry

BOMBER Command's last great show of strength before D-Day was a raid on Nuremberg on March 31st, 1944 when an air convoy of 795 set off on a round trip of 1,500 miles, which was to take eight hours for those who returned. But many didn't for this was a disaster similar to the Light Brigade's futile charge at Balaclava. Ninety five planes were lost and 545 aircrew died bringing the total of Allied crews lost in four months to a staggering 1,117.

Among the aircraft which left its British base on that tragic evening was a new Halifax bomber LK797E, piloted by Cyril Barton of Elm Road, New Malden. 'Cy' as he was known to his family and friends was 23 years old and the pride of Beverley Central School, St. John's Church and Parnells aircraft factory — all in New Malden — where he had studied, worshipped and worked before joining the RAF.

'Cy' with his crew of seven took off just after 10 pm on the long leg to Nuremberg in what was destined to be one of the most famous and bravest flights by a single bomber in wartime. Half-way along the 'long leg' searchlights snapped on and then fighter flares began to appear. But they were attacking the aircraft ahead and the Halifax passed between the flares.

About 70 miles from the target the bomber was attacked by a Junkers 88 which flew away into the darkness and then appeared again on the Halifax's port beam accompanied by a Messerschmitt 210. Barton took the necessary corkscrew action but the Halifax had been hit in the starboard inner engine, cannon shells were exploding in the navigator's compartment, some of the equipment was on fire, the intercom was dead and the bomber's machine guns out of action.

The Halifax still flew on and Barton gave the "resume course" signal but as fighters continued to attack and confusion reigned the signal was misinterpreted by the navigator, the wireless operator and bomb aimer who thought the order was to bale out. Barton and his remaining three colleagues checked the damage which included a ruptured fuel tank and the loss of some 400 gallons. They flew on to the target area, dropped their bombs and turned for home.

The starboard inner engine which had been vibrating furiously suddenly tore loose and flew away into the night like an enormous catherine wheel. Using his captain's map and steering by the stars and compass Cy Barton flew across enemy territory and through more flak and searchlights. He crossed France, turned north and headed for the emergency aerodrome at Woodbridge, Suffolk. The Halifax was badly damaged and there was no navigator or proper navigational aid. Suddenly the crew were lost. They saw a Beaufighter and fired a distress signal but the pilot flew into the mist and out of sight.

As the grey light of dawn became brighter they crossed the English coast and were alarmed when ground defences opened fire having failed to recognise this single lame English bomber. One of the crew, Timber Wood signalled SOS but it was too late. A petrol tank had been severed and the fuel ran out instead of into the engines. Barton shouted to his crew that they were going to crash land and must take up positions, sitting on the floor with their backs against the rear spar and hands behind their heads.

They circled for a while and then crashed and as they did so the nose, the wings, the engines and half the fuselage tore off. In the remaining half were three of the crew, wounded but all alive. They had crashed into the area of a coalmine at Ryhope in Sunderland and were immediately rescued by miners and admitted to Cherry Knole Hospital where they learned that Cy Barton was dead.

Pilot Officer Barton had faced a situation of dire peril. With the port engine out of action, fuel dangerously low, his navigational team gone, too low to abandon the plane, he then found he was flying over houses. Somehow he managed to steer the falling bomber away from what could have been a terrible tragedy and clipped just the end house of West Terrace.

For his actions from beginning to end, Cy Barton was awarded the country's highest award for gallantry, the Victoria Cross.

The East Surreys entering Cassino in May 1944. A prelude to one of the toughest battles of the war.

Surreys defy Nazis in the battle of Cassino

THE Italian campaign, in which units of the 1/6th and 1st Surreys, continued to fight almost side by side lasted from September 1943 until May 1945. It was confusing, it was bloody and conditions were appalling but the two battalions of the county regiment held vital positions under constant fire, helped to breach the German line and played a crucial part in opening the road to Rome.

The battle of Monte Cassino was the vital stage. High on the mountainside, occupied by German troops, stood the smouldering remains of the historic monastery of St Benedict. It had been bombed by the RAF but still came to symbolise one of the toughest battles of the war. Here the Germans had an unimpeded view across the Liri valley to the west, the Castiglione to the south and the road and railway running up through central Italy to Rome.

The Surreys were fighting with the British Eighth Army and one of their tasks was to try to flush the enemy out of the monastery and off the hillside. There were numerous patrol clashes and at times the Surrey men were so close to the Germans that they could hear them singing *Lili Marlene* in the still night air.

The first battle of Cassino ended with the enemy still commanding the vital Highway 6. The 1/6th Surreys joined the fray and on the the night of May 11th, 1944 in the face of a thunderous barrage from a fanatical defence they crossed the aptly-named Rapido which was 80 feet wide and flowing fast with flood water. The river claimed many lives but the assault craft delivered the Battalion across it and the minefields beyond were systematically cleared. By the evening of the 18th, the 1/6th Surreys had taken the town of Cassino.

The vital hill, stormed by Polish troops, also fell, Kesselring's army retreated with more than 2,000 men taken as prisoners and the road to Rome was opened.

There were many casualties but the tenacity of the East Surreys, many of the men from towns and villages throughout the county, gave other units the opportunity to advance and the indomitable Polish Corps to take Monte Cassino. It was a brilliant action and the Surrey newspapers were full of praise for the gunners, the tank men, the sappers, the signallers and the infantrymen who ran the gauntlet of shells and mortar bombs for so many weeks.

Monty's message at Albury Heath

SOUTH-Eastern Army Command headquarters was at Reigate and Field Marshal Bernard Montgomery was a regular visitor to the town where he often read the lesson in the parish church and inspected the troops in the area. In May 1944 he left his desk at Reigate and was driven to Albury Heath, where he spoke to more than 1,000 soldiers and told them that they would be under his command for the Second Front. It was the message that every soldier wanted to hear.

Among the men at Albury Heath that day was Walter A. Moir, serving with the Royal Canadian Engineers at Round Down, Gomshall. Walter, with 600 colleagues, marched from Gomshall via Silent Pool to meet the Field Marshal and attend the famous rally. He knew he would soon be going to France, but could only speculate on the date.

Suddenly there were rumours among civilians everywhere that a great liberation army was being prepared. Troops were recalled from North Africa, Sicily and Italy to join with the Canadians. Armies came from the Empire and eastern Europe but all were confined to camps and communication with local residents was discouraged. Long lines of vehicles under camouflage netting appeared on the A3, A29, A286 and the A24 dual carriageway between Dorking and Leatherhead. There were tank movements everywhere. The countryside, particularly around Thursley, Milford, Elstead and Haslemere became a vast military camp.

The troops took part in exercises. How to wade in rough waters in full kit. How to assemble a folding bicycle in a few seconds. Many took part in the "invasion" of Littlehampton and Hayling Island while others helped to strengthen and widen road and rail bridges to help with the build-up of traffic. At Mickleham a new road and Bailey Bridge over the river was built by the Canadians and out in the villages stretching towards the south coast were tanks and ambulances while ammunition and petrol was stored in the woods.

As the elaborate plans for the invasion continued, factories increased their productivity. Among the most important were the Churchill tanks, rolling off the production line at Dennis Brothers works in Guildford and landing barges made by Gales of Kingston. Elsewhere engineers were perfecting the production of artificial harbours — code-named Mulberry — made up of floating concrete units. It was planned to accommodate ships by enclosing sheltered water with a depth of at least nine metres and at least 18 metres high. Strategists had long appreciated the crucial importance of safe harbours for subsequent waves of troops and supplies.

The Mulberrys, described by Churchill as "majestic"

Monty spoke to the men on Albury Heath and told them he was tired of the war and it was time it was ended. Together, he said, we can win it this year. Today, a plaque marks the spot where he addressed the men.

needed to be defended and the Fourth Battalion of the Queen's Regiment — the Royal West Surreys — were chosen to provide the anti-aircraft defences on the harbours with two batteries — the 416th and the 440th. Another battery, the 439th was given instructions to man the light cruiser HMS *Despatch* as well as three old ships which were to be sunk to form the initial breakwater.

The Despatch was the control ship until the harbours were built and the Royal Navy could supply a shore base. The 439th placed 16 Bofors on board with selected officers and men while the other batteries took part in invasion exercises at Portsmouth Dockyard and Dungeness. Meanwhile, the rest of the 439th installed guns on three tramp steamers and set sail from Oban in Scotland, down the Irish Channel for Normandy.

In this eventful hour of British history, the Royal West Surreys were the first troops to sail for Normandy. As they did so General Eisenhower, Supreme Commander, was postponing *Operation Overlord* for 24 hours because of the weather. It was on the morning of Monday June 5th that he made his famous decision "OK, Let's go".

Dunsfold Aerodrome, in its short history, had received a few important visitors but the VIP personnel who landed in a Dakota on April 18th, 1944 included the Supreme Commander of the Allied Forces, General Dwight Eisenhower, Air Chief Marshal Sir Trafford Leigh-Mallory and top-brass representatives of the USAAF and US Army. The General addressed the crews of 98 and 320 Squadrons in a T2 hangar and told them to be prepared for the challenges ahead. A few days later Group Captain Larry Dunlap RCAF, Commanding Officer at Dunsfold and Wing Commander (flying) Alan Lynn were ordered to Northolt for a top-secret briefing on a cross-Channel invasion, code-named Operation Overlord.

Top secret codenames in Telegraph crossword

THE Allied team planning the invasion of France could not believe their eyes. The *Daily Telegraph* crossword for May 2nd contained the following two clues — for 17 across "One of US" and for 3 down "Red Indian on the Missouri". The answers were "Utah" and "Omaha", the secretly guarded codenames given for two of the American invasion beaches.

The compiler was Leonard Dawe, a 54-year-old teacher from Leatherhead who had also compiled another puzzle in which "Overlord" was the answer to a clue. Senior officers, convinced that invasion secrets were being leaked, passed the matter on to MI5. It turned out to have been a completely innocent coincidence.

The making of Mulberry. The giant concrete structures were towed to Normandy where they were defended by the Royal West Surreys. Picture shows the telescopic span being connected to inter-pontoon.

Royal West Surreys and the Mulberry Harbour

THE floating concrete units, from which the Mulberry Harbour was eventually formed, were called Phoenixes and it was the task of the Royal West Surreys to defend them while the harbours were constructed and then accompany the tugs which towed them across the Channel to Arromanches. During these anxious days one Phoenix was torpedoed and an officer and ten men killed.

By then the vast armada of more than 6,000 ships had already left for Normandy. Fifty miles wide and protected by scores of fast-moving torpedo boats the invasion fleet carried 185,000 men and 20,000 vehicles. Each man and landing craft was scheduled to arrive at a specific time.

As news of the Allied landings reached Surrey, Ministry of Information vans drove through town centres broadcasting the great news and asking people to ignore any other rumours or so-called "information". The *Sutton Times* wrote: "At mention of the name of Eisenhower tradesmen left their counters, shopkeepers their baskets and office girls their typewriters to catch every word of the momentous news. When the communiqué ended Suttonians were reminded of the golden opportunity they would have of honouring the Crusaders of the invasion force when the Borough's Salute the Soldier Week starts on Saturday".

At Cheam a special "invasion service" was held at St Dunstan's church, attended by representatives of civilian organisations throughout the parish. There were services in other towns and villages throughout Surrey, ministers outlining the stern resolve of the invasion force to see it through to a triumphant end and, above all, to avenge Dunkirk.

The tension in the county that had existed during the great military build-up had suddenly been lifted. Daily bulletins were followed with the greatest possible interest, there was an unprecedented demand for newspapers and wireless reports were relayed to workers in the great Surrey factories.

Some days after the landings the completed Mulberry Harbours were towed by tugs to Arromanches, ready to receive 12,000 tons of cargo and 2,500 vehicles a day. The Royal West Surreys mounted their guns and remained until the job was done.

RAF Horne — theD-Day airfield

THE hustle and bustle in the Surrey countryside during that big build-up towards D- Day was not confined to the military. The RAF was also preparing for the invasion by building additional runways on the established airfields and constructing more and more advanced landing grounds (ADG) for the huge numbers of Allied aircraft that would be involved in *Operation Overlord.*

The ADGs were crude airfields with grass tracts that were covered with steel mesh to withstand the pounding of aircraft continually taking off and landing. There were no proper hangars — the planes were serviced in the open — and both the air and ground crew were required to sleep in canvas tents. It was all very temporary but useful experience for pilots who would

Canadians of 402 Squadron at RAF Horne in May 1944. FO Bill 'Slim' Harvey sunbathes with FO Wally Lalonde, FO 'Mac' Macleod, FO Wally O'Hagan, who was soon to go missing, and PO Marty Naylor, (standing).

have to operate from similar places once a bridgehead in Europe had been established.

One such airfield was constructed on farmland close to the village of Horne, south of Redhill and just a few miles from the present London Gatwick International Airport. It was ready for use in early May and for seven crucial weeks became a vital cog in the build-up to the invasion and on D-Day itself. Then it reverted to a balloon site and was handed back to the farmer long before the end of the war.

In that short time more than 300 RAF personnel from five different nations ate, slept, worked and flew from RAF Horne. The local inhabitants were intrigued that so many men should operate in such primitive conditions and often wondered exactly what was going on. Not until the invasion had succeeded did they find out.

Three Spitfire Squadrons, No 130, commanded by Squadron Leader W.H.Ireson, No 303 (Polish) commanded by Squadron Leader T.Koc and No 402 (Canadian), commanded by Squadron Leader G.W.Northcott came together at Horne as 142 Wing, under the overall command of Wing Commander Johnnie Checketts (flying). They flew in or came by train or personal transport on April 30th and set up their tents while Flying Control was established in a caravan just to the west of Bones Lane, Horne.

From Monday May 1st until D-Day and then beyond, the pilots of 142 Wing participated as escorts to Douglas Boston medium bombers on 26 raids (or Ramrods as they were known). They provided fighter cover for a number of Beaufighters on anti-shipping strikes and they made low-level ground attacks (Sweeps) on various targets in Europe. There were many mishaps. Some were whisked to nearby Smallfield Hospital to have their injuries treated and others crashed in France and became PoWs.

On D-Day the first patrol was airborne at 3.42 am and over the beaches within the hour — one of the first to provide the vital cover on that day. Bill Ireson of 130 Squadron said of that day: "The scene of hundreds of ships below showed the scale of the enterprise, but the sight of filled body bags on the American beaches showed how tough and costly this endeavour really was".

The saddest day for RAF Horne was Saturday June 17th when Flight Sergeants Graham Ferguson and Jeep Hale collided over the Channel. Ferguson was killed and Hale made a forced landing at Tangmere.

When they were not flying, the pilots and the groundcrew frequented such pubs in the area as the Plough at Smallfield and the Blue Anchor (now the Parson's Pig) on the Balcombe Road. After their D-Day patrols the Polish pilots went to the Jolly Farmers where the locals, desperate for news of the invasion, bought them drinks and asked what it was like to look down on the beaches.

The Wentworth Bunker

THIS is the entrance to the extensive and little-known underground bunker which was built beneath the golf fairways at Wentworth. The bunker contained 44 rooms and was destined to become GHQ of the home forces for General Sir Alan Brooke and his staff if their headquarters at Storey's Gate in London became untenable following enemy action. In 1941 a practice evacuation from Storey's Gate to Wentworth, known as *Exercise Carter Paterson*, was carried out. It went well but some difficulty was experienced in carrying heavy equipment, such as duplicators, into the bunker.

In an article about military interest in the Wentworth area before and during the war local historian Mr Ron Davis of Virginia Water wrote: "Even as late as 1942 the Commander-in-Chief wished to retain Wentworth and new cabling was being installed, putting Wentworth in direct communication with other local military establishments such as Queenswood and Bellefields in Egham."

The bunker was constructed with the same heavy iron girders which were used to build the London underground stations and had London Transport printed on them. The golf clubhouse

and other houses on the Wentworth Estate were the home of the Army Tactical School and the area was defended by anti-tank mines, a store of grenades and several lines of barbed wire. During plans for the Second Front it was assumed that General Eisenhower might well use the bunker but, in fact, it was never necessary to abandon Storey's Gate and the Wentworth bunker became a fascinating "what might have been" story. The bunker is still there today but access is denied.

Redhill's introduction to the flying bomb came on June 19th, 1944 when one crashed in a garden at the angle of Earlsbrook Road and St John's Road, Earlswood. Scores of people were buried in the debris of their own homes and the death toll was eleven.

War was nearly won — then came the battle of the doodlebug

THE joyful news of the Normandy landings and the expectation that the war would be over by Christmas was to be short-lived. In the early hours of June 16th a strange stuttering noise, likened by some to that of a badly-tuned motor bike, was heard over Surrey. Red flames were spurting from the rear and it looked like a black cross in the sky.

The Observers on their lonely outposts in the Surrey hills knew this must be Hitler's much-vaunted pilotless plane or flying bomb which they had been told to look out for. One had landed in London a few days earlier but all details were strictly censored. The Observers passed the information to their headquarters and the sirens sounded. Unbeknown to them at the time the new Battle of Britain was about to begin.

A few miles away in Longfellow Road, Worcester Park — a smart residential area in the "stockbroker belt" — a mother heard the air raid warning and instinctively picked up her baby boy and carried him to a safe part of the house. As she put him down, the flying bomb, later to be christened "doodlebug", crashed with an enormous bang into the junction of two adjacent roads, Caldbeck Avenue and Browning Avenue.

The little boy was called John Major, destined to become Prime Minister, and he was not hurt by the blast which blew in the windows of his house and brought tragedy to his neighbourhood. On that day in Worcester Park 14 people were killed in the wreckage of their homes and two died later in hospital. Civil Defence workers, angry and puzzled, toiled through the night to bring out the dead and take the injured to hospital.

As more of these deadly, novel weapons, armed with an explosive nose and propelled by a pulse-jet engine, sped across the Surrey skies just above rooftop height, so more reports came in of death and devastation.

Twelve were killed in Cliveden Road, Wimbledon, the explosion destroying 17 homes and damaging property over a vast area. That was also June 16th. Two days later shoppers in Sutton High Street saw a bomb gliding silently over their heads. It crashed in Hamilton Avenue, North Cheam where nine people were killed. At Camborne Road, Sutton, rescuers toiled for hours to reach two women and four children buried in the ruins of a demolished house. The wife of Squadron Leader Thomas and their three children were dead but her friend and a four-year-old boy were still alive. The blast was so great that it actually uprooted trees in the garden.

The men on the anti-aircraft batteries in the suburbs could hardly believe their luck as wave after wave of enticing targets came over all flying a straight course. And they cheered madly when the sudden cut-out by the engine seemed to indicate they had been hit. One was shot down into the garden of a house at Earlswood, Redhill and ten people and a baby died. Shells rained down everywhere as gunners greeted the monsters with more enthusiasm than discrimination.

The campaign continued through June and into July but the fastest fighters which chased the monsters across the skies and the formidable gunners frequently got in each other's way — so the defences were redeployed. Fighters were instructed to patrol the area between Beachy Head and Dover and they were the first line of defence. The second was an enormous barrage of anti-aircraft guns ranged along the coast and on the coastal slopes of the Kent Downs. The third were more fighters which roamed inland and the fourth were the goalkeepers, the balloons, anchored on higher ground between the Thames and Redhill.

The doodlebugs were launched from mobile ramps in Pas de Calais and Picardy, set up in woods and villages. The busiest route was between Dungeness and Hythe so the greatest emphasis on air defence was placed there. But those that avoided the guns, slipped past the Tempests, Spitfires, Mustangs and night-fighting Mosquitos and evaded the balloons, created more and more havoc in London and the southern boroughs.

Schools, churches, hospitals and villages all suffered. In Headley, the Rector and his wife heard the approach of a doodlebug and just had time to dive under their Morrison shelter in the kitchen. The house collapsed around them but they were not injured. Outbuildings, trees and the gardener's cottage were ruined.

In Shirley, on July 26th, the children of St John's School heard the air raid warning and trooped obediently to the shelter. A V1 made a direct hit on their school, took out two cottages and the roof of the church. The children, uninjured, came out of their shelters to stare in astonishment at the ruins of their school. At Merstham, too, the children were lucky. About 100 were at morning assembly when a bomb exploded outside. Windows were shattered and a heavy frame fell below two lines of girls. Teachers and children were showered by glass fragments and the headmaster was struck on the back as the ceiling collapsed. In a highways depot in the road outside three workmen were killed.

St Helier Hospital, Carshalton was struck twice. The

The introduction of the doodlebug was followed by another great evacuation. By July 17th it was estimated that 170,000 evacuees had left the London boroughs and the numbers grew daily until they reached 1,450,000. Escorted by the WVS and other volunteers they went to Yorkshire, Scotland, Wales and the West Country. Here are the children from Ewell as they arrived in Wadebridge, Cornwall in July 1944. To the chagrin of some of the boys but to the great relief of their mothers they "missed" the excitement of 29 flying bombs falling in their borough.

first V1 landed on the morning of June 21st and injured many nurses who then became patients in their own hospital. Six days later, as if to finish the job, another one struck the hospital and two died.

The occupants of an isolated cottage in Sandy Lane, Dorking, which was surrounded by many acres of open countryside, must have heard the doodlebug of June 30th approach. It was flying so low that it struck the trees, demolished the cottage and killed two women and a boy in the house.

At Abinger, on September 15th, the vicar of the beautiful old Parish Church of St James, was just leaving the Rectory for the 8 o'clock service when a doodlebug impacted on the roof of the west end of the church. The vicar watched his church collapse before his eyes; within seconds the roof, the belfry, the spire, the south doorway and the porch were smouldering ruins amid blasted trees and broken tombstones. Other historic buildings nearby including the Manor House and the Abinger Hatch Inn also suffered.

One dramatic moment followed another and hardly a single parish in Surrey escaped the attention of the doodlebug. In the Dorking rural area, for example, five bombs fell in Abinger, Betchworth 5, Buckland 2, Charlwood 5, Capel 1, Headley 7, Holmwood 5, Horley 5, Leigh 1, Newdigate 6, Ockley 2, Wotton 5 — the majority in fields and woods.

Even at Guildford, much further away from the target area, doodlebugs fell in such areas as Foxburrow Avenue, Stoke recreation ground, East Shalford Lane, South Warren Farm and Aldersey Road. Homes were shattered, straw bales destroyed and animals maimed but there were no human casualties.

Between June 16th and September 7th, 1944, 295 flying bombs fell in Surrey — considerably less than Kent with 1,444, East Sussex 880 and Essex 412. It was a short-lived campaign but, nonetheless, this unique, brilliantly conceived, totally indiscriminate weapon had a devastating effect on morale at a time when everyone thought the war was nearly won.

Nos 51 and 53 Greenways, Hinchley Wood, near Esher after a V1 flying bomb exploded. Three people in these homes were killed.

The damage caused by the V1 which exploded on Myrtle Grove, Kingston on July 28th, 1944, destroying Nos 10, 12, 14 and 16. The milkman, however, still left a pint at the gate!

142 flying bombs crash in Croydon borough

CROYDON suffered grievously from the flying bomb attacks. For three terrifying months hardly a day or night went by without the Borough receiving a doodlebug and, on most occasions, they came in batches. There was scarcely a road in the town which escaped damage and, during one exceptional weekend, 15 crashed in residential areas. When the campaign ended the final reckoning made grim reading: 142 flying bombs killed 211 people, seriously injured 692 and slightly injured 1,277. Fifty nine thousand houses were damaged and, of these, 1,400 were completely destroyed.

The first V1 fell at the junction of Avenue and Warminster Roads and the Incident Officer's report was unusually detailed. Here is an extract: "The deep-throated roar was heard first. A blinding flash followed and an explosion that rocked the warden's post. The race to the scene was through a nightmare fog of mortar and dust, the road being carpeted with leaves, glass and rubble. Injured and uninjured were rushing out, dazed and bewildered in the dim dawn light.

"The scene itself was desolation; four large houses which were known to be occupied were down and dozens of others were sagging or broken in various ways. A rapid reconnaissance enabled express messages to be sent to the Control for help. First came soldiers from a searchlight site, then a party of Bedfordshires who were billeted in Aukland Road. They went at once to the work of releasing the trapped; work in which they were joined by a Light Rescue Party from Penge. The NFS arrived and, almost immediately, too, came the Housewives Service of the WVS who established their post in a broken garage...."

Throughout the ordeal, everyday life in Croydon was severely disrupted. Few Croydonians enjoyed a full night's sleep. They took it in snatches and sometimes declined to go to the shelter, even when the air-raid alert went off 11 times and death or terrible injury was imminent.

People died in groups. In one incident four of the Creswell family were killed and on other occasions three in each of the families of Denman, Dowland, Gibbs and Hanchett.

Alongside the tragedy was the great exodus. From this great peril nearly 26,000 left Croydon to find safer areas while those left behind toiled to repair the shattered homes. Members of the Home Guard on most evenings were seen with their bags of tools and materials rendering first aid repair whenever they could. Badly damaged homes were made weatherproof with more than 5,000 yards of tarpaulin. Schools were closed and furniture was stored in them. Houses in fringe areas were requisitioned for rest centres.

Everything that Croydon had envisaged and carefully planned during the days of the "phoney war" in 1939-40 had come a nightmare reality. When it was over the Borough was given a title that has lasted to this day. It was simple and to the point. Courageous Croydon.

The diary of flying bomb incidents

CENTRAL CROYDON AREA

June 16-17	Tennant's Nursery
29	Middle Whitgift School Grounds
July 8-9	Duppas Avenue
27-28	Cranmer Road
Aug 5-6	Duppas Hill Terrace
8-9	Bramley Hill

EAST CROYDON AREA

June 15-16	Selsdon Park Road
17-18	Addington New Golf Course
25-26	Addington Golf Course
28-29	Gascoigne Road
July 1-2	Yew Tree Way
3-4	Addington Palace Golf Course
20	Lodge Lane
20-21	Bishop's Walk
30	Featherbed Lane
31	Featherbed Lane
Aug 2-3	Addington Palace Golf Course
5	Addington New Golf Course
11-12	204, Yew Tree Way
16	Addington House Estate

ADDISCOMBE

Lower Addiscombe Road District

June 20-21	Chepstow Road
July 1	Dalmally Road
7-8	Beckford Road
27-28	Bredon Road and Jesmond Road
30-31	Beckenham Golf Course
Aug 11-12	Beckenham Golf Course

Upper Addiscombe Road District

June 25-26	Addiscombe Road
Aug 7-8	Ranmore Avenue

SHIRLEY

June 15-16	Upper Shirley Road
16-17	Shirley Residential School
18-19	Shirley Church Road
18-19	South Way
22-23	Woodmere Gardens
22-23	Gladeside
26	Parkfields
26	Bennett's Avenue
26	The Glade
26	Shirley Way
28	Oak Avenue
30-July 1	Ash Road
July 1	Shirley Residential School
3	Shirley Hills Road
15-16	Oak Avenue
21-22	Upper Shirley Road
26	Spring Park Road
27	Mead Way
Aug 1	Shirley Park Golf Club
2-3	Lorne Gardens
6	Royal Bethlem Hospital
6-7	Woodmere Avenue
13-14	Ash Road
16	Royal Bethlem Hospital

WEST CROYDON AREA

June 16-17	Pawsons Road
16-17	St James's Road
23	West Croydon Station. Direct hit on platform with damage there and on Oakfield Road and to the Ave Maria Convent in Wellesley Road.
30-July 1	Colvin Road
July 1-2	Windmill Road
3	Elmwood Road
5-6	Curzon Road
6-7	Canterbury Road
Aug 2-3	Lavender Road
2-3	Brading Road
4	Greenside Road
15	Milton Avenue

WOODSIDE

July 5	Estcourt Road
7-8	Handley's Brickworks
8-9	South Norwood Sewage Farm
21	Long Lane
21-22	Estcourt Road

NORTH CROYDON AREA SELHURST

June 16-17	Selhurst New Road
July 27-28	The Crescent

South Norwood

North of Selhurst Road District

June 15-16	Warminster and other roads
17-18	Stanley Halls
28-29	South Norwood Hill
30-July 1	Wrights Road
July 1-2	Warminster Road
2	Holmesdale Road
8-9	Lancaster Road
14	Saxon Road
Aug 10-11	Lancaster Road

South of Selhurst Road District

June 22-23	Southern Railway: burst on railway 50 yds south of Tennison bridge; damaged Davidson Road
July 4-5	Portland Road
7-8	Tennison Road (Handley's Brickworks - also affected Davidson Road)
9-10	Harrington Road

THORNTON HEATH

June 25-26	Stanley Road
30-July 1	Whitehall Road
30-July 1	Colvin Road
July 1	Nursery Road
1	Pridham Road
1	Haslemere Road
2	Chipstead Avenue
3-4	Woodville Road
4-5	Layard Road
4-5	Livingstone Road
4-5	Moffatt Road
11	Marion Road
12-13	Grange Road
15-16	Brigstock Road
31	Thornton Heath Recreation Ground
Aug 4	Grangewood Recreation Ground

NORBURY

East of London Road District

June 22	Hatch Road
27-28	North Surrey Golf Course
July 2	County Road
3-4	Norbury Crescent
5-6	Norbury Crescent
20-22	Norbury Avenue
29-30	North Surrey Golf Course
Aug 1-2	Norbury Crescent

West of London Road District

June 17-18	Norbury Court Road
19-20	Acacia Road
24	Pollards Hill East
28-29	Pollards Hill South
July 11-12	Pollards Hill South
15-16	Pollards Hill South

UPPER NORWOOD

June 15-16	Warminster Road
21	Ross Road
28-29	Central Hill; Convent of the Faithful Virgin
July 5	Biggin Hill
15	Spa Hill
16-17	Spurgeon Road
19	Ross Road
20	Moore Road
20-21	Gibson's Hill
24	Church Road
26-27	Sylvan Road
28	Sylvan Road
Aug 2-3	Beulah Hill
5-6	Ryecroft Road

SOUTH CROYDON AREA

East of Brighton Road District

June 15-16	Junction of Croham Road and Campden Road
17-18	Winchelsea Rise
20-21	Coombe Road
25-26	Croham Valley Road
27-28	Coombe Farm
28-29	Pampisford Road
28-29	Lloyd Park
July 1-2	Coombe Lane
9-10	Lloyd Park
9-10	Croham Valley Road
17-18	Brighton Road
31-Aug 1	Hurst Way
Aug 4	Croham Road
Nov 14-15	Castlemaine Avenue

West of Brighton Road District

Aug 2-3	Haling Park Road

Air raid wardens, the light rescue squad, old men and tin-hatted small boys take a break from sifting the debris at Croydon Road, Beddington to enjoy a snack provided by the good ladies of the WVS. This was June 16th, 1944 and one of the first flying bomb attacks. Left: A sad sight for the owner of this car at Grosvenor Road, Wallington in July 1944.

This was the damage caused by the doodlebug which landed in a garden at South Croydon and completely demolished a number of homes. Miss M.G. Hayman who loaned the picture and was away at the time says that her father and brother were in the shelter when the bomb fell and her mother was just about to enter. She was slightly injured but the blast ripped her clothes to shreds and she was badly shocked. In all this devastation there were no fatalities or serious injuries and that included the dog who was in the house in his basket under the steel draining board.

The Anderson shelter which was like a small bicycle shed, partly buried, really came into its own during the flying bomb campaign, providing wonderful protection against falling masonry and blast. Here is the Anderson which saved lives in Spring Park Road, Shirley on July 26th, 1944.

Glider pilots tell of the "hell hole at Arnhem"

OF the 10,000 hungry, battle-stained and weary men who took part in *Operation Market Garden* — the attempt to capture bridges over the Rhine near the German border — only 2,000 returned home to England, and among them were two glider pilots from Beddington who told their story to the *Sutton Times.*

Staff Sergeant Harry Gustard of Sandhills and Sergeant Terry Mooney of Lavington Road said they were among those who landed at Arnhem with the brief to by-pass the fortified Siegfried Line, seize the Rhine bridges and defend them.

Staff Sgt Gustard said: "My section landed smoothly and pushed on through the streets of Arnhem, penetrating the network of snipers and mortar-gun fire. When we left the town for the woods it was just a blazing inferno. Everything was on fire. During the fighting which followed I lost count of time. I couldn't even tell what day it was. We were being shelled, sniped at and mortared constantly. Hundreds were dying. The German barrage was terrible.

"Food supplies were low. Most of us had finished the 24-hour pack. Dutch peasants gave us their garden produce and fruit and they were kind. By this time British planes were hovering over the battle area and dropping containers with fresh supplies of food and ammunition. However, we didn't get them. The Germans shot them down and stole them."

The men holding the bridgehead against overwhelming odds remained there for nine days — the last three without water and little food. The order to abandon the operation was given by Montgomery and the withdrawal took place on the night of September 25th-26th, 1944. Of the 10,000 who took part, 1,200 were killed and 6,642 taken prisoner.

"When the order came through from Monty", said Staff Sgt Gustard "we made our way down to the river bank and some dived in and tried to swim across. A few of us found a couple of boats but everytime we tried to push out the Germans sprayed the banks with machine gun bullets. We eventually took a chance and crossed and just managed it."

Another local man to return safely from Arnhem was Captain C.P. Scott-Malden, Intelligence Officer of the famous 1st Airborne Division. Captain Scott-Malden, of Downs Lodge, Western Road, Sutton was taken to a military hospital to recover from a leg wound.

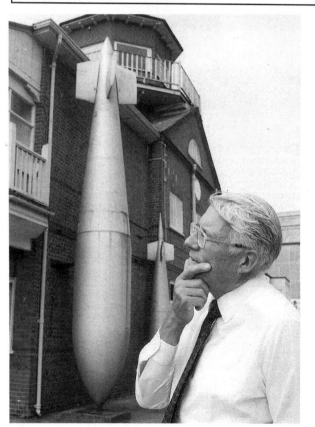

The biggest bomb of all

THE Chief Designer of Structures at Vickers, now better known as Barnes Wallis, the Dambuster, had been working from his home in Effingham on another extraordinary bomb. This one was nicknamed "tallboy", a 12,000 pounder with offset fins which spun as it penetrated the ground and then erupted like an earthquake.

One of the first successful "tallboy" attacks was against Germany's only remaining super battleship, the *Tirpitz.* A formation of Lancasters found the ship in the Russian seas and one direct hit went straight through the forecastle and peeled back the deck like the lid of a sardine can. That was on September 15th. A few weeks later, 21 "tallboys" breached the sea wall protecting the Dutch island of Walcheren where heavy guns were threatening Allied shipping.

Meanwhile RAF bombers in northern France were pounding away at sites and depots where it was suspected that Germany had their rocket factories. Two of them, in the Foret d'Eperlecques and at Wizernes were so badly smashed by tallboys that construction work had to be abandoned.

Photograph shows Jack de Coninck of British Aerospace with the "tallboy family" which were displayed after the war outside the Brooklands clubhouse in Weybridge.

Sunnybank, South Norwood where a V2 rocket killed six people and trapped many beneath the ruins.

Double thunderclap as the rocket arrived

AS the flying bomb attacks diminished and the Allied armies rolled eastwards through Belgium and towards the borders of Adolf Hitler's Fatherland there was a great deal of optimism. Everywhere there was talk of the end of the war before Christmas. The hope was short-lived.

As the people of Richmond dispersed from their offices, shops and factories on the fine autumn evening of Friday September 8th they were blissfully ignorant of the fact that fifty miles above their heads a long dark rocket, weighing 13 tons, armed with a ton of high explosive, was travelling at more than 3,000 miles an hour. It had come from the Dutch coast and, of course, no-one heard it and no-one saw it.

The rocket ended its deadly flight over the Thames and plummeted from the stratosphere at four times the speed of sound. Richmond heard the double explosion. People on buses, in trains and on the pavement felt the ground shake as it impacted on the other side of the river at Chiswick. The first sound was the explosion — like a thunderclap — the second was the noise of the rocket breaking the sound barrier.

This was the turning point in the history of warfare. The V2 rocket offensive had begun and from this moment military strategy was revolutionised. Hitler immediately boasted that this was a weapon that could win the war for Germany.

At first there was a conspiracy of silence and the official explanation for the thunderous noises was blamed on exploding gas mains. More rockets arrived. One landed at Sunbury on September 15th and then one at Coulsdon two days later. On November 10th Mr Churchill admitted in the House of Commons that Britain was under attack by another of Hitler's secret weapons, the V2. "Although there has been no panic", he said, "action against the V2 depends on Allied forces destroying the rocket bases in the Netherlands. He was right. There was no other defence against the rocket for they took just five minutes from launch to impact and travelled too high and too fast to be tracked down.

Croydon's turn, inevitably, came on October 20th. It fell behind houses in Sunnybank, South Norwood making a crater, 40 feet wide and 20 feet deep. The rescue squads found several people trapped in the ruins but some were so deep that they could not be found. It was necessary to call for a detector dog from Chelsea and, in the glare of floodlights, silence was called as the dog nosed his way over the ruins becoming intensely excited when he came near a live casualty. When the search was completed it was found that six people had died, three from one family. A V2 landed at Thames Ditton in October and on November 2nd three people were killed at Banstead.

Only one more rocket fell on Surrey before the end of 1944 and that was again in Croydon, on the north side of the Croham Valley Road at the foot of Conduit Lane. It struck a house called Undercliff, killing Keith Jackson, a popular Croydon solicitor, his wife Gertrude and a friend Eleanor Fishpool.

Throughout the early months of 1945 explosions could be heard at intervals, day and night but they became fewer. One fell at Barnes on January 2nd and Titsey Hill, Oxted on January 4th and two, way off course, at Manor Farm, East Shalford and near the Hogs Back, Guildford on January 6th. Banstead was hit again on January 16th, Oxted on February 10th and Leatherhead on the 12th. This fell close to the City of London Freeman's School and the windows of 50 houses were shattered but there was only one casualty. In March the Allies finally gained the initiative and the rocket pads were overrun but not before there were explosions at Woking on March 2nd, Richmond on March 15th and Nutfield on March 19th.

Posthumous VC for another New Malden pilot

THE second Victoria Cross to be awarded posthumuously to a New Malden bomber pilot was followed by an official announcement in the *London Gazette* outlining the bravery of Acting Squadron Leader Ian Willoughby Bazalgette of Elm Road during a raid on a V1 storage depot at Trossy, St Maxim, France on August 4th.

Bazalgette was the master bomber of 635 Squadron who were laying pathfinder marker flares to illuminate the target. His Lancaster was hit by flak from anti-aircraft guns and two starboard engines, the starboard wing and the fuselage burst into flames. Both the bomb aimer and the mid-upper gunner were killed.

The pilot somehow regained control, released the markers, then flew the blazing Lancaster on for another 30 miles before ordering the crew to bale out at 1,000 feet. Bazalgette attempted to land the aircraft in a field but it exploded as it touched down and the 26-year-old was killed.

At the time 635 Squadron were stationed at Downham Market in Norfolk and a plaque in the local church was unveiled in his honour. The people of New Malden named a road after their second hero with the highest known award for gallantry.

Surrey says farewell to its great Citizens' Army

HOME Guard units throughout Surrey were stood down at the end of November 1944 and throughout the county there were parades to mark the occasion. On this rainy, windy day the various Colonels, most of them still emblazoned with 1914-18 war medals, made their speeches and then gave the order for the last time. "Home Guards and Auxiliaries, dismiss". The rigid lines broke and dissolved into a horde of now-ordinary civilians seeking shelter from the driving mist and sleet.

The men had mixed emotions. In 1940 as the remnants of a beaten Army came home from Dunkirk this citizens' army was rising, prepared to fight in the fields and in the streets to secure the breathing space the nation so urgently required. In the years that followed they gave many hours to military training and war office manuals. Now, instead of lying behind hedges with rifles they could read books and pursue peacetime activities.

Many of the battalions of the Surrey Home Guard were affiliated to the Queen's Regiment. Among them was the 1st Surrey formed in Camberley and Farnham which had a strength of 1,200. The 5th Battalion started at Godalming and was reorganised to cover a large country area stretching from Effingham through Shere and Cranleigh to Chiddingfold with more than 2,000 recruits. The 12th was formed as a railway unit with headquarters at Woking and looked after 100 stations of the Southern Railway with more than 3,500 men passing through the Battalion.

When the men of the Surrey Home

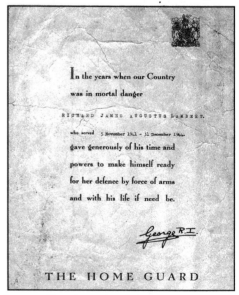

In the years when our Country was in mortal danger

RICHARD JAMES AUGUSTUS LAMBERT

who served 5 November 1941 - 31 December 1944

gave generously of his time and powers to make himself ready for her defence by force of arms and with his life if need be.

George R.I.

THE HOME GUARD

Guard took off their caps on that damp November Sunday afternoon bald heads gleamed, silver heads shone and grey heads glowed. The great citizens' army was no more.

1945

Berlin falls, Hitler commits suicide: VICTORY

January 17th: Russia's Red Army defeated the Germans and marched into Warsaw.

January 27th: The Russians entered Auschwitz and discovered the horrors of the Nazi's biggest extermination camp.

January 31st: The Red Army crossed the German frontier and captured Driesen, 95 miles from Berlin. The Burma Road from India to China reopened, allowing supplies through to Nationalist China.

February 11th: The Yalta conference took place when Stalin, Roosevelt and Churchill met to discuss the future of post-war Europe.

February 14th: The city of Dresden in Germany was devastated by RAF bombers amid much criticism.

February 16th: Street lighting returned to Surrey, but only on an experimental basis for one week only.

February 23rd: US forces captured the island of Iwo Jima after four days of fierce battle.

March 10th: Massive US fire bomb attack on Tokyo killed more than 80,000.

April 12th: President Franklin D. Roosevelt died suddenly aged 63. He was succeeded by Harry S.Truman.

April 28th: Mussolini was killed by partisans in Italy.

Road blocks, constructed in early 1940 to deter Hitler's panzers, when an invasion seemed likely, are taken down — a sign that Croydon could at last sleep easy.

April 30th: After a nine-day battle the Red Army captured Berlin. Hitler and Eva Braun committed suicide.

May 3rd: The Burmese capital of Rangoon was captured by the Allies.

May 8th: VE Day. In a broadcast from Downing Street, Churchill announced the war was over in Europe.

May 9th: The Germans surrendered the Channel Islands after five years of occupation.

May 10th: Many Surrey units of the Civil Defence Services were stood down and on the 13th, big parades were held in most of the towns in Surrey.

May 28th: Lord Haw Haw (William Joyce) was captured near Hamburg.

June 18th: The demobilisation of British troops began, each man being entitled to a 'demob' suit and other civilian clothing.

July 26th: The Labour Party won a sensational victory in the general election. Churchill resigned and Clement Attlee moved into 10 Downing Street.

August 6th: The Americans dropped the Atomic bomb on Hiroshima causing devastation and loss of life on a scale the world had never known.

August 14th: Japan surrendered, and the second world war ended.

August 15th: The Allied nations celebrated VJ Day.

August 31st: Harrowing tales emerged of cruelty suffered by Allied PoWs in Japanese camps.

September 12th: A small detachment of Air Ministry scientists arrived at Kenley to organise the storage and evaluation of captured German aircraft equipment being sent over from the Continent.

September 21st: The "Stand Easy" canteen for the Forces in West Street, Dorking closed. It had remained open every evening, including Sundays, holidays and Christmas days for five years.

Germany surrenders: Surrey celebrates

THE winter of 1944/5 was bitterly cold. There was ice, frost, fog, seemingly endless queues and fuel shortages. The rockets kept coming and now the doodlebugs were launched, not from ramps in France, but from the bellies of Heinkel aircraft. A woman from Surbiton wrote in her diary. "I have heard bangs from rockets, sirens every evening and two doodles droning over the house. People in the office have colds, pains and aches in their limbs. With only cardboard and mica windows to keep out draughts, it seems our legs will never be felt again. When will this blessed war end?"

The end wasn't far away. Dashed by Hitler's last great offensive in the Ardennes and those infernal vengeance weapons, hopes of a speedy victory had faded but, by April 1945, the news from Europe was unbelievably good. The Nazi retreat was becoming a rout as the Allied armies advanced. The concentration camps at Belsen and Buchenwald were taken by the British. The Russians had a stranglehold on Berlin. Mussolini was executed. The survivors of the Dachau death camp were liberated. German forces in Italy surrendered and Hitler retreated to his bunker to be joined by Eva Braun.

On April 30th, 36 hours after marrying Miss Braun, Hitler dined then retired to his quarters. A single shot rang out and the body of Hitler, dripping blood, was found slumped on a couch. Beside him was Eva Braun; she had taken poison. With Russian shells exploding all around the bodies were doused with petrol and set alight.

Four days later, on May 4th, the German forces in western Europe surrendered. General Montgomery read the capitulation terms and announced that the Third Reich was dead. May 8th was to be VE Day. The official announcement came from Churchill from 10 Downing Street.

Right across Surrey there was a rush to buy flags and bunting. Banners appeared everywhere bearing portraits of the King and 'welcome home' flags appeared in almost every street ready for the repatriated prisoners of war. Revellers lit bonfires, danced and sang. There were fireworks, thanksgiving services and the pubs had special late night extensions.

In Guildford the mayor, Mr Wykeham Price appeared on the balcony of the Guildhall on the morning of May 8th and announced that he would put the microphone onto the wireless so everyone could hear the Prime Minister's speech. When Mr Churchill finished and the National Anthem was sung, 2,000 people stood to attention with officers at the salute. It was an impressive sight.

It was followed by dancing in the street, a colourful, swirling mass of soldiers, sailors, airmen and civilians with hundreds of women wearing red, white and blue dresses, costumes and jumpers. The *Surrey Advertiser* described the scene: "There were diversions; one was the appearance of the drums of the 5th Cadet Battalion of the Queen's, another was when fire engines came clanging down the street and one when a procession of youth made its way to Mount Farm where a huge bonfire was lighted on the hilltop.

"The dominant note beneath the gaiety was gratitude. Hysterical festivity does not become people whose nerves have withstood the test of total war and this merrymaking had a warmer glow. The subtler difference was the enhanced significance of light, for the blackout had become the symbol of the struggle. To see the floodlights shining out over Guildford High Street and illuminating happy faces was a source of delight to all."

Godalming also heard Mr Churchill's speech and this was followed by a victory peal from the parish church bells. The ringers were led by their captain, Mr C.Childs who had rung the victory peals after the South African war and the 1914-18 war. In the evening many residents from Godalming and adjacent villages were the guests of Canadian troops at Witley Camp and transport was provided free.

In Woking they danced in the street outside the Albion Hotel until after midnight and in Chertsey an effigy of Hitler, burned on a huge bonfire, was followed by a fair in Free Prae Road. Children in Camberley were given Princess Elizabeth birthday cards with savings stamps attached and, in Leatherhead, an open-air thanksgiving service was held on the terrace of Elm Gardens led by ministers of all denominations. Farnham called a special meeting of the urban council and the chairman, Mr J.Chuter, moved a resolution of thanks to God for the deliverance of the nation and then expressed his thanks to all those who had served, his admiration for the courage and endurance shown by the people of Farnham and his heartfelt sympathy with the families of those men and women who had laid down their lives.

There were celebrations in Surbiton where the National Fire Service held a dance for allcomers on the forecourt of the Ewell Road fire station. The proprietor of the Toby Jug hotel, Kingston by-pass, Tolworth had a pig roasted outside his premises and hot roast pork sandwiches were distributed free. In Walton, a piano was brought into the street and in Weybridge extra emergency seating had to be found to accommodate all those who thronged into the parish church for a special service.

It was a day to be remembered but tinged with sadness for there was a realisation that many men and women were not yet home from various fighting fronts and the Japanese had still to be conquered. Above all, there were thousands throughout the county who would not return.

VE Day street parties in Holly Tree Road, Caterham (above) and Richmond Park Road, Kingston (below).

Street parties were organised throughout Surrey and enjoyed by all ages. This one (left) was held in Landsdowne Road, Shirley, and (below left) in Dorking.

Men and women of the fighting forces who returned home to the village of Elstead were each given a copy of this certificate (below) during a special ceremony in the village to honour their contribution to the Defence of Freedom.

The People of Elstead gratefully record their appreciation of the services rendered by ... Jack Collyer ... to King and Country during the great fight for freedom which began in 1939. No words or action can adequately express our heartfelt thanks for those services; the hardships endured and the sacrifices made in the Defence of Freedom

You answered the call to duty With courage and devotion. May God bless and help you always.

V for Victory. Stoughton Infants School, Guildford.

33 die as transport plane hits pylon at Hindhead

Aeroplane crashes continued to happen despite the war ending. On Sunday May 6th an American transport Curtis Commando flying wounded servicemen from France hit the radio location mast on Gibbet Hill, Hindhead and crashed onto a hut in the station grounds below. All 32 occupants were killed.

There was rain and mist over the district at the time and the aircraft was heard flying low over the Devil's Punch Bowl. It collided with the tallest pylon. Flying Officer Emerson Parrish who was in the hut was also killed.

Two of the men in the aircraft were British, one French-Canadian and the remainder American.

The tragedy followed an incident near Dorking, a few days earlier, when an RAF reconnaissance Hudson returning from Germany dived onto the by-pass in the early hours of the morning and immediately caught fire with bursting shells adding to the drama. The four occupants

all baled out safely, one landing less than 100 yards from the Hudson.

A few days later it transpired that the pilot, Flight Lieutenant D.B.Webb, had ordered his men to abandon the stricken plane so he could remain at the controls until the last possible moment, gallantly manoeuvring the aircraft to prevent it falling on houses. He then jumped and residents of Deepdene saw him descending in his parachute against a background of flames. He was only slightly hurt.

In an expression of gratitude a 14-year-old Dorking girl, Barbara Worsfold, of Marlborough Road collected money from neighbours in order to buy cigarettes for the plane's crew. Flight Lieutenant Webb wrote to her mother with his thanks for the reception they received, "the excellent attention at your hospital leaves me with very pleasant memories of Dorking. The crew are safe and well, and I myself sustained four broken bones in the left foot".

Residents of William Road, Sutton pose for a VE Day picture knowing that many men from their locality were still in PoW camps in the Far East.

Atom Bomb saved 200 East Surreys

AS the war with Japan continued, British and American scientists were working on a plan "to implode segments of plutonium to form a critical mass in which neutrons would split the atomic nuclei". In other words the Atom Bomb was nearing completion.

The first successful test was held in the Mexican desert. The weapon exploded with a force equivalent to 20,000 tonnes of TNT. It fused sand into glass, sent a mushroom cloud 40,000 feet into the sky and released enormous energy in a chain reaction. It was a bomb capable of crippling Japan, forcing them to surrender and ending the war. The decision lay, not with the scientists, but the politicians.

On August 6th, the USAAF B-29 *Enola Gay* dropped the first atom bomb on Hiroshima killing 80,000 people and maiming more than 200,000 from blast, burns and radiation. Three days later the target was the shipbuilding port of Nagasaki and, on this occasion, Wing Commander Leonard Cheshire was a British observer. Tokyo condemned the acts as "atrocities", demanded peace talks and, on August 14th, Japan surrendered unconditionally.

By now Churchill was no longer Prime Minister. In the General Election of July, Labour had won an overwhelming majority, although in Surrey their only gains were at Mitcham and Croydon. It was Clement Attlee who made the announcement just before midnight that "the last of our enemies has been laid low".

The atom bomb was a device that cast a shadow over the world but it brought a reprieve for thousands of Japanese prisoners of war who, though they may not have realised it, were virtually under sentence of death. Among them were 200 men of the East Surreys who later held a reunion celebration at Chelsea Town Hall and heard their CO, Lieutenant Colonel C.E.Morrison explain: "After the Japanese surrender it was found that the commander in Bangkok had given orders to dispose of all his PoWs." The Lieutenant Colonel said: "You know what that meant. It was a warrant for the massacre of all the prisoners in Siam and that was all of you".

As each man arrived for the reunion at Chelsea they were received personally by Major W.G.Gringell, former quartermaster of the 2nd East Surreys and one of the few to escape from Singapore when the British Battalion was forced to capitulate. Gringell and 23 other men managed to board a British ship but it was blown up and sunk. All but six of the party were drowned. These men found a boat and clung to its keel but were then machine gunned from a few feet above sea level. Many were wounded but they managed to push the boat through shark infested waters until, seven hours later, they reached a small island.

The small party was treated in hospital and then walked across Sumatra to Padang, living on pineapples. Finally Major Gringell and his party managed to scramble aboard the last ship from Padang and after another nightmare journey they reached Colombo.

Those who were left behind, about four-fifths of the British Battalion were to spend more than three years in PoW camps. Many of them died from dysentery, after years of eating rice, grass, cockroaches and even cats and dogs and from the filthy conditions in which they were housed. Many of the survivors managed to make the reunion in Chelsea. One man came from Dublin and another had hitch-hiked from St Albans. The Major shook hands with all of them but he had a special welcome for Lance-Corporal Clothier from Sutton who had clung with him under that upturned boat while under fire from the Japanese.

We want to end this book with a photograph of a war memorial. The British Legion Poppy Factory in Petersham Road, Richmond is a continuing memorial to those who gave their lives in all wars and those who survived. Our picture shows some of the workers.

The Poppy Factory was first established in 1922 by Major George Hewson MC, an officer in the 1914-18 war, who employed five disabled ex-servicemen and set up his factory in the Old Kent Road. The first Poppy Day was held on Novemember 11th of that year and raised £106,000.

In 1926 larger premises were required and Major Hewson found a perfect location in Richmond on the site of an old brewery where 58 flats were built on the adjoining four-acre estate of Cardigan House. By 1931 more than 300 men, women and children lived on the factory estate.

During the war the disabled employees, scarred physically and mentally by the 1914-18 war, redoubled their efforts knowing that another generation of servicemen and women would be needing the Legion's help. By 1945 they were producing 45 million poppies and more than 65,000 wreaths and, in that year, the Poppy Appeal raised £1 million for the first time.

By 1995 the factory at Richmond had changed and diversified but one thing remains constant — the dedication and enthusiasm of the employees who produce the nation's poppies.

Surrey men who won the Victoria Cross

Philip John Gardner
A/Captain Royal Tank Regiment, RAC
Born: Sydenham 25.12.1914

On 23rd November, 1941 at Tobruk Gardner took two tanks to the rescue of two armoured cars of King's Dragoon Guards which were under heavy attack. He managed to hitch a tow rope to one of the cars, but it broke; amidst heavy firing he returned to the car but was wounded in the arm and leg. Despite this he managed to transfer a wounded man to one of the tanks and returned to British lines through intense shell-fire.

George Gristock
Co. Sergeant Major Royal Norfolk Regiment
Born: 14.1.1905 South Africa
Connections: Sandhurst, Surrey

On 21st May, 1940 near the River Escaut in Belgium Gristock organised a party of eight riflemen to cover an area where the enemy had broken through. He went on with one man under heavy fire and was severely wounded in both legs. Despite this he carried on and refused to be evacuated until contact with the battalion had been established. He died of his wounds.

George Arthur Knowland
Lieutenant Royal Norfolk Regiment
att'd No 1 Commando
Born: Catford 16.8.1922
Connections: Croydon, Surrey

Knowland was in command of a forward platoon of a troop which was being heavily attacked near Kangaw, Burma on 31st January, 1945. When all the crew of one of the Bren guns had been wounded he manned it himself, standing up to fire at ten yards range until all casualties had been evacuated. He held his ground for twelve hours until mortally wounded.

John Neil Randle
T/Captain 2nd Battalion Royal Norfolk Regiment
Born: India. Memorial in St Peters Church, Petersham.

Randle took command of his company, in spite of being wounded, on 6th May 1944 in Assam, India. He led an attack and charged an enemy post single handed Although mortally wounded he silenced the machine gun by throwing a grenade through the bunker slit, then threw his body across the slit to completely seal it.

Robert Edward Dudley Ryder
Commander (later Captain) Royal Navy
Born: India 16.2.1908 Connections: Camberley, Surrey

On 28th March, 1942 in an attack on St Nazaire, France Ryder led *HMS Campbeltown* in under intensive fire. When the main objective had been accomplished and the ship had been beached he remained on the spot, evacuating men and conducting operations while exposed to heavy fire. His motor gun boat full of dead and wounded survived by a miracle and managed to withdraw through an intense barrage of gunfire.

Arthur Stewart King Scarf
Squadron Leader 62 Squadron RAF
Born: Wimbledon 14.6.1913

On 9th December 1941 all aircraft were ordered to make a daylight raid on Singora in Siam. As leader, Scarf had just taken off when enemy aircraft swept in destroying or disabling all the other planes. He flew on alone. Despite attacks he completed his bombing run. On his return he came under fire, was wounded and crash landed his Blenheim. He died two hours later.

Eric Charles Twelves Wilson
A/Captain (later Lieutenant Colonel)
The East Surrey Regiment att'd Somali Mounted Infantry
Born: Sandown, IOW October, 1912

From 11th - 15th August 1940 at Observation Hill, Somaliland, Captain Wilson kept machine gun post in action in spite of being wounded and suffering from malaria. He was taken prisoner but freed when Eritrea was conquered.

Two RAF bomber pilots, both from New Malden, also won the VC. The bravery of Pilot Officer Cyril Barton and acting Squadron Leader Ian Bazalgette are featured separately on pages 169 and 184.

Polish Memorial at Northolt

A monument devoted to the memory of Polish pilots who lost their lives stands beside the Western Avenue on the north-eastern edge of Northolt Aerodrome, where many of the Polish squadrons had been stationed during the war years.

The monument is selective in that only the names of 1,241 Polish airmen are inscribed on the surrounding wall. More than 2,400 were killed in the war, including 31 in the Battle of Britain.

The memorial was unveiled in 1948 by Marshal of the Royal Air Force, Lord Tedder.

Brookwood, Surrey also played a significant role as a memorial for here a temporary cemetery was opened for the United States. It was dismantled in 1948, the remains either being transferred to the permanent American cemetery at Madingley, near Cambridge, or repatriated to the States.

There is another cemetery at Whyteleafe, near Caterham where many of the pilots from the Kenley Squadrons were buried.

Among the many people who contacted us with information about Surrey in the war years, I would especially like to thank the following: Mr R.T.Harding of Godstone, Mrs Anna Parkhurst of Ham, Richmond, Mrs Margaret Allen of South Norwood, Mr Maurice Jones of Walton-on-Thames, Mr Ron McGill of Worplesdon, Guildford and Mr Derek Moore of the Bletchingley Historical Society.

Surrey men who won the George Cross

Wallace Launcelot Andrews
2nd Lieutenant (later Major) 22/23
Bomb Disposal Sections, Corps of
Royal Engineers
Born: 13.3.1908

At Crohamhurst Golf Course near Croydon on 26th August, 1940 Andrews was in charge of Nos 22 and 23 Bomb Disposal Sections when a bomb fell near the aerodrome and failed to explode. It was necessary to extract fuse to forward it to the Department of Scientific Research but several attempts were made to remove it without success. He told his men to take cover and after tying a piece of cord to the ring of the fuse discharger, pulled, with the result that the bomb exploded. He was blown a considerable distance and two of his men received splinter wounds.

Kenneth Alfred Biggs
Major Royal Army Ordnance Corps
Born: 26.2.1911 Connections: Ewhurst,
Surrey

On 2nd January, 1946 Biggs, together with A/Staff Sergeant Rogerson were in Savernake Forest, Wiltshire where ammunition was being loaded onto a train. Suddenly there was an explosion and two wagons and a 3-ton lorry just disappeared. There were 96 more wagons in the area and another 27 blew up, as well as two lorries. With complete disregard for their own safety the two men worked all night, uncoupling and moving wagons and managed to prevent more from catching fire.

John Noel Dowland
Flight Lieutenant (later Wing Commander)
Born: 6.11.1914 Connections:
Wokingham, Surrey

This was the first action for which the George Cross was awarded. On 11th February 1940 the steamship *Kildare* was hit by two bombs, which failed to explode. With two civil instructors Dowland went on board to dismantle them — the crew had put a mattress underneath one to stop it rolling about. He successfully accomplished his mission.

Roy Thomas Harris
ARP Engineers Service
Born: Croydon, 1903

Harris dismantled unexploded bombs at Langdale Road School, Thornton Heath on 18th September, 1940. He showed a conspicuous bravery in dealing with these exceptionally dangerous devices. He later joined the Royal Engineers and attained the rank of Lieutenant Colonel.

Sidney George Rogerson
A/Staff Sergeant Royal Army Ordnance
Corps
Born: Mitcham 14.5.1915

See under entry for Kenneth Alfred
Biggs

Jenkin Robert Oswald Thompson
Captain Royal Army Medical Corps
Born: 13.7.1911 Memorial, The
Brookwood, Surrey Connections:
Claygate.

Thompson spent most of the war aboard hospital carriers. He was awarded the George Cross posthumously for conspicuous gallantry and devotion to duty, particularly in HM Hospital Carrier *Paris* at Dunkirk in May 1940; in the *St David* at Sicily in July 1943; Salerno in September 1943 and Anzio in January 1944.

St John Graham Young
Lieutenant Royal Tank Regiment
Born: Esher 16.6.1921

On 23rd July 1944 while commanding night patrol in Italy he rendered harmless three mines. He then knelt on one, severing his right leg. Despite this he reached one of his injured men and dressed his wounds. For five hours he gave encouragement to his men. He died that evening.

The RAF memorial at historic Runnymede

THE Runnymede Memorial, designed by Sir Edward Maufe, records the names of 20,547 airmen (including Czechs and Belgians but not Poles) who went missing serving with the Royal Air Force during the Second World War. The names are engraved on a cloister and nearby is a tower reminiscent of an aerodrome watch office and a vaulted shrine as a place for contemplation.

The memorial was built on Cooper's Hill, part of a wooded ridge that sweeps down to the Thames at historic Runnymede and was unveiled by a young Queen Elizabeth in 1953. The cloisters have curved wings terminating in two lookouts, one facing towards Windsor and the other towards Heathrow (the Great West Aerodrome as it was known during the Battle of Britain). A balcony, with gallery above, gives a fine view of the Thames Valley and seven counties.

The memorial and the gardens were created on six acres of land donated by Sir Eugen and Lady Effie Millington-Drake.

Visitors come from all over the world to see the names of the missing inscribed on stone in the cloister. In the centre rests the Stone of Remembrance containing the inscription: "In this cloister are recorded the names of twenty thousand airmen who have no known grave. They died for freedom in raid and sortie over the British Isles and the land and seas of Northern and Western Europe".

Of the 537 airmen who were killed in the Battle of Britain, 175 have no known grave.

Civilian casualties, damage and bombs

(in the Eastern Emergency Area) — Damage to property

Local Authority	killed	Seriously injured	Slightly injured	Total	Incidents	High explosives	Flying bombs	Rockets	Demolished	Badly damaged
Banstead UD	15	66	171	252	204	591	38	2	97	138
Barnes B	73	140	213	426	143	221	10	1	288	2,215
Beddington & Wallington B	68	214	389	671	190	203	38	0	242	2,932
Carshalton UD	40	115	371	526	156	192	27	0	332	1,867
Coulsdon & Purley UD	98	184	285	567	700	1200	57	1	290	1,825
Epsom & Ewell B	36	93	299	428	261	440	28	0	194	411
Esher UD	39	66	269	374	460	582	36	1	114	100
Kingston B	74	140	323	537	31	83	8	1	260	6,000
Malden and Coombe B	80	148	200	428	253	549	21	0	332	373
Merton & Mord UD	142	277	342	761	203	404	35	0	525	3,726
Mitcham B	124	398	669	1,191	249	276	50	0	743	2,642
Richmond B	94	137	209	440	230	547	11	2	297	272
Sutton & Cheam B	137	463	328	928	278	320	35	0	399	2,561
Surbiton B	51	125	211	387	198	228	22	0	223	527
Wimbledon B	166	380	465	1,011	649	367	35	0	587	2,267
TOTAL	1,237	2,946	4,744	8,927	4,205	6,203	451	8	4,923	27,856
Croydon	716	1,600	2,662	4,978	2,621	2,527	144	4	2,323	95,177
TOTAL	1,953	4,546	7,406	13,905	6,826	8,730	595	12	7,246	123,033

How Surrey suffered

THESE figures of civilian casualties, the number of projectiles and the damage to property were given in a comprehensive report by the Special War Executive of Surrey County Council and filed at County Hall in Kingston. It includes Group Nine of the Metropolitan Police Area — that part of Surrey in the London region — and the Surrey Constabulary Area. The report defines them as the Eastern emergency and the Western emergency areas.

The total number of casualties during the war for both areas were 2,300 killed, 5,216 seriously injured and 8.905 slightly hurt — a total of 16,421. The total UK casualty figures were 60,595 killed and 86,182 injured — a total of 146,777.

Compared to neighbouring counties including Kent, which earned the nickname of Hell Fire Corner, Surrey suffered badly. The number of people killed were as follows: Kent (2,974), Sussex (1,008), Essex (855).

The Surrey figures are perhaps a little misleading because they include Croydon which was easily the worst-hit borough in London. The town's ordeal was such that 716 were killed and 1,600 seriously injured. 2,323 properties were completely demolished and 95,177 damaged. The figures include those slightly damaged which are missing from the rest of the table.

In the western area it can be seen that Walton and Weybridge lost 120 civilians, more than a third of those killed in the other urban or rural areas. The big raid on Brooklands in 1940 when 89 died and the attention which the Luftwaffe continued to show to the great aircraft factories in the locality were the reason for pounding received in that area.

A relatively quiet war, in terms of fatalities, was experienced by those who lived in Farnham, Woking, Frimley and Camberley, Godalming and Haslemere although each area had terrifying attacks and many properties were damaged. On the other end of the scale Godstone Rural suffered badly from the V1 flying bomb with 95 crashing in the area — most of them harmlessly, in open country.

Civilian casualties, damage and bombs

(in the Western Emergency Area)

Damage to property

Local authority	killed	Seriously injured	Slightly injured	Total	Incidents	High explosives	Flying bombs	Rockets	Demolished	Badly damaged
Bagshot RD	4	19	24	47	42	190	5	0	7	16
Caterham & Warlingham UD	34	15	232	281	293	879	21	0	125	268
Chertsey UD	19	36	48	103	100	202	4	1	21	179
Dorking UD	25	20	56	101	123	267	19	0	15	65
Dorking & Horley RD	6	36	101	143	266	578	49	0	29	83
Egham UD	18	27	50	95	49	45	2	1	28	87
Farnham UD	0	0	2	2	13	45	0	0	7	61
Frimley & Camberley UD	1	1	14	16	17	87	1	0	5	1
Godalming B	0	2	17	19	23	29	2	0	5	32
Godstone RD	25	44	169	238	684	1,726	95	4	54	160
Guildford RD	13	25	65	103	240	629	33	0	35	86
Guildford B	5	10	63	78	31	109	3	0	25	125
Hambledon RD	13	51	64	128	195	529	14	0	8	71
Haslemere UD	1	10	12	23	17	32	1	1	0	10
Leatherhead UD	11	61	77	149	91	594	16	1	71	282
Reigate B	50	80	81	211	184	498	17	0	98	317
Walton& Weybridge UD	120	233	372	725	217	392	19	0	108	364
Woking UD	2	0	52	54	90	311	7	1	39	79
TOTAL	347	670	1,499	2,516	2,675	7,142	308	9	680	2,286

The Thanksgiving Parade which was held in Croydon at the end of the war. The Civil Defence Services were disbanded and all officials thanked for their faithful work. It was a memorable moment in the town's history.

The author

BOB Ogley lives near Westerham but close enough to the Surrey border to be aware that the Battle of Britain was not exclusive to Kent and neither was the title of "front-line county". The people of Surrey shared the experience of war with a whole range of memories and emotions, both happy and sad.

Bob was born in Sevenoaks in July 1939 — too young to remember the excitement a year later when incendiary bombs destroyed cottages in his road and he and his family had to flee their home in the middle of the night, dodge the burning debris and seek refuge in another part of town.

However, he remembers the doodlebugs and he remembers his older brother's wartime souvenirs which were buried carefully at the bottom of the garden.

In later years Bob became editor of the *Sevenoaks Chronicle* where he took a great interest in local history. His life took a dramatic turn in 1987

when he wrote and published a book on the great storm which was entitled *In The Wake of the Hurricane*, after being rejected by a publisher. The book went into the national bestseller list and was followed by a national edition which climbed to number two in the country. Through these two books and regional editions which followed Bob, and his partner Fern , have raised more than £60,000 for environmental charities.

Since 1989 when he left the news-

paper, Bob has written *Biggin on The Bump*, a history of the famous RAF fighter station, which raised £15,000 in author's royalties for thre RAF Benevolent Fund and *Doodlebugs and Rockets* — now in its third reprint. He also published *Flying Bombs over England*, a lost manuscript which he discovered in the Public Record Office. This had been written more than 50 years ago by the late novelist H.E.Bates and then embargoed under the "30-year rule".

Bob has also teamed up with Ian Currie from Coulsdon and Mark Davison from Reigate to research, write and publish the illustrated history of the weather in English counties. So far they have written Surrey, Kent, Essex, Norfolk and Suffolk, Hampshire and the Isle of Wight and Berkshire.

As well as his writing and publishing, Bob has discovered a supplementary career as speaker to clubs and organisations.

Photograph credits

We acknowledge with thanks the following who supplied photographs:

Imperial War Museum: 5 (top), 16 (top), 18, 26, 28, 33, 40, 50 (bottom), 59, 72, 95, 103, 108, 133, 145, 146, 165, 170, 171, 173. Croydon Local History Services: 5 (bottom), 7, 13, 19, 24, 31, 41, 42, 44, 46, 48, 52, 55, 58, 63 (bottom), 67, 85, 90, 94, 101, 102 (bottom), 136, 137 (top), 138, 159 (bottom), 181 (bottom), 183, 185, 188 (top), 195. Croydon Advertiser Group: 96. East Surrey Museum (Caterham): 8, 27 (top), 106 115 (top), 134.Surrey Local Studies Library: 10, 22, 33 (top), 73, 75, 102 (top), 128 (top), 135 (top), 168, 187 (top). Chrispics (Farnham): 74, 105, 124, 126, 131 (top), 154 155, 156 (bottom), 158, 164, 175 (top). Kingston Heritage: 161 (bottom), 169, 178 (top), 184 (top), 187 (bottom).

Elmbridge Museum: 71, 99 (top), 104 (top), 135 (bottom), 167 178 (bottom). Bourne Hall Museum, Ewell: 14, 17, 69, 99 (bottom), 116. Sutton Local History: pages 39, 49, 61, 159 (top), 180 (both), 190. The Wimbledon Society Museum: 11, 37 (both), 111.Shere Museum: 98, 121, 127, 163. Kent Messenger: 115 (bottom), 129 (bottom), 143, 153. Merton Heritage Centre and Library Services: 63 (top) 77, 120, 139. John Topham Ltd: 15, 30, 38, 56, 84. National Archives of Canada: 148, 149, 172. Hulton Deutsch Collection: 81 (top), 91. Brooklands Museum:20, 21, 150, 151, 152, 182. Dorking and District Museum: 32 (bottom), 119 (bottom), 147, 188 (bottom). The Egham Museum Trust: 100 (both). Chertsey Museum: 33 (bottom), 88, 97, 129, 132 (botom), 137 (bottom). Richmond Poppy Factory: 191. After the

Battle Magazine: 50, 60, 79, 81 (bottom). The London Transport Museum: 112. Cossack Association: 118, 119 (top). Cornwall Local History Services: 177. Surrey Record Office: 86 (bottom), 87, 122. Shamley Green History Society 9. Quadrant Picture Library: 12. The Biggin Hill Collection 68. Evening News: 54. Surrey Comet: 57, 62. Strode's College: 132 (top). Jack Sales: 16 (bottom), 80, 89, 109, 176 (bottom), Andy Saunders: 64, 65, 83. Joan Nicholson: 36, 142. Pat Lelliott: 32 (top), 104 (bottom), 131 (bottom), 157, 188 (bottom right). John Gent: 110, Bill Harvey: 174. Phyllis Barnes: 156 (top). Reg Payne: 157. Ken Anscombe: 161 (top). Olga Kendall 113. Air Vice Marshal Peter Brothers: 114. John Haybittle: 117, 125. Miss Colleen Jacobs 189. Frank Danne: 66. Miss Hayman 181 (top).

Acknowledgements

THIS book would not have been possible without the co-operation of many people and I would like to thank those who responded to my appeal for information, reminiscences and photographs. Practical help came from many quarters including The British Library, the Imperial War Museum, the London Transport Museum, the Surrey County Record Office at Kingston, the Public Record Office, the Queen's Royal Surrey Regiment Museum at Clandon Park, Guildford Munitions Room and the chief executive and staff of the Richmond Poppy Factory.

I would particularly like to thank museum curators and staff especially Julian Temple of Brooklands, Jeremy Harte of Bourne Hall, Ewell, Mary Turner of Dorking, Sarah Gould of Merton Heritage Centre, Viv McKenzie of Elmbridge, Amanda of Chertsey, Elizabeth Rich of Shere, Matthew Alexander of Guildford, Keith Shawcross of Sutton and John Mills of Egham Museum Trust. Great assistance came from the local history department of many libraries notably Steve Round of Croydon, John Janaway of Guildford, Paul Bowness of Wimbledon Society.

Individuals who gave practical help were Andy Saunders of Hastings, Paul McCue of Godalming, Pat Lelliott of Worcester Park, Chris Shepheard of Farnham, Jack Sales of Reigate, Olga Kendall of Croydon, Phyllis Barnes of Addlestone, Mrs A. Coles of Esher, Ron and Dorothy Davis of Egham-by-Runnymede Historical Society, Bert Martin of Dorset, Reg Doring of The Cossack Association, Winston Ramsay of After the Battle Magazine, Gloria Patten of Strode's College, Egham, Derek Moore of Bletchingly Historical Society, Sylvia Langden and Colleen Jacobs, Marian May of Shamley Green, Colin Prateley of Croydon, Joan Nicholson of Weybridge, Ken Anscombe, Karen Fielder of Sainsbury Ltd, Peter Willoughby of Leigh, Kent, D.P.Brummell, of Farncombe, London EC1, Cecilia Gerrard, chairman of Surrey County Council, A.L.Vice of Woking History Society, Ray Webb of Richmond.

Finally I would like to thank the editors of newspapers throughout the county and, in particular, their predecessors. The appetite for news in wartime was almost insatiable and a glance at the newspaper files confirms the desire of all editors to report as much as possible. But they had a problem for so much at the time was secret, there was so much propaganda and so much confusion in the "fog of war" that truth was rather elusive. Added to that was the policy of censorship. No locations could be given apart from the rather inadequate "somewhere in the south of England". Thanks to the help I received, almost everywhere, I have managed to report what actually happened, track down locations, give the exact date and, in many cases, name the people involved.

Surrey at War would not have been possible without this wonderful voluntary help.

Bibliography

Chronicle of the Second World War *(Longman)*

Churchill, Martin Gilbert

Men of the Battle of Britain, *Kenneth Wynn*

Born Leader, *Alan Cooper*

Most Secret War, R.V.Jones

Battle of Britain, *Richard Hough and Denis Richards*

Operation Sealion, Peter Fleming

How we Lived Then, *Norman Longmate*

The Blitz (Volumes 1,2 and 3) *(After the Battle)*

The Battle of Britain, Then and Now *(After the Battle).*

Fear Nothing (501 Squadron), *David Watkins*

RAF Kenley, *Peter Flint*

East Surrey Regiment, *Michael Langley*

Safe as Houses, *Norman Plastow*

Cyril Barton VC, *W.W.Lowther*

Henry Strode's Charity, *Pamela Maryfield*

Doodlebugs and Rockets, *Bob Ogley*

Brockham Village Remembers, *Editor Tony Hines*

RAF Horne, *Brian Buss*

Hurricane, Clouded by Legend *(British Aerospace)*

Dunsfold, Surrey's Most Secret Airfield, *Paul McCue*

Croydon and the Second World War. *Berwick Sayers*

Farnham in War and Peace

The History of Reigate

Surrey Within Living Memory *(Women's Institutes of Surrey)*

Croydon Airport and the Battle of Britain *Douglas Bluett*

Dorking in the War, *David Knight*

Kent at War, *Bob Ogley*

RAF Redhill, *Geoffrey Tait*

Raiders Overhead, *Stephen Flower*

Action Stations 9 *Chris Ashworth*

Nova Scotians *Thomas H. Randall*

INDEX

This list does not contain all the pilots who are mentioned in the text but lists chief personalities together with towns, villages and other place names.